TAROT UNIVERSAL

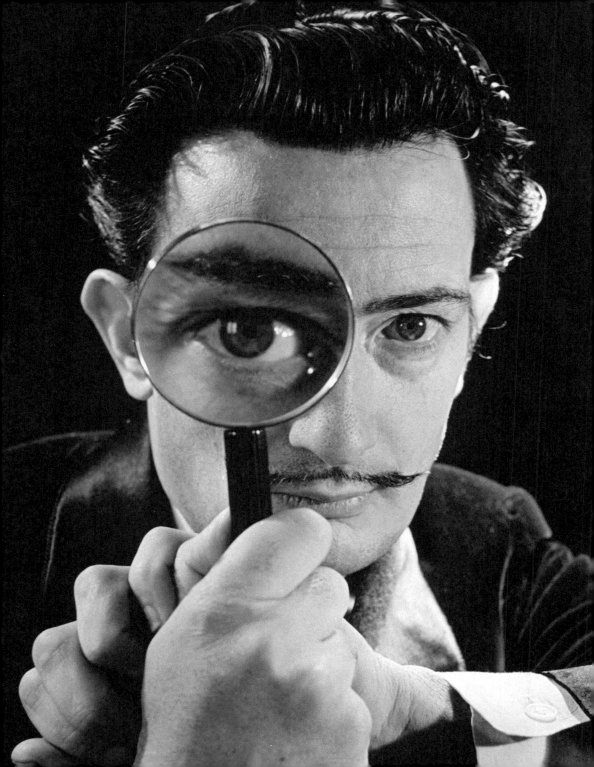

Johannes Fiebig

TAROT UNIVERSAL

Introduction/Vorwort/Préface
Annette Köger

German Playing Card Museum
Deutsches Spielkartenmuseum
Musée allemand de cartes à jouer

ᴇᴠᴇʀɢʀᴇᴇɴ

Contents
Inhalt
Sommaire

Introduction
Vorwort
Préface

Annette Köger

In the mid-1970s, Salvador Dalí created the *Tarot Universal Dalí*, which was originally published as a limited-edition signed artwork. Based on the age-old tradition of the Tarot, Dalí created a new artistic version by drawing on nearly 78 masterpieces of Western civilization from antiquity to modernity, including some of his own.

He thus, at the age of 70, became one of the many great names in art history to surrender to the magic of playing cards. The Tarot has fascinated not only Dalí, but many other artists as well—ranging from Andrea Mantegna (ca. 1465) and Albrecht Dürer to Giuseppe Maria Mitelli (1664) and Niki de Saint Phalle (2000).

Many artists have used the medium of playing cards as an experimental arena for the portrayal of dramatic or lascivious scenes. The following list of names, which is by no means complete, reflects the rich artistic variety and the creative use of playing cards: Konrad Witz (1440-1445), Sebastian Brant (1494), Virgil Solis (1540-1545), Jost Amman (1588), Henri de Saint-Simon (1793), Philipp Otto Runge (1810), Max Ernst (1941), Sonia Delaunay (1958-1959), Jean Dubuffet (1968), Karl Korab (1973), Jean Vérame (1991), and many more.

A traveler through the universe of the *Tarot Universal Dalí* will be confronted repeatedly with three stylistic elements. Artistic ability is sharply contrasted with provocative crudeness, thereby creating a mood that is surprisingly surreal. With a light stroke of his brush, Dalí often added a human figure or a human head to the cards, as if he were trying to emphasize the meaning of the card with this ghostly being or shadowy figure. Appearing on many of the cards is a butterfly—traditionally a symbol of the psyche—or a crutch. According to Dalí, the crutch has a double meaning and represents the dualism of consciousness and unconsciousness, of outer and inner worlds. The crutch helps to connect the two worlds and to open up a window between two realities.

Annette Koeger, PhD, Director of the German Playing Card Museum Leinfelden-Echterdingen

Das *Tarot Universal Dalí* entstand Mitte der 1970er Jahre und wurde zunächst als signierte Grafikserie in limitierter Auflage veröffentlicht. Basierend auf der jahrhundertealten Tarot-Tradition gestaltete Dalí ein neues Künstler-Tarot mit 78 Bildzitaten aus der abendländischen Kunst, die von der Antike bis zur Neuzeit, zu seinen eigenen Kunstwerken, reichten.

Dalí, der zu jenem Zeitpunkt das 70. Lebensjahr fast vollendet hatte, reihte sich damit in die Reihe der großen Namen der Kunstgeschichte ein, die die künstlerische Gestaltung von Spielkarten reizte. Die Tarot- oder Tarok-Karten übten nämlich nicht nur auf Dalí eine große Faszination aus. Der Bogen spannt sich von Andrea Mantegna (um 1465) und Albrecht Dürer über Giuseppe Maria Mitelli (1664) bis zu Niki de Saint Phalle (um 2000).

Spielkarten bieten Künstlern seit jeher Freiräume für die Darstellung drastischer oder gar obszöner Szenen. Eine Auswahl an Namen – ohne Anspruch auf Vollständigkeit – vermittelt einen Eindruck von der künstlerischen Vielfalt und dem fantasievollen Umgang mit der Gestaltung von Spielkarten: Konrad Witz (1440-1445), Sebastian Brant (1494), Virgil Solis (1540-1545), Jost Amman (1588), Henri de Saint-Simon (1793), Philipp Otto Runge (1810), Max Ernst (1941), Sonia Delaunay (1958/59), Jean Dubuffet (1968), Karl Korab (1973), Jean Vérame (1991) und viele andere.

Drei wiederkehrende Stilkriterien begleiten die Betrachter auf ihrer Reise durch das *Tarot Universal Dalí*. Künstlerische Fertigkeit steht im Kontrast zu provokanter Derbheit und setzt damit überraschende surreale Akzente. So fügte Dalí auf zahlreichen Karten eine mit leichtem Pinselstrich gezeichnete menschliche Figur, Köpfe oder Gesten hinzu, als ob eine Art Geistwesen oder eine Schattenfigur die Bedeutung der Karte erhöht. Ferner taucht häufig sowohl das Motiv des Schmetterlings – traditionell Symbol der Psyche – wie auch das der Krücke auf. Die Krücke ist für Dalí ein doppeldeutiges Symbol. Sie repräsentiert den Dualismus von Bewusstem und Unbewusstem, von äußerer und innerer Welt. Sie hilft, zwei Welten zu verbinden und ein Fenster zwischen zwei Realitäten zu öffnen.

Dr. Annette Köger, Direktorin Deutsches Spielkartenmuseum, Leinfelden-Echterdingen

Le *Tarot Universel Dalí* fut créé au milieu des années 1970 et fut publié, dans un premier temps, en tant que série graphique dans une édition limitée. En se basant sur la tradition ancienne du tarot, Dalí créa une nouvelle version artistique des soixante-dix-huit lames issues de l'ensemble de l'art occidental, de l'Antiquité jusqu'à sa propre performance artistique.

Vers la fin de sa soixante-dixième année, Dalí compte parmi les plus grands noms de l'histoire de l'art qui ont de tout temps été attirés par la création artistique de cartes à jouer. Le jeu de tarot fascina non seulement Dalí, mais aussi une multitude d'artistes comme Andrea Mantegna (vers 1465), Albrecht Dürer, ou encore Guiseppe Maria Mitelli (1664) et Niki de Saint Phalle (vers 2000).

Les cartes à jouer ont offert à de nombreux artistes un espace libre de création pour représenter des scènes violentes et même obscènes. Une sélection d'artistes-peintres – sans avoir la prétention d'être exhaustive – donne une impression de la riche palette créative et de l'inventivité des artistes avec les cartes à jouer : Konrad Witz (1440-1445), Sébastian Brant (1494), Virgil Solis (1540-1545), Jost Amman (1588), Henri de Saint-Simon (1793), Philipp Otto Runge (1810), Max Ernst (1941), Sonia Delaunay (1958-1959), Jean Dubuffet (1968), Karl Korab (1973), Jean Vérame (1991), et bien d'autres encore.

Trois critères stylistiques répétitifs accompagnent l'observateur dans son voyage à travers le *Tarot Universel Dalí*. Le talent artistique contraste avec la grossièreté provocatrice et propose ainsi une nouvelle orientation surprenante vers le surréel. À l'aide d'un léger trait de pinceau, Dalí ajouta sur de nombreuses cartes une silhouette humaine, des têtes ou des gestes comme pour renforcer la signification de la carte par la présence d'un certain esprit ou l'ombre d'une silhouette.

De plus, le papillon – symbole traditionnel de l'âme – ainsi que la béquille sont des motifs qui sont représentés à plusieurs reprises. La béquille est pour Dalí un élément ambigu. Elle représente la dualité entre le conscient et l'inconscient – le monde extérieur et le monde intérieur. Elle aide à faire le lien entre deux mondes et à ouvrir une fenêtre sur deux réalités.

Dre Annette Koeger, Conservatrice du musée allemand de cartes à jouer, Leinfelden-Echterdingen

Tarot Universal Dalí
Tarot Universal Dalí
Le Tarot Universel Dalí

When the unprecedented tarot boom started in the early 1970s, Dalí created his version of the 78 cards—the *Tarot Universal Dalí*. Some famous poets and writers such as T. S. Eliot and Italo Calvino had already incorporated the Tarot into their works, but Dalí was the first well-known painter to create a completely new set of cards. Other famous painters, sculptors, and filmmakers would soon follow. One of them was the French-American artist Niki de Saint Phalle, who created her famed Tarot Garden in the south of Tuscany in Italy.

This booklet will help to shed light on the subject of the great artistic importance of Dalí's tarot.

The tarot cards of Salvador Dalí provide a stupendous kaleidoscope of art history. Dalí combined artistic genius, knowledge of the meaning of symbols, and creative finesse with skillfully chosen pictorial sources taken from the entire history of European art.

The result is an inimitable series of images, a new vision, which brilliantly engages the spirit of the first tarot cards.

The Making of the Dalí Tarot

It is no surprise that legends concerning the making of the Dalí Tarot have emerged. It can be said with certainty that several people assisted Dalí in the preparation of his tarot cards. Isidor Bea, who worked with Dalí for several years, is one of his better-known collaborators. She contributed to Dalí's bigger pictures, but not to his tarot. Some people claim that Dalí's friend Amanda Lear created one or even several of the cards. But this has not been substantiated by reliable sources. It is, however, certain that Dalí's wife, Gala, was an avid card reader (even during the Franco years, when this practice was outlawed). It is also certain that in 1941, a circle of Surrealists created a deck of 22 cards in Marseilles, and that a Paris-based publishing house issued a deck of playing cards (consisting of two sets of 54 cards) by Salvador Dalí in 1966.

The biographers agree that Dalí signed a contract for 78 tarot cards in the 1970s, after which time, his contract partners changed a number of times. Eventually, a New York publisher bought it. When Dalí delayed the delivery of the deck—or stopped working on the cards altogether—he was sued in a New York court and a rather large amount

Anfang der 1970er Jahre, als der beispiellose Tarot-Boom der Gegenwart gerade erst begann, schuf Salvador Dalí seine Version der 78 Karten – das Tarot Universal Dalí. Bis dahin hatten namhafte Dichter und Erzähler wie T. S. Eliot oder Italo Calvino die Tarot-Symbole bereits kunstvoll bearbeitet. Salvador Dalí war der erste prominente Bildkünstler, der einen kompletten Satz von 78 Tarot-Karten neu schuf. Etliche bekannte Maler, Bildhauer und Filmemacher sollten ihm folgen. Eine von ihnen ist die französisch-amerikanische Künstlerin Niki de Saint Phalle, die im Süden der Toskana ihren berühmten Tarot-Garten aufbaute.

Die künstlerische Bedeutung des Dalí-Tarots verdeutlicht der vorliegende Band. Die Karten von Salvador Dalí bieten ein erstaunliches Kaleidoskop der abendländischen Kunstgeschichte. Malerisches Genie, Wissen um die Be- deutung von Symbolen und gestalterische Raffinesse verbinden sich mit geschickt gewählten Bildzitaten aus der gesamten europäischen Kunstgeschichte.

Das Ergebnis ist ein einzigartiger Bilderreigen, eine neue Vision, die dem Genie der ersten Tarot-Karten ebenbürtig gegenübertritt.

Zur Entstehung des Dalí-Tarots

Um die Entstehung von Salvador Dalís Tarot ranken sich, wie nicht anders zu erwarten, manche Legenden. Sicherlich haben Assistenten Dalí bei der Vorbereitung von Gemälden geholfen. Namentlich bekannt ist etwa Isidor Bea, der etliche Jahre mit Dalí arbeitete. Doch dieser wirkte bei Großgemälden mit, nicht bei Dalís Tarot. Manche behaupten, Dalís Freundin Amanda Lear habe einige dieser Karten gemalt. Doch dafür gibt es keine seriöse Quelle. Sicher ist allerdings, dass Dalís Frau Gala ihr Leben lang eine eifrige Kartenlegerin war (auch zu Franco-Zeiten, als dies verpönt und verboten war). Bemerkenswert ist ferner, dass im Kreis einiger Surrealisten bereits 1941 in Marseille ein Tarot mit 22 Karten neu gezeichnet wurde und dass Dalí 1966 ein Deck Spielkarten (mit zweimal 54 Blatt) in einem Pariser Verlag veröffentlichte.

Übereinstimmend berichten die Biografen, dass Dalí Anfang der 1970er Jahre einen Vertrag über den

Au début des années 1970 alors que l'engouement sans précédent pour le tarot actuel commençait à se développer, Salvador Dalí créa sa propre version des soixante-dix-huit lames : le Tarot Universel Dalí. Jusque-là, seuls des poètes et auteurs réputés comme T. S. Eliot ou Italo Calvino avaient finement introduit les symboles du tarot dans leurs œuvres. Salvador Dalí fut le premier artiste-peintre célèbre qui recréa un jeu complet de soixante-dix-huit lames de tarot. De nombreux peintres, sculpteurs et producteurs de films célèbres le suivront dans cette entreprise. Parmi eux se trouve l'artiste franco-américaine Niki de Saint Phalle, qui construisit son célèbre jardin des tarots dans le sud de la Toscane italienne.

L'objectif de ce livret est de participer à réaliser cette tâche depuis longtemps indispensable, qui consiste à remettre en valeur la grande signification artistique du Tarot de Dalí.

Les cartes de Salvador Dalí nous proposent un kaléidoscope remarquable de l'histoire de l'art occidental. Le génie pittoresque, la connaissance des significations des symboles ainsi que le raffinement artistique sont associés à des références artistiques, habilement choisies et issues de l'histoire complète de l'art européen.

Le résultat est une ronde d'images unique en son genre, une nouvelle vision qui est à pied d'égalité avec le génie des premières cartes de tarot.

L'origine du Tarot de Dalí

L'origine de la création du Tarot de Salvador Dalí est bien entendu entourée de légendes. Certes, Dalí se faisait assister pour peindre ses tableaux, et l'on connaît de nom Isidor Bea qui travailla pendant de longues années auprès de Dalí. Cependant, Isidor Bea assista Dalí pour ses grands tableaux et non pour son tarot. Selon certaines rumeurs, Amanda Lear, l'amie de Dalí, aurait peint certaines cartes de tarot, mais il n'existe aucune preuve à ce sujet. Ce qui est toutefois certain, c'est que la femme de Dalí, Gala, aima tirer les cartes tout au long de sa vie (bien qu'à l'époque de Franco cette activité fût mal vue et interdite). De plus, un cercle de quelques surréalistes dessina à Marseille, en 1941, vingt-deux cartes de tarot et, en 1966, Salvador Dalí publia un jeu de cartes à jouer dans une édition parisienne (deux fois cinquante-quatre cartes).

of money in his American accounts was frozen. On January 30, 1975, the *Diario de Barcelona* reported: "Lawsuit in the US: Publisher demands the delivery of 78 gouaches [color drawings] by Dalí."

The case was settled out of court, but Dalí had to sign about 20,000 print sheets (250 for each card) in 1976-77. Around that time, Dalí engaged a new secretary by the name of Enrique Sabater, who succeeded in regaining control of the tarot drawings and integrating them into the firms Distribucions d'Art Surrealista and Dasa (Dalí–Sabater).

Whereas the New York gallery of Gertrude Stein distributed the prints, Naipes Comas, the well-established Catalan printer of playing cards (located near Barcelona), published the work in 1983-84 as a complete deck of tarot cards. In 2010, the owners sold Naipes Comas to Cartamundi, the leading European playing card manufacturer.

The Life of Salvador Dalí

Salvador Felipe Jacinto Dalí i Domènech was born on May 11, 1904, at 8:45 a. m. in Figueres, Catalonia, Spain. His artistic talent had already become evident in his early school years. In 1918, the first works of the then 14-year-old Dalí are shown in the municipal theater. He also tries his hand at writing, an interest he will pursue throughout his life.

After his mother's death, he moves to Madrid in October 1921 and enrolls at the art academy of San Fernando. In the student dormitory, he makes the acquaintance of Federico García Lorca (who later becomes his friend and confidant) as well as Luis Buñuel, Pepín Bello, and others. In 1923, Dalí is expelled for a year after harshly criticizing the competence of his professors. In 1926, he is expelled for good. On his first trip to Paris, in April 1926, he meets Pablo Picasso. For the premiere of the play *Mariana Pineda* by his friend García Lorca, Dalí designs the set as well as the costumes. In 1929, during his second stay in Paris, he makes the film *An Andalusian Dog* with Buñuel and meets the Surrealists André Breton and Paul Éluard. He falls in love with Éluard's wife, Gala, who becomes his lover, wife, and muse.

After a solo exhibition of his works in Paris, he has his first American exhibition, in 1933. In 1934, Dalí

Entwurf von 78 Tarot-Karten unterzeichnete. In der Folgezeit wechselte mehrfach sein Vertragspartner; schließlich war es ein New Yorker Verleger, der nicht unbedingt den besten Ruf in der Kunstszene besaß. Als Dalí die Arbeit an den Karten verschleppte bzw. ganz einstellte, wurde er in New York verklagt und eine große Summe auf seinen amerikanischen Konten eingefroren. „Anklage in den USA: Verlag fordert von Dalí die Lieferung von 78 Gouaches", meldete die Tageszeitung *Diario de Barcelona* am 30. Januar 1975.

Es kommt zu einem außergerichtlichen Vergleich, in dessen Zuge Dalí in den Jahren 1976/77 etwa 20 000 Druckbogen unterzeichnet (250 für jede Karte). Zu jener Zeit hatte Dalí gerade einen neuen Sekretär, Enrique Sabater, eingestellt. Sabater gelingt es, die Rechte an den Dalí-Zeichnungen für die Tarot-Karten zu klären und sie in die Firmen Distribucions d'art surrealista und Dasa (Dalí-Sabater) einzubringen.

Während die Drucke über die New Yorker Galerie Gertrude Stein vertrieben werden, legt die alte katalanische Spielkartendruckerei Naipes Comas (L'Hospitalet de Llobregat bei Barcelona) um 1983/84 die Tarot-Entwürfe als Tarot-Karten auf. 2010 verkaufen die Inhaber aus Altersgründen Naipes Comas an Cartamundi, den großen europäischen Spielkartenhersteller, der seitdem dieses Erbe weiterführt.

Aus dem Leben des Salvador Dalí

Salvador Felip Jacint Dalí i Domènech wurde am 11. Mai 1904 um 8.45 Uhr im katalanischen Figueres geboren. Früh fällt in der Schule seine künstlerische Begabung auf. Erste Bilder des damals 14-Jährigen werden 1918 im heimischen Stadttheater ausgestellt. In dieser Zeit betätigt er sich auch bereits als Autor.

Nach dem Tod seiner Mutter Felipa geht Dalí im Oktober 1921 nach Madrid, wo er an der Kunsthochschule San Fernando sein Studium aufnimmt. Im Studentenwohnheim Residencia de Estudiantes lernt er seinen späteren Freund und Vertrauten Federico García Lorca sowie Luis Buñuel, Pepin Bello und andere kennen. Nach heftiger Kritik an der Kompetenz seiner Professoren wird Dalí 1923 zunächst für ein Jahr, 1926 jedoch endgültig von der Akademie verwiesen. Im April 1926 lernt er dann wäh-

Les biographes s'entendent sur le fait que Salvador Dalí signa un contrat au début des années 1970 pour créer l'esquisse de soixante-dix-huit cartes de tarot. Ce contrat fut repris par plusieurs éditeurs et se retrouva finalement dans les mains d'un éditeur de New York dont la réputation était douteuse dans le milieu artistique. Dalí travaillant peu sur la création de ses cartes et cessant même son travail, il fut poursuivi en justice à New York, et une grosse somme d'argent fut gelée sur son compte américain. « Plainte aux États-Unis : maison d'édition réclame de Dalí la livraison de 78 gouaches », titrait le quotidien *Diario de Barcelona*, le 30 janvier 1975.

Finalement, les deux parties s'accordèrent, et Dalí signa entre 1976 et 1977 environ 20 000 reproductions (250 pour chaque carte). À cette époque, Dalí venait juste d'engager un nouveau secrétaire, Enrique Sabater, et ce dernier réussit à préserver les droits des ouvrages de Dalí pour le tarot et à les introduire dans les sociétés Distribucions d'art surrealista et Dasa (Dalí-Sabater).

Tandis que les reproductions étaient écoulées par Gertrude Stein de la galerie de New York, une ancienne imprimerie de cartes à jouer catalane, Naipes Comas (à l'Hospitalet de Llobregat près de Barcelone), édita vers 1983/84 les esquisses de tarot en tant que véritables cartes de tarot. En 2010, les propriétaires de Naipes Comas, en raison de leur âge avancé, vendirent l'imprimerie à Cartamundi, le grand fabricant européen de cartes à jouer, qui assure, depuis, cette succession.

La vie de Salvador Dalí

Salvador Felipe Jacinto Dalí i Domènech naît à Figueras, en Catalogne, le 11 mai 1904 à 8h45. Très tôt, son talent artistique se remarque à l'école. Les premières œuvres de Dalí, alors âgé de quatorze ans, sont exposées dans le théâtre municipal de sa ville natale en 1918. À cette époque, il commence déjà à écrire, comme il continuera de le faire tout au long de sa vie.

Après la mort de sa mère Felipa, Dalí part pour Madrid en octobre 1921, où il commence des études d'art à l'Académie des Beaux-Arts de San Fernando. Dans la résidence d'étudiants « Residencia de Estudiantes », il fait la connaissance de son futur ami Federico García Lorca, de Luis Buñuel, de Pepin Bello et de bien d'autres personnalités.

travels to the United States for the first time. Other exhibitions in New York and London follow and are triumphal successes. In 1935, Dalí lectures at the Museum of Modern Art in New York on the art of Surrealism. He makes the front page of *Time*. He designs *Dream of Venus, a* pavilion for the 1939 New York World's Fair. Fleeing the chaos of World War II in Europe, Dalí and Gala move to the United States in 1940. In 1941, the first retrospective of his works is shown and his autobiography *The Secret Life of Salvador Dalí* is published. Other texts, novels, and plays are published as well. In 1948, the Dalís return to Spain.

In the following years, Dalí paints, writes, and produces tirelessly. His paintings alone number more than 1,600. Major exhibitions all over the world add to Dalí's fame and the prices of his works reach astronomical figures. Because of his genius, Dalí is considered to be one of the greatest artists of the 20th century; because of his eccentric lifestyle, he becomes a favorite of the media.

During his last years, he withdraws more and more and suffers from depression and other ailments of old age. He never quite recovers from Gala's death in 1982. That same year, he receives the title of Marqués de Dalí de Púbol. In 1984, Dalí suffers severe burns resulting from a fire in his bedroom. He dies on January 23, 1989, in the Torre Galatea. In keeping with his wishes, he is buried in a crypt below the stage of the Dalí Theatre-Museum in Figueres.

Surrealism—The Reality of the Otherworld

The Paris-based Dada movement was the forerunner of Surrealism, which includes all genres. André Breton (1896-1966) broke with Dada after an unsuccessful attempt to reorganize the movement. Breton then created a theoretical and methodical foundation, which was to become the basis of Surrealism.

The term *Surrealism* was coined by Guillaume Apollinaire (1880-1918), who gave his 1917 play *Les Mamelles de Tirésias* the subtitle "A Surrealist Drama." In his 1924 manifest *Premier Manifeste du surréalisme*, Breton defined the term as a spontaneous verbal expression of the unconscious.

rend seiner ersten Paris-Reise Pablo Picasso kennen. Für die Uraufführung (1927) des Theaterstückes *Mariana Pineda* seines Freundes García Lorca entwirft Dalí Bühnenbild und Kostüme, mit Buñuel dreht er 1929 während seines zweiten Paris-Aufenthalts den Film *Ein andalusischer Hund*. Dabei trifft er mit den Surrealisten André Breton und Paul Éluard zusammen. Er verliebt sich in dessen Frau Gala, die fortan seine Geliebte, Frau und Muse ist.

Nach einer Einzelausstellung mit seinen Werken in Paris hat er 1933 die erste US-amerikanische Einzelausstellung. 1934 reist Dalí dann selbst in die USA. Weitere große Ausstellungen in London und New York sind außerordentlich erfolgreich. Am New Yorker Museum of Modern Art hält er 1935 einen Vortrag über die surrealistische Malerei. Sein Gesicht erscheint auf dem Titelbild der *Time*. Für die Weltausstellung 1939 in New York entwirft er den *Traum der Venus*. 1940 flüchten Salvador und Gala vor den Kriegswirren in Europa und gehen nach Amerika, wo 1941 eine erste Retrospektive seiner Werke gezeigt wird und seine Autobiografie *The Secret Life of Salvador Dalí* erscheint. Weitere Texte, darunter auch einige Romane und Theaterstücke, erscheinen. 1948 kehrt das Ehepaar Dalí nach Spanien zurück.

Dalí malt, schreibt, inszeniert in den folgenden Jahren unermüdlich. Allein sein malerisches Œuvre umfasst über 1600 Werke. Große Ausstellungen in aller Welt machen Dalí berühmt und lassen die Preise für seine Bilder in schwindelerregende Höhen schnellen. Dalí wird aufgrund seiner Genialität zu einem der größten Maler des 20. Jahrhunderts und aufgrund seines exzentrischen Lebens zu einem Liebling der Medien.

In den letzten Jahren wird es ruhiger um ihn, insbesondere der Tod Galas im Juni 1982 ist ein schwerer Schlag für den von Alter, Depression und Krankheit Gezeichneten. 1984 erleidet er bei einem Brand in seinem Schlafzimmer schwere Verbrennungen. Am 23. Januar 1989 stirbt Salvador Dalí, der im Juli 1982 zum Marquès de Púbol geadelt worden war, im Torre Galatea. Er wird auf seinen Wunsch hin unter der Bühne seines Museums in Figueres beigesetzt.

Après avoir sévèrement critiqué les compétences de ses professeurs, Dalí est renvoyé de l'Académie une première fois en 1923 pour un an, puis définitivement en 1926. En avril de la même année, lors de son premier voyage à Paris, il fait la connaissance de Pablo Picasso. En 1927, pour la représentation de la pièce de théâtre *Mariana Pineda* de son ami Garcia Lorca, Dalí crée le décor et les costumes. En 1929, lors de son deuxième séjour à Paris, il réalise avec Buñuel le film *Un chien andalou*. C'est à cette période qu'il rencontre les surréalistes André Breton et Paul Éluard. Dalí tombe amoureux de la femme d'Éluard, Gala, qui deviendra désormais sa maîtresse, sa femme et sa muse.

Après une exposition individuelle à Paris en 1933, il expose à New York pour la première fois. En 1934, Dalí se rend lui-même aux États-Unis. D'autres grandes expositions suivent à Londres et à New York et connaissent un énorme succès. Au Museum of Modern Art de New York, il tient un discours en 1935 sur la peinture surréaliste, et son portrait est en couverture du *Time*. Pour l'exposition universelle de 1939 à New York, il crée *Le Rêve de Vénus*. En 1940, Dalí et Gala fuient la guerre et s'installent en Amérique où une première rétrospective des œuvres de l'artiste est exposée en 1941. Son autobiographie *La Vie secrète de Salvador Dalí* est publiée ainsi que d'autres textes, romans et pièces de théâtre. En 1948, les Dalí retournent en Espagne.

Les années suivantes, Dalí travaille d'arrache-pied : il peint, écrit et met en scène. Son œuvre picturale compte à elle seule déjà plus de 1600 ouvrages. Des grandes expositions dans le monde entier rendent Dalí célèbre et font monter très vite et très haut les prix de ses tableaux. En raison de son génie, il devient l'un des plus grands peintres du XXᵉ siècle, mais aussi la coqueluche des médias pour sa vie excentrique.

Dalí vit une vie tranquille pendant ses dernières années, mais la mort de Gala en juin 1982 est un coup dur pour cet homme, marqué par la vieillesse, la dépression et les maladies. La même année, il est anobli par le roi d'Espagne et nommé marquis de Púbol. En 1984, il est gravement brûlé lors d'un incendie dans sa chambre à coucher. Le 23 janvier 1989, Salvador Dalí meurt à Torre Galatea. Il est inhumé selon sa volonté dans la crypte de son théâtre-musée à Figueras.

Surrealism is based on the belief of existence of a higher reality, the importance of the spontaneous stream of consciousness, the absolute power of dreams, and the free play of thoughts. Everyone is a poet—if one would only listen to hints from the unconsciousness.

Surrealism becomes a way of life. "The Surrealists do not intend to destroy literature and art, but rather to integrate them into a practice, in which art and life are no longer opposites." (Surrealist Manifesto, 1924) "I firmly believe that the seemingly opposite states of dreams and reality can dissolve into a form of absolute reality—if you will, into surreality." (ibid.)

Therefore Surrealism may be defined as wa psychic automatism, through which one tries to express one's current stream of thoughts—whether verbally, in writing, or by any other means.

Dreams serve as catalysts of the merging of inner and outer worlds and the workings of chance play an important role in Surrealism. Contrary to the scientific interpretation of dreams by Sigmund Freud, the Surrealists do not attempt to shed light on the unconscious by subjecting it to the scrutiny of consciousness. For the Surrealists, the unconscious always has first priority. Breton defined chance as the meeting of outer causality and inner finality and, therefore, as an important aspect of every creative attempt.

Dalí is often equated with Surrealism itself, but in reality, he was more on the sidelines of the movement. He invented his own method, which he termed "paranoid-critical." By systematizing chaos and confusion, one may outdo reality. The paranoid-critical method is based on a "critical and systematic objectification of delusionary association and interpretation." It is Dalí's "spontaneous method of irrational knowledge."

The Importance of the Dalí Tarot

In a sense, we are all artists: masters of the art of life. Today, many people relate to the "way of the artist" or the "way of the pilgrim." The concepts of art and pilgrimage now represent methods of designing your own life, discovering your destiny, and choosing, creating, and meeting personal challenges.

Tarot and fairy tales, myths and dreams—what Erich

Surrealismus – die Realität der Anderswelt

Der alle Kunstgattungen umfassende Surrealismus entstand aus der Pariser Dada-Bewegung, genauer aus dem Bruch mit dem Dadaismus, den André Breton (1896-1966) im Jahre 1922 nach dem Scheitern eines zum Zwecke der Neuorientierung einberufenen Dada-Kongresses eingeleitet hatte. Breton führte eine konstruktive Wendung, einen theoretischen und methodischen Unterbau ein, der als Basis des Surrealismus dienen sollte.

Die Bezeichnung Surrealismus geht auf Guillaume Apollinaire (1880-1918) zurück, der sein Theaterstück *Les Mamelles de Tirésias* (1917) mit dem Untertitel „surrealistisches Drama" versah. Bei Breton bezeichnet der Begriff eine spontane verbale Schöpfung aus dem Unbewussten heraus, wie er dies in seinem *Premier Manifeste du surréalisme* (1924) definiert.

Der Surrealismus beruht auf dem Glauben an eine „höhere" Wirklichkeit, an die Bedeutung der spontanen, freien Assoziation, an die Allmacht des Traumes und das zweckfreie Spiel des Denkens. Jeder ist Poet, wenn er den Hinweisen des Unbewussten Beachtung schenkt: Surrealismus als Lebensform. „Nicht Zerstörung der Literatur und der Kunst intendieren die Surrealisten, sondern deren Aufhebung in einer Praxis, in der Kunst und Leben keine Gegensätze mehr sind." (*Erstes Surrealistisches Manifest*, 1924)

„Ich glaube an die künftige Auflösung dieser scheinbar so gegensätzlichen Zustände von Traum und Wirklichkeit in einer Art absoluter Realität, wenn man so sagen kann: der Surrealität." (Ebenda)

Surrealismus ist demnach ein *psychischer Automatismus*, mit dem man mündlich, schriftlich oder auf jede andere Weise den aktuellen Ablauf des Denkens auszudrücken sucht.

Hier spielen vor allem der *Traum* als Katalysator zur Vereinigung der inneren und der äußeren Welt sowie der Zufall eine Rolle. Im Unterschied zur wissenschaftlichen Anwendung (Freud) richten die Surrealisten ihr Traumprogramm nicht auf die Erhellung des Unbewussten durch das Bewusste, sondern geben dem Unbewussten den ausdrücklichen Vorrang. Den Zufall definiert Breton

Le surréalisme ou la réalité de l'autre-monde

Le surréalisme est un mouvement artistique qui comprend tous les genres de l'art et qui est né du dadaïsme parisien, et plus précisément de la rupture avec le dada, menée par André Breton (1896-1966) en 1922. Après l'échec d'un nouveau congrès du dadaïsme dont l'objectif était une nouvelle réorientation, Breton s'oriente vers une recherche constructive, à savoir une théorie et une méthode, une base sur laquelle naîtra le surréalisme.

Le terme « surréalisme » est employé pour la première fois par Guillaume Apollinaire (1880-1918) dans le sous-titre de sa pièce de théâtre *Les mamelles de Tirésias* (1917), intitulé « Drame surréaliste ». Chez Breton, ce terme indique une création spontanée et verbale provenant de l'inconscient, comme il le définit dans son *Premier Manifeste du surréalisme* (1924).

Le surréalisme repose sur la croyance en la réalité supérieure, en l'importance des associations spontanées et libres, en la toute-puissance du rêve ainsi qu'au jeu désintéressé de la pensée. Tout le monde est poète, il suffit d'accorder son attention aux signes de l'inconscient : le surréalisme devient un mode de vie. « Les surréalistes n'aspirent pas à détruire la littérature et l'art, mais à les rapprocher de la vie quotidienne où l'art et la vie réelle ne s'opposent plus », et « Je crois à la résolution future de ces deux états, en apparence si contradictoire que sont le rêve et la réalité, en une sorte de réalité absolue, de surréalité, si l'on peut dire ainsi » (*Premier Manifeste du surréalisme*, André Breton, 1924).

Le surréalisme est un automatisme psychique pur pour lequel on se propose d'exprimer, soit verbalement, soit par écrit, soit de toute autre manière, le fonctionnement réel de la pensée.

Le rêve ainsi que le hasard jouent un rôle prépondérant en tant que catalyseur pour allier le monde intérieur et extérieur. À la différence des méthodes scientifiques (Sigmund Freud), les surréalistes ne concentrent pas leurs méthodes à éclairer le conscient par l'inconscient, mais ils accordent toujours à l'inconscient une priorité explicite. Breton définit le hasard comme la rencontre d'une causalité extérieure et d'une finalité intérieure, et par conséquent comme un aspect important de toute création artistique.

Fromm called "symbolic languages"—are precious and oftentimes irreplaceable companions because they provide an effective and safe training ground for the exploration of utopias and alternative realities. One of the most beautiful results of this training is a growth of consciousness: you experience the conscious handling of the unconscious.

Since his youth, Dalí had been a great admirer of Sigmund Freud. In July 1938, he finally visited him (Dalí was 34 years old then, and Freud was 82). Dalí wrote in a letter to André Breton that meeting Freud had deeply impressed him and that Freud had said: "If you look at the paintings of the old masters, you are immediately inspired to look for the unconscious aspect. But if you look at a surrealistic picture, you are immediately inspired to look for the conscious aspect." (From the estate of André Breton, quoted by Ian Gibson, p. 402.)

This bon mot of Freud shows us a meaningful way, effective still today: from the conscious to the unconscious and back to a new and holistic consciousness, thus including conscious life and existence.

The *Tarot Universal Dalí* builds a bridge from the Renaissance to the masters of early modern art of the 20th century and into the 21st. In many ways, it is a focal point and one of the most beautiful expressions of diverse artistic efforts that are committed to overcoming boundaries: the borders between life and art, between spirit and handiwork, between possibility and reality. The tarot cards of Salvador Dalí with their pictorial enigmas and allusions ultimately present a mirror: you are the *Magician*, an original—unique, talented, and creative.

The Structure of the Dalí Tarot

Major and Minor Arcana: Like any other tarot deck, the Dalí Tarot consists of 78 cards. Of these, 22 are considered trump cards or Major Arcana, and 56 are minor cards or Minor Arcana. The word *arcana* is the plural of the Latin word *arcanum*, meaning "secret." The major or trump cards represent major aspects of life—like love, death, or the Devil. The minor cards are no less important; they represent character traits, personality types, temperaments, and other aspects.

The Four Suits: The 56 cards of the Minor Arcana are

als Begegnung einer äußeren Kausalität und einer inneren Finalität, kurz als bedeutenden Faktor jeder kreativen Produktion.

Dalí wird oft mit dem Surrealismus gleichgesetzt, steht jedoch eher am Rande dieser Bewegung. Er erfindet seine eigene Methode, die „paranoisch-kritische Methode". Durch Systematisierung des Verworrenen könne die Realität überboten werden: Die paranoisch-kritische Methode beruhe auf „kritischer und systematischer Objektvierung wahnhafter Assoziationen und Interpretationen", sie ist seine „spontane Methode irrationaler Erkenntnis".

Zur Bedeutung des Dalí-Tarots

In gewisser Weise sind wir *alle* Künstler – *Lebenskünstler*. Der „Weg des Künstlers" ist ebenso wie der „Weg des Pilgers" für viele Menschen heute keine unbekannte Größe, sondern eine lebendige Erfahrung. Kunst und Pilgerschaft stehen für Methoden, einen eigenen Lebensentwurf zu gestalten, eine persönliche Bestimmung zu entdecken und selbst gewählte Aufgaben zu verwirklichen.

Tarot und *Märchen, Mythen und Träume* – diese „Symbolsprachen", wie Erich Fromm sie nannte – sind auf diesen Wegen wertvolle und oft unverzichtbare Begleiter; sie stellen ein wirkungsvolles (und letztlich gefahrloses) Training für die Erkundung von Lebensutopien und alternativen Wirklichkeiten dar. Eines der schönsten Ergebnisse dieses Trainings ist eine Bewusstseinserweiterung: Man macht Erfahrungen im bewussten Umgang mit dem Unbewussten.

Seit seiner Jugend war Salvador Dalí ein großer Verehrer Sigmund Freuds. Im Juli 1938 konnte Dalí Freud endlich persönlich kennenlernen (Dalí war zu diesem Zeitpunkt 34 und Freud 82 Jahre alt). In einem Brief an André Breton berichtete Dalí, dass ihn dieses Treffen sehr beeindruckt habe. Sigmund Freud habe unter anderem ausgeführt, dass „man bei den Bildern der alten Meister dazu neigt, sofort nach dem Unbewussten zu suchen, während man, wenn man ein surrealistisches Bild betrachtet, sogleich den Drang verspürt, nach dem Bewussten zu fragen." (aus dem Nachlass von André Breton, zitiert nach I. Gibson, S. 402 f.)

Freuds vielsagende Bemerkung weist einen interessan-

Bien que souvent associé au surréalisme, Dalí s'est tenu à l'écart de ce mouvement, mais il inventera sa propre méthode, la « méthode paranoïa-critique ». La réalité peut être dépassée en systématisant le délire : la méthode paranoïa-critique repose sur « l'objectivation critique et systématique des associations et interprétations délirantes », elle est la « méthode spontanée de connaissances irrationnelles » de Dalí.

Ce qu'il ressort du Tarot de Dalí

Nous sommes tous en quelque sorte des artistes, des artistes de la vie. De nos jours, la voie de l'artiste, tout comme la voie du pèlerin, représente pour beaucoup de personnes non pas un chemin inconnu mais une expérience vivante et créative. L'art et le pèlerinage sont des méthodes pour tracer l'esquisse de sa vie, découvrir son propre destin et réaliser ses tâches personnelles.

Sur cette voie, le tarot, *les contes, les mythes et les rêves*, ces « langages symboliques », nommés ainsi par Erich Fromm, sont des accompagnateurs précieux et souvent irremplaçables. Ils permettent de bien s'exercer en toute sécurité à explorer les utopies de la vie et les réalités possibles. L'un des plus beaux résultats de cet exercice est l'élargissement de la conscience : faire des expériences en prenant conscience de l'inconscient.

Salvador Dalí était depuis sa jeunesse un grand admirateur de Sigmund Freud. En juillet 1938, Dalí eut enfin la possibilité de rencontrer Freud personnellement (Dalí avait alors trente-quatre ans et Freud, quatre-vingt-deux ans). Dans une lettre adressée à André Breton, Dalí raconte qu'il avait été très impressionné par cette rencontre et que Sigmund Freud avait notamment déclaré : « Dans les tableaux classiques, je cherche l'inconscient, dans les œuvres surréalistes, je cherche ce qui est conscient ! » (de la succession d'André Breton, cité par J. Gibson, p. 402).

Cette remarque déterminante de Freud indique une voie essentielle, et encore actuelle aujourd'hui, qui consiste à passer du conscient à l'inconscient pour revenir au conscient en atteignant ainsi un niveau insoupçonné de conscience intégrale où il s'agit d'être et de vivre consciemment.

Le *Tarot Universel Dalí* est à l'image d'un pont dont les arches s'étendent de l'époque de la Renaissance et des

divided into four suits (wands, cups, swords, and coins—also known as pentacles.)

The Numbered Cards (Pip Cards): Each suit consists of ten numbered cards ranging from ace (one) to ten.

The Court Cards: In addition, each suit has four court cards: queen, king, knight, and page (also known as knave or princess). They symbolize the shades of a "majestic" personality, which is able to rule over its respective elements: fire (wands), water (cups), air (swords), or earth (coins or pentacles).

ten Weg, der an Aktualität bis heute nichts verloren hat: Vom Bewussten zum Unbewussten und von dort wieder zurück zu einem neuen – integralen – Bewusstsein, das nun ein *bewusstes Leben und Sein* beinhaltet.

Das Tarot Universal Dalí bildete eine Brücke von der Renaissance und den Meistern der klassischen Moderne bis ins 20. und 21. Jahrhundert. Dalís Tarot stellt in vielerlei Hinsicht einen Brennpunkt dar, eine der schönsten Zusammenfassungen und Bestätigungen jener künstlerischer Wege, denen es um die Aufhebung von Grenzen geht – der Grenzen zwischen Kunst und Leben, zwischen Geist und Handwerk, zwischen Möglichkeit und Wirklichkeit. Dalís Tarot-Collagen mit ihren bildhaften Rätseln und Zitaten halten uns dabei auch den Spiegel vor: Du selbst bist der *Magier:* ein Original – einzigartig, auf eine bestimmte Art begabt und schöpferisch.

Der Aufbau des Dalí-Tarots

Große und kleine Arkana: Wie jedes Tarot-Spiel umfasst das Dalí-Tarot 78 Karten. Davon werden 22 als große Karten oder Arkana und 56 als kleine Karten oder Arkana bezeichnet. Arkana ist der Plural von Arkanum, lateinisch „Geheimnis".

Die großen Karten stellen große Stationen des Lebens dar – wie Liebe, Tod und Teufel. Die kleinen Karten sind allerdings nicht unwichtiger, sie bezeichnen Charaktere, Typen, Temperamente und vieles mehr.

Die vier Farbreihen: Die 56 kleinen Arkana teilen sich auf in die vier Farbreihen Stäbe, Kelche, Schwerter und Münzen (auch Pentakel genannt).

Zahlenkarten: In jeder der vier Farbreihen gibt es zehn Zahlenkarten, von Ass (= Eins) bis Zehn.

Hofkarten: In jeder der vier Farbreihen treten außerdem vier Hofkarten auf: Königin, König, Ritter und Page (auch Bube oder Prinzessin genannt).

Die Hofkarten stellen, in unterschiedlichen Nuancen, jeweils einen Idealtyp dar: eine Persönlichkeit, die „majestätisch" und souverän mit dem betreffenden Element (mit Feuer/Stäbe, Wasser/Kelche, Luft/Schwerter und Erde/Münzen) umgeht.

maîtres de l'art moderne classique aux XXe et XXIe siècles. Le Tarot de Dalí représente à tous les égards un axe central, il est l'un des plus beaux résumés et témoignages reflétant une voie artistique où les frontières se dissipent : celles qui se trouvent entre l'art et la vie, entre l'esprit et la matière, entre la possibilité et la réalité. Avec ses énigmes et ses citations illustrées, les collages du Tarot de Dalí sont comme un miroir dans lequel vous vous regardez pour découvrir que vous aussi êtes le « Magicien », un original, unique, talentueux et créateur.

La structure du Tarot de Dalí

Grands et petits arcanes : comme tous les jeux de tarot, le Tarot de Dalí contient soixante-dix-huit lames. Vingt-deux lames représentent les grands arcanes et cinquante-six lames représentent les grands petites lames ou les petits arcanes. Arcana est le pluriel du latin *arcanum* qui signifie secret.

Les grandes lames représentent les grandes étapes de la vie comme l'amour, la mort ou le diable.

Les petites lames sont tout aussi importantes puisqu'elles représentent les caractères, les types, les tempéraments et beaucoup d'autres aspects individuels.

Les quatre séries de couleur : les cinquante-six petits arcanes sont divisés en quatre séries de couleur : les bâtons, les coupes, les épées et les deniers (nommés également pentacles).

Les cartes numérales : chaque série de couleur contient dix cartes numérales, de l'as (un) au dix.

Les cartes de la cour : chaque série des quatre couleurs contient également quatre cartes de la cour : le valet (nommé également page ou princesse), le cavalier, la reine et le roi.

Chacune des cartes de la cour représente – de façon nuancée – un type idéal : une personnalité qui agit souverainement avec les quatre éléments (le feu / les bâtons, l'eau / les coupes, l'air / les épées et la terre / les deniers) et qui est donc en mesure de décider et d'agir avec souveraineté dans son propre royaume.

How to Read the Cards
Praxis des Tarot-Kartenlegens
Règles du tirage du tarot

Laying Out the Cards

Working with the Tarot involves interpreting the symbols, but you also need to summon the courage to face your own emotions and confront those unknown aspects of your being.

It is advisable to start with "a-card-a-day" routine. Draw a card in the morning or at night. This card will reveal the tasks of the day, motivate you for the day ahead, or help you reflect on the day gone by. Your interpretation of its meaning should be very personal and purely intuitive. Later, you might integrate other, more general readings.

Here are two (of many) spreads:

1—The current situation
2—The past or that which already is
3—The future or that which needs to be newly evaluated

Or:

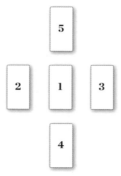

1—The key or main aspect
2—The past or that which already is
3—The future or that which needs to be newly evaluated
4—The root or foundation
5—The crown or chance

So legen Sie die Karten

Zum Tarot-Kartenlegen gehört neben der Symboldeutung auch der Mut, den eigenen Gefühlen und den Wirklichkeiten der eigenen Person ins Auge zu schauen.

Beginnen Sie am besten mit der „Tageskarte". Diese sollte möglichst morgens oder abends gezogen werden – als Symbol, als Motivierung oder als besinnlicher Reflex des persönlichen Tagesgeschehens. Die Bedeutungen dieser Tageskarten sollen zunächst individuell und intuitiv erfasst werden. Später können Sie zusätzliche Interpretationen aus der Tarot-Literatur zu Rate ziehen.

Im Folgenden werden zwei (der zahlreichen) Muster für das Tarot-Kartenlegen vorgestellt:

1 – Aktuelle Situation
2 – Vergangenheit oder bereits Vorhandenes
3 – Zukunft oder das, was neu zu beachten ist

Oder:

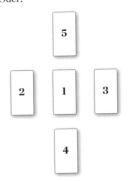

1 – Schlüssel oder Hauptaspekt
2 – Vergangenheit oder bereits Vorhandenes
3 – Zukunft oder das, was neu zu beachten ist
4 – Wurzel oder Basis
5 – Krone oder Chancen

Étalez les cartes

Pour jouer au tarot, en plus de l'interprétation des symboles, il faut avoir le courage de faire face à ses sentiments et aux réalités de sa personnalité.

On commence de préférence par la « carte du jour ». Celle-ci doit être tirée si possible le matin ou le soir – comme symbole, comme motivation ou comme réflexion personnelle sur les événements de la journée. Les interprétations des cartes du jour doivent être d'abord considérées sur un plan individuel et intuitif. Plus tard, des interprétations complémentaires peuvent être consultées dans des ouvrages de littérature du tarot.

Ci-dessous sont présentés deux (des nombreux) modèles pour le tirage de cartes du tarot :

1 – Situation actuelle
2 – Passé ou ce qui est déjà là
3 – Avenir ou ce qu'il faut reconsidérer

Ou :

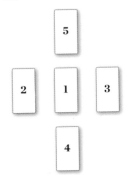

1 – Clé ou aspect principal
2 – Passé ou ce qui est déjà là
3 – Avenir ou ce qu'il faut reconsidérer
4 – Racine ou base
5 – Couronne ou chances

Practical Tips

– Always use all 78 cards of the deck.

– Think of a question that you would like to ask the cards. There are no set rules governing the subject matter of these questions.

– It is important to understand that each card functions like a mirror. You might want to ask questions about other people, but the answer will always include your own perception of them. If you ask questions about others, you are always part of the equation.

– Shuffle the cards the way you are used to. All rules— such as drawing with the left hand, shuffling by mixing the cards on a table, etc.—are nonsense. If you like, you can create your own ritual, without worrying about any set rules.

– Decide how you want to lay out the cards beforehand. You might use traditional spreads as well as personal ones. It is important to decide which one you want to use before you shuffle the cards.

– Draw the cards the way you are used to. Lay them upside down on a table.

– (Usually) you should turn the cards over one by one. Finish the interpretation of one card before turning over the next one.

– Everything that happens while working with the cards is part of the answer you are seeking.

– The sum of all the cards is the answer to your question.

Zum praktischen Vorgehen

– Verwenden Sie alle 78 Karten eines Tarot-Spiels.

– Überlegen Sie sich eine Frage, die Sie an die Tarot-Karten richten möchten. Für die Art der Frage gibt es keine zwingenden Ge- und Verbote.

– Beachten Sie: Die Karten wirken wie ein Spiegel. Sie können auch Fragen über andere Personen stellen. Die Antwort der Karten schließt dabei stets Ihr Verhältnis zu diesen Personen mit ein.

– Mischen Sie die Karten, wie Sie es gewohnt sind. Es gibt keine Vorschriften, wie die Karten gemischt werden sollen.

– Legen Sie die Karten nach einem Legemuster aus, das Sie zuvor ausgewählt haben. Sie können dazu Legemuster aus der Literatur benutzen, aber auch eigene entwerfen. Eigene Legemuster sollten vor der Kartenbefragung entworfen werden.

– Ziehen Sie die Karten, wie Sie es gewohnt sind und legen Sie sie verdeckt in Form des Legemusters vor sich hin.

– Decken Sie die Karten nun einzeln auf. Erst wenn die Betrachtung und Interpretation einer Karte beendet ist, sollte die nächste aufgedeckt werden.

– Alles, was während einer Kartenbefragung geschieht, kann zum Inhalt der gesuchten Antwort gehören.

– Die Antwort auf Ihre Frage geben alle Karten einer Auslage zusammen.

Règles pratiques

– Utilisez toutes les 78 cartes d'un jeu de tarot.

– Méditez une question que vous aimeriez adresser aux cartes de tarot. Il n'y a ni règlements ni interdits quant à la nature de la question.

– Attention : Les cartes sont comme un miroir. Vous pouvez aussi poser des questions par l'intermédiaire d'autres personnes. La réponse des cartes implique toujours votre relation avec ces personnes.

– Mélangez les cartes comme vous avez l'habitude de le faire. Aucune règle ne prescrit la façon dont les cartes doivent être mélangées.

– Étalez les cartes selon un arrangement que vous aurez choisi auparavant. Vous pouvez, pour ce faire, consulter la littérature spécialisée, mais aussi suivre votre propre inspiration. Vous devez fixer votre arrangement avant d'interroger les cartes.

– Tirez les cartes comme vous le faites habituellement et posez-les devant vous, face cachée, dans la forme de l'arrangement.

– Retournez maintenant les cartes l'une après l'autre. Ne retournez une carte qu'après avoir lu et interprété la précédente.

– Tout ce qui advient durant l'interrogation de la carte peut être un élément de la réponse attendue.

– La réponse à votre question est fournie par l'ensemble des cartes étalées.

MAJOR
ARCANA

GROSSE
ARKANA

GRANDS
ARCANES

The Magician
Der Magier
Le Magicien

Personal Magic

There is a kind of magic that really works and is not merely a matter of trickery, sleight of hand, hocus-pocus, or stage illusions. Magic, the "possibility of the impossible," is nothing more than becoming one with yourself, with God, and the world. The number of this card—one—cannot be divided by any other number in Tarot. Significantly, the term "indivisible" has the same Latin root as "individual."

We are all artists and magicians. On this card, Dalí himself poses as a "magus," as THE MAGICIAN, displaying paraphernalia from some of his best-known works on the table. He thus draws attention to himself and yet we realize that each individual is being invited to take part—according to their own individual talents and qualities.

On your personal journey, you go through unique experiences and come up with solutions that no one has ever arrived at previously, as if under a wonderful spell. But your personal magic is not really supernatural. It is merely a matter of successfully fashioning your own unique existence by drawing on your special talents and qualities.

The flames in the picture symbolize the life force, the fire of creation and transmutation lying dormant in each of us.

The bread and wine (on the table) stand for the individual's participation in the divine act of creation. The "soft" clock represents the elasticity and uniqueness of your personal life-time, while the scroll on the table implies that you should take command of your own life by making plans and determining your own role.

Like the columns in the composition, all aspects of your personality should complement each other and unite in serving a higher purpose. To this end, it is important to stay open (blue background), to go beyond your current limitations (just as the picture breaks through the upper frame), and to see your work within a larger context (taking into account the upper corners of the image).

Practical advice: *No one can misappropriate or take away your special talents and qualities. Use your imagination, creativity, and communication skills! Make your very own distinctive contribution.*

Persönliche Magie

Es gibt eine Zauberkraft, die tatsächlich funktioniert, die sich nicht in Phantastereien, Tricks oder Gaukeleien erschöpft: Diese Magie, die „Möglichkeit des Unmöglichen", besteht darin, mit sich, mit Gott und der Welt eins zu werden. Die Zahl der Karte, die Eins, ist auf der Ebene der Zahlen des Tarot nicht teilbar, und „unteilbar" heißt auf lateinisch „individuum".

Wir alle sind Künstler und Magier. In diesem Bild inszeniert sich Dalí als Magus und zitiert in den Gegenständen auf dem Tisch einige seiner bekanntesten Werke. Das Bild lenkt unsere Aufmerksamkeit zunächst auf die Person Dalís, verdeutlicht aber auch, dass es darum geht, die eigene Person ins Spiel zu bringen – mit ihren individuellen Begabungen und Möglichkeiten, auf diesem individuellen Weg einzigartige Erfahrungen zu machen und eigene Lösungen zu finden. Das erscheint wie ein wundervoller Zauber, doch ist dieser persönliche Zauber nichts Übernatürliches. Es handelt sich einfach um die erfolgreiche Gestaltung des eigenen Lebens mit all den individuellen Talenten und Eigenarten.

Die Flammen im Bild zeugen von der Lebensenergie, der Erfindungs- und Verwandlungskraft, die in jedem von uns schlummern. Brot und Wein (auf dem Tisch) symbolisieren die persönliche Anteilnahme am göttlichen Schöpfungsprozess, die „weiche" Uhr steht für die Elastizität und Besonderheit der persönlichen Lebenszeit, und die Papierrolle auf dem Tisch versteht sich als Aufforderung, einen Lebensentwurf zu formulieren: einen Plan zu machen und die eigene Rolle zu definieren.

Alle Bausteine der Persönlichkeit sollen sich ergänzen und in einem übergeordneten Ziel vereinigen, wie die Pfeiler im Bild. Dabei gilt es, persönlich offen zu bleiben (blauer Hintergrund), über sich hinauszuwachsen (das Bild durchbricht den oberen Rahmen) und das eigene Werk in einen größeren Kontext zu stellen (siehe obere Bildecken).

Praxistipps: *Ihre ganz persönlichen Chancen kann Ihnen niemand vorenthalten oder wegnehmen. Hier zählen Erfindungsgeist, Kreativität und die Fähigkeit, sich mitzuteilen. Leisten Sie Ihren unverwechselbaren Beitrag!*

Magie personnelle

Il existe une force magique qui fonctionne réellement sans se réduire à des fantasmagories, trucs et autres tours de passe-passe : cette magie, la « possibilité de l'impossible », consiste à ne faire qu'un avec soi, Dieu et le monde. Le chiffre de la carte, le un, n'est pas divisible dans le domaine des chiffres du tarot, et « indivisible » signifie « individuum » en latin. Nous sommes tous des artistes et des magiciens. Dans cette image, Dalí se met lui-même en scène comme magicien et évoque à travers les objets posés sur la table plusieurs de ses œuvres les plus connues. L'image attire d'abord l'attention sur la personne de Dalí tout en soulignant l'importance d'entrer soi-même en jeu – avec ses dons et facultés individuelles –, de faire sur cette voie individuelle des expériences uniques et de trouver des solutions personnelles. Cela semble être un fabuleux sortilège, toutefois cette magie personnelle n'a rien de surnaturel. Il s'agit simplement de l'accomplissement de sa propre vie avec tous ses talents et caractéristiques.

Les flammes expriment l'énergie vitale, le pouvoir d'invention et de métamorphose qui sommeillent en chacun de nous. Le pain et le vin (sur la table) symbolisent la participation personnelle au processus divin de création, la pendule représente l'élasticité et la particularité du temps à vivre, le rouleau de papier traduit l'invitation à formuler un projet de vie : échafauder un plan et définir son propre rôle.

Tous les éléments de la personnalité doivent se compléter et s'unir vers un but supérieur, telles les colonnes sur l'image, tout en restant ouvert (fond bleu), en se dépassant soi-même (l'image transperce le cadre supérieur) et en plaçant sa propre action dans un plus grand contexte (voir les coins supérieurs de la carte).

Conseils pratiques : *Nul ne peut vous révéler vos chances personnelles ou vous les retirer. Seuls comptent ici l'esprit d'invention, la créativité et le sens de la communication. Contribuez vous-même à votre réussite personnelle !*

The High Priestess
Die Hohepriesterin
La Papesse

Inner Voice

High priestesses are encountered throughout human history and mythology as oracular authorities, exemplified by the Pythia of Delphi, sibyls, or prophetesses like Cassandra. Being a mirror, this card counsels you that it is quite correct and effective to seek guidance first and foremost within yourself.

Many tarot decks depict THE HIGH PRIESTESS holding a holy book. She is reading the "script" of her own life. Dalí gives her a scroll to hold, expressing the same idea. This card is all about your own role and your personal way of life, personal taste and style, and about expressing your own opinion.

The predominantly blue hues and the crescent moon symbolize the power of your soul, your inner voice, and your moods—as changeable as the phases of the moon—which decide your success in life.

It is interesting how Dalí depicts the clothing of THE HIGH PRIESTESS. The outer garment (a kind of cloak) is reminiscent of a nun's habit as found in many portrayals of the Mother Mary. But underneath her cloak, the figure wears a black and blue sequined evening gown, imparting a mundane and feline look. Like the cat statue in the left-hand foreground, the big head at the left margin—the "child's head"—represents the unconscious, libidinous mind feeding and tempting the soul with its long tongue.

In sum, THE HIGH PRIESTESS encourages you to develop the power of your own soul and your own inner perceptions in order to mediate between piety and frivolity, nun-like devotion and cat-like instincts. The script of your life should be unrolled and evolved.

Practical advice: *Listen. Become aware of your inner voice and be open to sounds and timbres as well as to silence. Create a space just for yourself. Train your voice and express what matters most to you.*

Eigen-Sinn

In der Geschichte und der Mythologie begegnen uns Hohepriesterinnen als Orakelwesen wie die Pythia von Delphi, als Sibyllen oder als Seherinnen wie Kassandra. Als persönlicher Spiegel sagt uns diese Karte, dass es gut und richtig ist, sich Rat zu holen – und zwar zuerst und zuletzt bei sich selbst!

Viele Tarot-Versionen stellen DIE HOHEPRIESTE-RIN mit einem heiligen Buch dar. Sie liest im „Script", im „Drehbuch" ihres Lebens. Dalí gibt ihr eine Schriftrolle in die Hand und drückt damit den gleichen Gedanken aus: Hier geht es um die eigene Rolle, um eine persönliche Lebensgestaltung, um Geschmack, Stil und Eigen-Sinn, um die Formulierung der eigenen Meinung.

Die vorherrschenden Blautöne und die Mondsichel verweisen darauf, dass es dabei vor allem die Kraft der Seele, die innere Stimme und die persönlichen Stimmungen sind, die über ein gutes Gelingen entscheiden, die sich aber wie die Phasen des Mondes wandeln. Beachtenswert ist die Kleidung der HOHEPRIESTERIN: Das äußere Gewand (ein Umhang) erinnert an die Ordenstracht einer Nonne und an bekannte Marien-Darstellungen, darunter trägt die Bildfigur ein schwarzblaues Abendkleid, das ihr eine mondäne und zugleich katzenhafte Note verleiht. Dieser Eindruck wird durch die Katzenfigur links im Bild unterstrichen. Wie die Katzengestalt steht auch der große Kopf am linken Bildrand, der „Kindskopf", für das Unbewusste, das Triebhafte, das mit seiner großen Zunge das Seelenleben gleichsam füttert und auf die Probe stellt.

Zusammengefasst stellt uns DIE HOHEPRIESTERIN damit die Aufgabe, zwischen Frömmigkeit und Frivolität, zwischen nonnenhafter Andacht und katzenhafter Triebhaftigkeit unsere Seelenkräfte zu aktivieren und unseren Eigen-Sinn zu entwickeln. Die Schriftrolle soll ausgerollt, ent-wickelt werden.

Praxistipps: *Lauschen Sie – achten Sie auf ihre innere Stimme und seien Sie offen für Klänge und Geräusche von außen ebenso wie für die Stille. Richten Sie einen Raum für sich allein ein. Pflegen Sie Ihre Stimme und drücken Sie aus, was Sie bewegt.*

Propre initiative

Dans l'histoire et la mythologie les grandes prêtresses nous apparaissent comme des vestales, telle la Pythie de Delphes, comme des sibylles ou prophétesses, telle Cassandre. Miroir personnel, cette carte nous enseigne qu'il est juste et bon de chercher conseil – d'abord et enfin auprès de soi-même !

De nombreuses versions de tarot représentent LA PAPESSE avec un livre sacré. Elle lit le « script », le « scénario » de sa vie. Dalí met dans sa main un parchemin pour exprimer la même idée : il est question ici de rôle personnel, de la réalisation individuelle de sa propre vie, de goût, de style et de persévérance, de la formulation de son opinion profonde.

Les tons dominants de bleu et le croissant de lune indiquent qu'avant tout la force de l'âme, la voix intérieure et les humeurs passagères influent sur la réussite, mais qu'elles sont variables comme les phases de la lune. L'habit de LA PAPESSE est remarquable : sa cape rappelle le vêtement ecclésiastique d'une nonne et les représentations traditionnelles de Marie, tandis qu'en dessous elle porte une robe du soir bleu-noir, qui lui confère une note à la fois mondaine et féline. Cette impression est renforcée par la présence d'un chat, à gauche de l'image. Comme la figure du chat, la grande tête au bord de l'image à gauche, la « tête d'enfant », représente l'inconscient, l'instinctif, qui à la fois nourrit de sa grande langue la vie de l'âme et la met à l'épreuve.

En résumé, LA PAPESSE nous assigne la mission d'activer nos forces spirituelles entre piété et frivolité, recueillement religieux et érotomanie féline et d'épanouir notre ego profond. Le parchemin doit être littéralement déroulé.

Conseils pratiques : *Écoutez attentivement – suivez votre voix intérieure et restez attentif aux sons et bruits extérieurs comme au silence. Aménagez un endroit pour vous seul. Cultivez votre voix et exprimez tout ce qui vous touche.*

The Empress
Die Herrscherin
L'Impératrice

Your Own True Nature

THE EMPRESS represents the many empresses and queens of yesteryear and today. She is also the Great Goddess of ancient history, the threefold Godhead of Christianity and other religions, the mothers of gods, such as Isis and Mary, and last but not least, the goddesses of love and fertility like Astarte, Aphrodite, and Venus.

The card is a mirror of your own femininity (or of the female qualities in a man), reflecting your personal experiences as a woman and/or with other women, the heritage of your mother, your grandmothers, and your foremothers.

THE EMPRESS has the face of Gala Dalí. Much has been written about the degree to which Gala dominated Dalí. But this card goes way beyond any biographical anecdotes. The expansive, open-ended background locates the central figure—taken from a picture by Delacroix—within a vast realm in front of a sea of possibilities. The imperial orb in her left hand symbolizes fertility as well as the globe, and thus represents the challenge to claim this vast land for oneself and to take command of it. The lily scepter in her right hand is an early symbol of fertility and virility. White stars dancing around the head of the figure elevate her above the blue water and the grayish mountains. This card is all about living a fruitful, flourishing, and star-studded life. Women as well as men are encouraged to become rulers of their own destiny and to take responsibility for their own well-being and fortune.

Practical advice: *In order to be happy and feel good, it is important to create your own realm, and to establish and follow rules that underpin your well-being and the pleasure you experience. Take charge of your daily well-being. Ban false goddesses and foreign empresses from your life!*

Persönliche Natur

DIE HERRSCHERIN erinnert an Kaiserinnen und Königinnen aus Geschichte und Gegenwart. Sie steht auch für die Große Göttin der Frühgeschichte, die dreifache Gottheit im Christentum und anderen Religionen, für Gottesmütter wie Isis und Maria und nicht zuletzt für die Göttinnen der Liebe und der Fruchtbarkeit wie Astarte, Aphrodite und Venus.

Schließlich ist die Karte ein Spiegel der eigenen Fraulichkeit (und der weiblichen Seite im Mann). Sie reflektiert persönliche Erfahrungen als Frau und/oder mit Frauen, das Erbe der Mutter, Großmütter und Ahninnen.

Gala Dalí hat dieser HERRSCHERIN ihr Gesicht geliehen. Es ist manches darüber geschrieben worden, wie sehr Gala über Dalí geherrscht hat, doch bei dieser Karte geht es um mehr als ein rein biografisches Abbild. Der offene, weite Hintergrund zeigt die Bildfigur (angelehnt an ein Bild von Delacroix) inmitten eines großen Reichs und vor einem Meer von Möglichkeiten. Der Reichsapfel in der linken Hand steht für Fruchtbarkeit; er symbolisiert eine Weltkugel und damit die Aufgabe, dieses große, weite Land als eigenes Reich, als eigene Welt in Besitz zu nehmen und zu regieren. Das Lilienzepter in der rechten Hand ist ein altes Fruchtbarkeits- und Potenzsymbol. Um den Kopf der Figur tanzen weiße Sterne, sie erheben sie über das blaue Wasser und die weißgrauen Berge. Es geht hier um ein fruchtbares, blühendes und sternenklares Leben. Für Frauen wie für Männer heißt dies, selbst Herrscherin zu sein, und das bedeutet, das eigene Wohlbefinden in die Hand zu nehmen und dem Glück ein persönliches Antlitz zu verleihen.

Praxistipps: *Damit es Ihnen gut geht und Sie sich wohlfühlen, ist es wichtig, dass Sie Ihr Reich einrichten, Regeln festsetzen und einhalten, die Ihnen Wohlbehagen und Freude garantieren. Übernehmen Sie die Fürsorge für Ihr tägliches Wohlbefinden. Verbannen Sie falsche Göttinnen und fremde Herrscherinnen aus Ihrem Leben!*

Nature personnelle

L'IMPÉRATRICE évoque les impératrices et reines du passé et du présent. Elle représente aussi la Grande Déesse de la préhistoire, la Sainte Trinité du christianisme et d'autres religions, les mères de Dieu comme Isis et Marie et bien sûr les déesses de l'Amour et de la Fécondité comme Astarté, Aphrodite et Vénus.

Enfin, la carte est un miroir de la propre féminité (et de la face féminine enfouie dans l'homme). Elle reflète les expériences personnelles vécues en tant que femme et/ou avec des femmes, l'hérédité transmise par les mères, grands-mères et aïeules.

Gala Dalí a prêté ses traits à L'IMPÉRATRICE. Beaucoup d'encre a coulé à ce sujet, à quel point Gala aurait dominé Dalí, mais cette carte est plus qu'un portrait autobiographique. L'arrière-plan ouvert et vaste présente le personnage (à l'instar d'un tableau de Delacroix) au centre d'un grand empire et devant une mer de possibilités. L'orbe (dans la main gauche du personnage) représente la fécondité ; il symbolise un globe terrestre et par là même la mission de prendre possession de ce pays immense pour en faire son empire, son univers personnel, et le gouverner. Dans la main droite, le sceptre à fleur de lys est un symbole ancien de fécondité et de puissance sexuelle. Autour de la tête de L'IMPÉRATRICE flottent des étoiles blanches et la font s'élever au-dessus de l'eau bleue et des montagnes blanchâtres. Ici étincelle une vie féconde, florissante et limpide. Pour les femmes comme pour les hommes, cela signifie être soi-même impératrice, prendre en main son bien-être personnel et conférer à la chance un visage individuel.

Conseils pratiques : *Pour être en forme et vous sentir bien, il est important de créer un empire, de fixer des règles qui vous garantissent bien-être et bonheur et de s'y tenir. Chassez de votre vie les fausses déesses et les usurpatrices !*

The Emperor
Der Herrscher
L'Empereur

Self-Motivated Pioneer

Emperors and kings, Zeus and Jupiter, and many other father figures have informed this image. It is a mirror of your own masculinity (or of the male qualities in a woman), reflecting your personal experiences as a man and/or with other men, the heritage of your father, your grandfathers and your forefathers. This card is not only a symbol of external (family or public) order, but also of your ability to take charge of your own destiny.

The message of THE EMPEROR should be heeded by both men and women, encouraging the art of self-rule and self-motivation. The lily scepter in the left hand of the figure is a symbol of might and virility, of the life force and fertility. Yet the colorful figure in the foreground, in all its magnificence and vitality, is presented in sharp contrast to the pale desert and dark ruins in the background. The meaning? Our greatest talents will come to nothing, if they are used destructively or if we don't succeed in creating something new out of dereliction. The wasteland must be turned into a garden! Every one of us brings something original into the world, which is waiting to be explored and developed. THE EMPEROR represents the pioneering spirit in us all and the ability to open up new possibilities in life or love.

Dalí shares this interpretation with many other depictions of THE EMPEROR. What is different is the remarkable and unique position of the right hand. This gesture can evoke indecisiveness, or weakness. But by the same token, it may suggest a teasing and coquettish, even camp playfulness. The impact is underscored by the two little birds (symbols of spirit, Eros, willpower, and imagination).

Practical advice: *Put your pioneering spirit to use. Explore your current situation. Don't imitate, innovate! Create your own facts. Be the master of your own game!*

Pionier in eigener Sache

Kaiser und Könige, Zeus, Jupiter und viele andere Vater-
figuren gehören zu den Paten dieser Bildgestalt. Sie ist ein
Spiegel der eigenen Männlichkeit (und der männlichen
Seite in der Frau). Die Karte betrifft die persönlichen
Erfahrungen als Mann und/oder mit Männern, das Erbe
des Vaters, der Großväter und Ahnen. Diese Karte ist
nicht alleine Abbild einer äußeren (familiären oder staat-
lichen) Ordnung, sondern auch ein Symbol für persönliche Selbstbestimmung.

DER HERRSCHER hat Bedeutung für Männer wie
für Frauen und steht für die Kunst, sich selbst zu regieren
und zu motivieren. Das Lilienszepter in der linken Hand
der Bildfigur ist ein Zeichen von Macht und Potenz, von
Lebenskraft und Fruchtbarkeit. Doch der Buntheit,
Pracht und Lebendigkeit der Figur im Vordergrund stehen Wüste, Farblosigkeit und Ruinen im Hintergrund
entgegen. Das bedeutet: Auch die größten Talente sind
wertlos, wenn sie Zerstörug anrichten und aus Ruinen
nichts Neues entstehen lassen. Hier gilt es, „die Wüste in
einen Garten zu verwandeln"! Jeder Mensch bringt etwas
Neues in diese Welt. Dieses Neue will erschlossen werden. Der HERRSCHER ist auch der Pionier, der in uns
allen steckt, die Kraft, die neue Lebens- und Liebesmög-
lichkeiten eröffnet.

Diese Inhalte hat das Dalí-Tarot mit anderen Bildver-
sionen des HERRSCHER gemeinsam. Worin sich das
Dalí-Tarot jedoch unterscheidet, ist die auffallende und
einzigartige Haltung der rechten Hand der Bildfigur.
Diese Geste kann Unentschlossenheit oder Schwäche
darstellen; gleichzeitig aber auch eine neckende, kokette,
auch manierierte Verspieltheit ausdrücken. Die beiden
kleinen Vögel unterstreichen diesen Eindruck (Bedeutung: Geist, Eros, Wille, Phantasie).

Praxistipps: *Setzen Sie Ihren Pioniergeist ein. Untersuchen
Sie die Lage. „Don't imitate, innovate": Schaffen Sie eigene
Tat-Sachen. Machen Sie Ihr Spiel!*

Pionnier dans son propre domaine

Les empereurs et les rois, Zeus, Jupiter et nombre d'autres
figures patriarcales ont inspiré ce personnage. Il est le
reflet de la propre virilité (et de la face virile enfouie dans
la femme). Cette carte renvoie aux expériences personnelles vécues en tant qu'homme et/ou avec des hommes,
l'hérédité transmise par les pères, grands-pères et aïeuls.
Elle n'est pas seulement la reproduction d'un ordre (familier ou étatique) extérieur, mais aussi le symbole d'une
autonomie personnelle.

L'EMPEREUR a de l'importance pour les hommes
comme pour les femmes et incarne l'art de se maîtriser et
de se motiver soi-même. Le sceptre à fleur de lys qu'il tient
dans la main gauche est un signe de pouvoir et de puissance sexuelle, d'énergie vitale et de fécondité. Cependant,
désert, fadeur et ruines à l'arrière-plan font contraste avec
les couleurs, la magnificence et la vivacité du personnage
au premier plan. En d'autres termes : même les plus grands
talents sont sans valeur s'ils sèment la destruction et ne
laissent derrière eux que des ruines. Ici, le mot d'ordre
est : « transformer le désert en un jardin ! », chaque être
humain apporte quelque chose de nouveau dans ce
monde. Cette nouveauté ne demande qu'à être découverte.
L'EMPEREUR est aussi le pionnier en chacun de nous, la
force qui libère les nouveaux sillons de vie et d'amour.

Le Tarot de Dalí partage ces thèmes avec d'autres versions de L'EMPEREUR. Ce qui fait la différence ici est la
position étonnante et originale de la main droite du personnage. Ce geste peut être synonyme d'hésitation et de
faiblesse ; mais il peut également exprimer une coquette-
rie espiègle et ludique. Les deux petits oiseaux soulignent
cette impression (signification : esprit, érotisme, volonté,
imagination).

Conseils pratiques : *Utilisez votre esprit pionnier.
Examinez la situation. « Don't imitate, innovate » : Créez
vos propres champs d'action. Faites vos jeux !*

The High Priest
Der Hierophant
Le Pape

Personal Quintessence

All HIGH PRIESTS of the most diverse religious traditions have one thing in common: the task of interpreting the mysteries of life and organizing the appropriate rites. It is your task today to recognize this power within yourself. The key is right in front of your very own eyes!

The staff with the triple cross points to the Christian pope. In a much broader sense, it is a symbol of a bond, of the interconnections between heaven and earth. The staff is like an antenna, which enables you to receive messages from near and far and transmit others.

The challenge is addressed to the whole person. The differences in scale of the various figures is a metaphor for personal strengths and weaknesses. Both should be utilized, stretching out beyond existing boundaries. The circles and rays around the figure's head symbolize a higher consciousness, which transcends individual personality. For religious-minded people, this card refers to finding one's way to God and making peace with Him. In a broader sense, this card is all about teaching and learning, initiation and understanding. In order to know others, we have to know ourselves and thus become able to appreciate the purpose of our own existence.

What is so special about Dalí's interpretation is that it focuses on the mutual initiation and communication processes between people (or between different aspects of the personality). Aside from the three figures, there is no church and no hint of religious dogma to be seen. But the halo around the head expands the dimensions at issue. Dalí shows that the sacred manifests itself in our daily human interaction. Each person can be a spiritual teacher for every other person.

Practical advice: *Initiate others into your mysteries. Be open to the needs of others.*

Persönliche Quintessenz

Gemeinsam ist den Hierophanten der verschiedensten Glaubensschulen die Aufgabe, Lebensgeheimnisse zu deuten und Riten zu organisieren. Heute kommt es darauf an, diese Kraft in jeder/jedem von uns zu erkennen. Der Schlüssel liegt vor uns!

Der Stab mit dem dreifachen Kreuz verweist auf den Papst im Christentum. In einem allgemeinen Sinn ist er Zeichen der Verbindung, der Übergänge zwischen Himmel und Erde. Der Stab gleicht einer Antenne, mit der man Botschaften von nah und fern empfangen oder dorthin versenden kann.

Der ganze Mensch ist gefragt: Die unterschiedlichen Größen der Bildfiguren stehen für persönliche Stärken und Schwächen. Beide sollen berücksichtigt werden und auch das, was über die eigenen Grenzen hinausgeht: Die Kreise und Strahlen um den Kopf der großen Bildfigur stehen für ein Bewusstsein, das die eigene Person transzendiert. Für religiöse Menschen bedeutet diese Karte, einen Weg zu Gott zu finden und Frieden mit ihm zu schließen. Aber unabhängig davon, ob man von „Gott" spricht oder nicht, geht es bei diesem Bild um Lehren und Lernen, um Einweihung und Verständnis. Ein funktionierendes Selbstverständnis ist die Grundlage dafür, andere zu verstehen, und es hilft uns, den Sinn der eigenen Existenz zu verstehen.

Das Besondere an diesem Dalí-Bild besteht darin, dass es sich auf den wechselseitigen Einweihungs- und Verständigungsprozess zwischen Menschen (oder verschiedenen Seiten der eigenen Person) konzentriert. Denn außer den drei Bildfiguren ist keine Kirche, kein Dogma oder anderes zu erkennen. Der Heiligenschein, der Strahlenkranz, betont zugleich, dass es um größere Dimensionen geht. So macht die Darstellung deutlich, dass sich die Offenbarung des Göttlichen zwischen uns Menschen im Alltag ereignet. Jeder Einzelne kann spiritueller Lehrer sein für andere.

Praxistipps: *Teilen Sie Ihre Geheimnisse und öffnen Sie sich für die Bedürfnisse anderer.*

Quintessence personnelle

Le point commun entre les hiérophantes des confessions les plus différentes est la mission d'interpréter les mystères de la vie et d'organiser des rites. Aujourd'hui, il s'agit de détecter ce pouvoir en chacune et chacun de nous. La clé est à nos pieds!

La crosse à triple croix renvoie au pape de la chrétienté. Dans un sens plus général, elle est signe de liaison, des passages entre le ciel et la terre. La crosse ressemble à une antenne avec laquelle on peut recevoir ou envoyer des messages de près ou de loin.

C'est l'homme dans sa totalité qui est interpellé : les grandes et petites figures de tableaux sont autant de métaphores des forces et faiblesses personnelles. Les deux aspects doivent être pris en considération ainsi que tout ce qui dépasse nos propres limites : les cercles et rayons autour de la tête matérialisent une conscience qui transcende la personne en elle-même. Pour les gens attachés à la religion cette carte aide à trouver le chemin de Dieu et à faire la paix avec Lui. Mais qu'on parle de « Dieu » ou non, cette gravure parle d'enseignement et de leçon, d'initiation et de compréhension. Une image de soi satisfaisante est le fondement pour la compréhension d'autrui et nous aide à comprendre le sens de notre propre existence.

L'originalité de cette image de Dalí réside dans le fait qu'elle se concentre sur le processus d'initiation et de compréhension réciproque entre les hommes (ou entre les diverses facettes de la personnalité). Car à part les trois personnages, aucune Église, aucun dogme ou autre n'est représenté. L'auréole, la couronne de rayons, souligne en même temps qu'il s'agit d'autres dimensions plus élevées. Ainsi, la représentation souligne que la révélation du divin entre nous les humains se révèle au quotidien. Chacun de nous peut être un maître spirituel pour son prochain.

Conseils pratiques : *Partagez vos secrets et ouvrez-vous aux besoins des autres.*

The Lovers
Die Liebenden
Les Amoureux

Paradise and the Shadow

Many of us remember the expulsion from Paradise as recorded in the Bible and in many other traditions. Less well known and yet also a part of our Occidental tradition is the story of man's return to Paradise, of the eternal life beginning on the Day of Judgment. Well, your day of judgment is today!

We long for love, but we may also be afraid to love and/or to be loved. Whether or not love makes us happy depends greatly on what hopes and expectations we hold about "love." As long as you are looking for your "better half," you risk being only half a person. Or we may be looking for someone who is most like ourselves. Ask yourself if this is what you are seeking. For if you are looking for the one who resembles you in every respect, who knows and understands you intimately, that person can only be yourself.

The more pronounced the distinctions, the more precious the points of harmony. Once you have learned to love the differences, the doors to a new paradise will open. However, many shadows and dark clouds will create obstacles on your path. Only love based on the individuality and originality of each partner will lead to this new paradise and be fulfilled (as in the image of the angel), in flights of inspiration and peak experiences going beyond the reach of each individual.

Practical advice: *The little angel in the picture represents the child of the two lovers. This hints at a real child or could be understood in a figurative sense. Every kind of relationship—even the one with yourself or with a business partner—needs a metaphoric "child": a productive result or outcome that bears witness to your partnership, and lives and grows.*

Paradies und Schatten

Viele Menschen kennen die Geschichte von der Vertreibung aus dem Paradies, wie sie in der Bibel und anderen Überlieferungen enthalten ist. Weniger bekannt, jedoch ebenfalls Teil der abendländischen Tradition ist die Geschichte von der Rückkehr ins Paradies, vom ewigen Leben, das am Jüngsten Tag beginnt. Dieser Jüngste Tag ist heute!

Wir sehnen uns nach Liebe, aber wir fürchten uns vielleicht insgeheim auch davor, lieben zu können und/oder geliebt zu werden. Ob wir mit der Liebe glücklich werden, das hängt stark davon ab, welche Ziele und Vorstellungen wir mit „Liebe" verbinden. Solange wir nach unserer „besseren Hälfte" suchen, besteht die Gefahr, dass wir uns halbieren. Oder wir suchen nach einem Maximum an persönlicher Gleichheit: Schauen Sie, wie weit diese Vorstellung Sie trägt.

Wenn Sie einen Menschen suchen, mit dem Sie in jeder Hinsicht übereinstimmen, der Sie genau kennt und versteht, dann gibt es dafür jedenfalls nur einen: Sie selbst. Je deutlicher die Unterschiede, desto fruchtbarer die Gemeinsamkeiten! Sobald wir in der Lage sind, die Unterschiede zu lieben, öffnet sich uns ein neues Paradies! Manch Schatten und manch dunkle Wolke sind auf diesem Weg zu durchdringen. Erst die Liebe auf der Basis von Individualität und Originalität des Einzelnen erreicht das neue Paradies und findet ihren Höhepunkt (wie im Bild in Gestalt des Engels) in beflügelnden Gipfelerlebnissen, die über die Reichweite des einzelnen Menschen hinausführen.

Praxistipps: *Der kleine Engel im Bild steht auch für das Kind der beiden Liebenden. Das kann im konkreten, aber auch im übertragenen Sinne gelten. Jede Art von Beziehung, auch die Beziehung zu sich selbst oder etwa zu Geschäftspartnern, braucht im übertragenen Sinne ein „Kind": produktive Ergebnisse – ein lebendiges Zeugnis einer partnerschaftlichen Zusammenarbeit – mit Leben und Zukunft.*

Paradis et ombre

Beaucoup se souviennent de l'histoire de l'Expulsion du Paradis telle qu'elle est décrite dans la Bible et dans d'autres récits. L'histoire du Retour au Paradis, de la Vie éternelle qui commence le jour du Jugement Dernier, est en revanche méconnue et appartient pourtant à la tradition occidentale. Ce jour du Jugement Dernier est aujourd'hui !

Nous aspirons à l'amour, mais en secret nous avons peut-être peur de pouvoir aimer et/ou d'être aimé. Notre bonheur en amour dépend beaucoup des objectifs et représentations que nous lions au mot « amour ». Tant que nous sommes à la recherche de notre « moitié », nous courons le risque de nous réduire de moitié. Ou bien nous recherchons un maximum de ressemblance personnelle : réfléchissez dans quelle mesure cette idée vous porte.

Si vous cherchez quelqu'un avec qui vous êtes d'accord à tout point de vue, qui vous connaît exactement et vous comprend, une seule personne remplit ces conditions : vous-même. Plus les différences sont marquées, plus les points communs sont enrichissants ! À partir du moment où nous sommes capables d'aimer les différences, un nouveau paradis s'ouvre alors à nous ! Sur ce chemin, ombres et nuages noirs doivent être transpercés. Seul l'amour basé sur l'individualité et l'originalité de l'individu arrive au nouveau paradis et atteint le paroxysme (comme la silhouette de l'ange sur l'image) dans des moments de bonheur suprême qui outrepassent la portée de chaque homme.

Conseils pratiques : *Le petit ange de la carte incarne aussi l'enfant des deux amoureux. Cela peut être pris au sens propre comme au sens figuré. Tout type de relation, y compris la relation avec soi-même ou la relation avec des partenaires commerciaux, porte au sens figuré un « enfant » : des résultats productifs – preuve vivante d'une collaboration collégiale – porteurs de vie et d'avenir.*

The Chariot
Der Wagen
Le Chariot

Chart Your Own Course

THE CHARIOT stands for experiencing and developing one's own personality, which has two aspects: deliberate choice, on the one hand, and the forces of the unconcious, on the other. The Sphinx represents the mysteries of life while the fiery ring stands for ordeals of fire, probably also hinting at burning ambition and fiery commitment.

The large central figure has its back to the viewer. One should pay careful attention to one's other side and explore one's true face and profile. The three red flames blazing in front of the head, chest, and abdomen of the central figure represent energy centers and the three levels of body, mind, and soul that make up the personality.

This card symbolizes the "way of desire," which is the path towards fulfillment of sensible desires and the ability to let go of unfounded fears. Everything you do on the way is worth your while, even if it requires a lot of effort or (apparent) detours. And even the greatest achievements mean nothing, if they do not help you on your way of desire—as wisely coined in the phrase "the journey is its own reward." In many other contexts, the difference between journey and destination is of the utmost importance.

Practical advice: *Assume full responsibility for the shaping of your life path. You cannot get off the chariot, nor relinquish your own karma, but you can strike out in a new direction. The right attitude helps you to accept and develop the positive aspects you encounter but also empowers you to avoid and let go or, alternatively, to integrate and master the "bad." Accept the light and the shadows and turn your darkest fears into golden opportunities and self-fulfillment.*

Einen eigenen Kurs wagen

DER WAGEN steht für die Erfahrung und Entwicklung der eigenen Persönlichkeit, die sich sowohl durch bewusste Steuerung als auch durch Einflüsse des Unbewussten ausbildet. Die Sphinx steht für die Rätsel des Lebens, der Feuerring für Feuerproben, möglicherweise auch für eine Aura mit brennendem Eifer einerseits und flammender Hingabe andererseits.

Die große Bildfigur wendet dem Betrachter den Rücken zu. Man soll sich nicht auf das vordergründig Sichtbare beschränken; auch das eigene Gesicht gilt es, von allen Seiten zu betrachten.

Die drei roten Flammen an Kopf, Brust und Unterleib stehen für die Energiezentren und für die Persönlichkeitsebenen von Körper, Geist und Seele.

So steht diese Karte auch für den „Weg der Wünsche", den Weg zur Erfüllung sinnvoller Träume und der Aufhebung unberechtigter Ängste. Solange man darauf unterwegs ist, lohnt sich alles, was man tut, auch wenn es mit Mühen oder (scheinbaren) Umwegen verbunden ist. Umgekehrt bleiben auch die schönsten Errungenschaften wertlos, wenn sie auf dem Weg der Wünsche nicht weiterhelfen, hier gilt: „Der Weg ist das Ziel"; in vielen anderen Zusammenhängen ist stattdessen der Unterschied zwischen Weg und Ziel entscheidend.

Praxistipps: *Übernehmen Sie Verantwortung für die Gestaltung Ihres Lebensweges. Sie können aus Ihrem Wagen, Ihrem „Karma", nicht aussteigen, aber Sie können ihn in eine neue Richtung lenken. Mit der richtigen Einstellung können Sie das Gute, das Ihnen widerfährt, annehmen und ausbauen, das Schlimme aber entweder vermeiden und loslassen oder integrieren und bewältigen. Akzeptieren Sie Licht und Schatten und verwandeln Sie ihre Ängste in Zuversicht und Selbstentfaltung.*

Oser suivre sa propre voie

LE CHARIOT est synonyme d'expérience et d'évolution de la personnalité qui se forme autant à travers un contrôle conscient que sous l'influence de l'inconscient. Le sphinx incarne les mystères de la vie, le cercle de feu symbolise les épreuves du feu, sans doute aussi un halo de zèle brûlant d'une part et un don de soi enflammé d'autre part.

Le personnage géant tourne le dos à l'observateur. Il faut regarder de près ce dos ; le visage et le profil restent invisibles. Les trois flammes rouges de la tête, de la poitrine et du ventre représentent les centres d'énergie et les niveaux de personnalité du corps, de l'esprit et de l'âme. Aussi la carte figure-t-elle la voie des désirs, le chemin vers l'accomplissement de rêves sensuels et l'évanouissement de peurs infondées. Tant que nous sommes en route, tous nos actes valent la peine, même si des efforts ou d'apparents détours sont nécessaires.

À l'inverse, les plus belles conquêtes restent vaines si elles ne nous font pas progresser sur la voie des désirs. « Le chemin est le but », tel est ici le slogan ; en revanche, dans beaucoup d'autres situations la différence entre chemin et but est déterminante.

Conseils pratiques : *Aménagez vous-même votre chemin de vie. Vous ne pouvez pas descendre de votre chariot, de votre « karma », mais vous pouvez le conduire vers une nouvelle direction. Doté d'une saine attitude, vous pouvez accepter le bien qui vous est fait et l'amplifier, mais aussi éviter le mal et lâcher prise ou bien l'intégrer et le surmonter. Acceptez la lumière et l'ombre et transformez vos peurs en confiance et en épanouissement.*

Justice
Gerechtigkeit
Justice

Mindfulness

It is but a small step from the right attitude associated with THE CHARIOT to JUSTICE, a cardinal virtue known from antiquity. How can we manage to do what is right for us and abstain from that which is false?

The land on the card represents familiar territory and the water, the uncharted territories beyond. In order to judge wisely, you have to connect the known with the unknown—and learn to distinguish one from the other. The scales of justice measure what is only vaguely known. Unclear feelings, thoughts, and physical sensations have to be evaluated, prejudices have to be overcome.

Dalí adapted the woman from one of Lucas Cranach the Elder's famous paintings. Her wild mane represents an abundance of life force, but also the invincible spirit of JUSTICE. Her maidenly body encourages a reappraisal of virginity (a theme already addressed by the card THE HERMIT). Some people consider virginity and innocence to be lost forever with the first sexual encounter. Others regard these virtues as being goals of personal growth that we have to work towards. "Innocence is not something that can be lost, it is something to be gained." (Bertolt Brecht) This kind of virginity and innocence is exemplified by mindfulness and the ability to get involved while avoiding entanglements and overidentification.

Practical advice: *"The more knowledge is contained within a thing, the greater the love." (Paracelsus) Be prepared to criticize and have the courage to praise, but above all, be willing to shed the discerning light of love on every person and event, on both the high and the low points of your life.*

Achtsamkeit

Von der richtigen Einstellung, auf die es beim WAGEN ankommt, ist es nicht weit bis zur Frage der Gerechtigkeit, einer schon aus der Antike bekannten Kardinaltugend: Wie können wir das Richtige tun und das Falsche lassen?

Land und Wasser symbolisieren bekanntes Terrain und unberührte Kontinente jenseits davon. Gerade die Verbindung und Unterscheidung von Bekanntem und Unbekanntem, von Wissen und Nichtwissen ist die Basis der Urteilsbildung. Die Waage misst das Vage. Gefühle, Gedanken und Empfindungen müssen geklärt, mögliche Vorurteile überwunden werden. Die Zahl der Karte, die Acht, klingt auch im deutschen Wort der Achtsamkeit an.

Die Frauenfigur hat Dalí den bekannten Darstellungen bei Lucas Cranach nachgebildet. Die unbändige Mähne steht für eine große Lebenskraft, aber auch für den offenen, unbezwingbaren Geist der Gerechtigkeit. Ihr mädchenhafter Körper gibt Anlass, über den Begriff der Jungfräulichkeit nachzudenken (ein Thema, das bereits auf die Karte des EREMITEN hinweist). Für manche stellen Jungfräulichkeit und Unschuld etwas dar, das wir mit der ersten sexuellen Erfahrung verlieren. Für andere aber geht es um persönliche und charakterliche Entwicklung: „Die Unschuld ist nichts, was man verlieren, sondern eher etwas, was man gewinnen kann" (Bertolt Brecht). Diese Art von Unschuld und Jungfräulichkeit besteht eben in der Achtsamkeit, in der Fähigkeit, Anteil zu nehmen und sich zugleich aus Verstrickungen und Identifikationen zu befreien.

Praxistipps: *„Je mehr Erkenntnis einem Ding innewohnt, desto größer ist die Liebe ..." (Paracelsus). Zeigen Sie Mut zu Kritik und Mut zu Lob, besonders aber die Bereitschaft, jeden Menschen, jedes Ereignis, die Höhepunkte und die Abgründe des Lebens mit Liebe und Kritik zu durchleuchten.*

Vigilance

La saine attitude, si importante dans le cas du CHARIOT, n'est pas très éloignée de la question de la justice, une vertu fondamentale déjà dans l'Antiquité : comment pouvons-nous faire ce qui est juste et nous détourner de ce qui est faux ?

La terre et l'eau symbolisent terrain conquis et continents vierges lointains. La relation entre connu et inconnu, savoir et ignorance est bien la base de notre faculté de jugement. La balance mesure l'indéfini. Sentiments, pensées et sensations doivent être définis, d'éventuels préjugés surmontés. (En allemand, le huit, chiffre de la carte « Acht » se retrouve dans le terme « Achtsamkeit », vigilance. N. d. T.)

Dalí a peint le personnage féminin d'après les fameuses œuvres de Lucas Cranach l'Ancien. La crinière sauvage symbolise une grande vitalité, mais aussi l'indomptable esprit de justice. Son corps de jeune fille donne à réfléchir sur le terme de virginité (un thème qui annonce déjà la carte de L'ERMITE). Pour beaucoup la virginité et l'innocence représentent quelque chose que nous perdons lors de la première expérience sexuelle. Mais pour d'autres une transformation personnelle et caractérielle se produit alors : « L'innocence n'est pas ce que l'on peut perdre, mais plutôt quelque chose que l'on peut gagner » (Bertolt Brecht). Cette forme d'innocence et de virginité consiste bien en une vigilance, en la faculté à la fois de prendre part et se libérer des complications et identifications.

Conseils pratiques : *« Plus la reconnaissance est innée à une chose, plus grand est l'amour... » (Paracelse). Osez la critique et l'éloge, mais surtout l'aptitude à éclairer chaque individu, chaque événement, les hauts et les bas de l'existence par l'amour et la critique.*

The Hermit
Der Eremit
L'Ermite

Healing

It is no accident that the lantern in the picture reminds us of the Biblical parable of the wise and the foolish maidens. (Wise maidens are on the alert and keep their light at the ready.) Dalí drew on a portrait of Luca Pacioli, a Renaissance scholar, a mathematical genius, and the inventor of modern bookkeeping, whose actual life shows some parallels to the symbolic meaning of THE HERMIT.

This card is all about evaluating the sum of your experiences and constantly reorganizing your life accordingly. Every human being brings something original and novel into the world, represented by the embryo in the lantern, the homunculus. Above the head of the figure, we see jewels, some of them egg-shaped. Like the embryo, the egg is a symbol of fertility and of the growth of something new.

Your light gets stronger as you resolve your own contradictions. If you do not assume responsibility for your life or if you retreat into incompetence or irresponsibility, you will fail to approach the magnificent power of THE HERMIT. He exemplifies rather a person who tackles his problems when appropriate and solves them. As such, this card is all about using your own light to heal and sanctify your world and to transform the earth back into its "virginal" state.

Practical advice: *This card sometimes signals a need for rest and withdrawal, but more often, for commitment and effort and for accepting responsibility. Pay your debts—in a material as well as a moral sense. Increase your own wealth, wellness and well-being as well as that of your fellow human beings.*

Heilung

Die Laterne im Bild erinnert nicht zufällig an das biblische „Gleichnis von den klugen und den törichten Jungfrauen" (die klugen Jungfrauen sind wachsam und halten ihr Licht bereit). Dalí hat das Bildnis von Luca Pacioli verwendet, eines Renaissancegelehrten, der als Rechenkünstler und Erfinder der modernen Buchhaltung einige Parallelen zum allgemeinen, sinnbildlichen Gehalt des EREMITEN aufweist.

Diese Karte fordert nämlich dazu auf, die Summe aus den eigenen Erfahrungen zu ziehen und sein Leben immer wieder neu zu ordnen. Jeder Mensch bringt etwas Einzigartiges, Neues in die Welt; dieses Neue stellt sich als Homunkulus, als Embryo in der Laterne dar. Über dem Kopf der Bildfigur sehen wir Juwelen, einige in Form eines Eis. Wie der Embryo ist auch das Ei ein Symbol für Fruchtbarkeit und das werdende Neue.

In der Aufarbeitung der Widersprüche in uns und um uns herum verstärkt sich das Licht. Nicht die Flucht vor der Verantwortung in Unzuständigkeit oder Unzurechnungsfähigkeit bringt uns der überragenden Kraft des EREMITEN näher. Er verkörpert vielmehr einen Menschen, der sich seinen Problemen stellt und sie löst. So gesehen geht es auch darum, mit unserem „Licht" unsere Welt in Ordnung zu bringen, sie zu heilen und zu heiligen, die Erde in einen „jungfräulichen" Zustand zu versetzen.

Praxistipps: *Manchmal signalisiert diese Karte Ruhe und Rückzug, öfter jedoch engagierte Bemühungen, ein höheres Maß an Verantwortung und Bereinigung. Lösen Sie Schulden ab, materielle wie moralische. Vermehren Sie den Wohlstand, das Wohlsein und das Wohlbehagen für sich und für möglichst viele Ihrer Mitmenschen.*

Guérison

La lanterne n'est pas sans rappeler la parabole biblique des « vierges sages et folles » (les vierges sages sont vigilantes et ont toujours leurs lampes près d'elles). Dalí s'est servi du tableau de Luca Pacioli, savant de la Renaissance, génie du calcul et inventeur de la comptabilité moderne, qui présente quelques parallèles avec le caractère général et symbolique de L'ERMITE.

Cette carte invite en effet à tirer les conséquences de ses propres expériences et à remettre sans cesse sa vie en ordre. Chaque être humain apporte quelque chose d'unique, de nouveau en venant au monde ; cette nouveauté se présente comme homoncule, comme embryon dans la lanterne. Au-dessus de la tête du personnage nous voyons des bijoux, certains en forme d'œuf. Comme l'embryon, l'œuf est un symbole de fécondité et de la nouveauté en devenir.

En surmontant les contradictions en nous et autour de nous, nous amplifions la lumière. La force extraordinaire de L'ERMITE ne nous enseigne pas la fuite loin de la responsabilité dans la veulerie et l'ineptie. Il incarne au contraire un homme qui fait face à ses problèmes et les résout. Il s'agit aussi de mettre notre univers en ordre à l'aide de notre « lumière », de le guérir et de le sanctifier, de rendre à la terre son état « virginal ».

Conseils pratiques : *Parfois la carte signalise calme et retrait, mais le plus souvent engagement et efforts, un plus grand sens de responsabilité et de purification. Payez vos dettes, matérielles comme morales. Augmentez le confort, le bien-être et la sérénité pour vous-même et pour le plus grand nombre des personnes de votre entourage.*

Wheel of Fortune
Rad des Schicksals
La Roue de Fortune

Great Resolution

If you submit yourself to the hands of fate, your individual life will be enriched with universal components: "You only live twice!" Do not exhaust your energy by simply trying to get by. Your life is meant to be much more than plain day-to-day survival or a heroic struggle for existence.

The picture shows the zodiac, reminding us of a witch board. Outside the circle, five figures can be seen based on well-known depictions of the four evangelists and also representing the four elements earth, fire, air, and water. On top of the wheel, there is an Oriental man holding a scimitar.

The disc in the middle is divided into two parts, indicating human consciousness and the unconcious mind. Both parts of the image complement each other, but differences are also apparent. The lower section is full of symbols and signs, while the upper areas are empty. This might suggest that the messages of the unconscious are conveyed through symbols alone.

The Greek word "symbol" in a general sense means, "that which has been thrown together," an appropriate concept for this card. The wholeness of the self can only be achieved by uniting consciousness and the unconscious mind. If the individual is reconciled with his destiny, he will be in harmony with the world and experience synchronicity and resonance.

Practical advice: *You learn to work in harmony with your destiny by lovingly—and critically—accepting "chance" and correlations that are beyond your comprehension. Tarot constitutes an ideal training ground, as it allows you to make use of coincidences. For the next ten days, draw a card every day!*

Große Lösung

Im Zusammenspiel mit dem Schicksal wird das individuelle Leben um die universelle Komponente bereichert, es wird gleichsam verdoppelt: „Du lebst nur zweimal!" Verausgaben Sie Ihre Kräfte nicht darin, das Überleben zu sichern. Weder das bloße Überleben noch ein heroisches „Über-Leben" stellt den Gipfel Ihrer Möglichkeiten dar.

Das Bild zeigt einen Tierkreis, dieser erinnert an ein „sprechendes Tischchen", ein sogenanntes Witchboard. Außerhalb des Kreises sind fünf Figuren zu sehen, die eine Variation bekannter Darstellungen der vier Evangelisten und der vier Elemente Feuer, Wasser, Luft und Erde darstellen; oben auf dem Rad befindet sich eine orientalische Gestalt mit Krummsäbel.

Die Scheibe in der Mitte ist in zwei Teile geteilt, womit das Bewusste und das Unbewusste im Menschen angedeutet werden. Beide Hälften ergänzen sich, wenngleich sich auch Unterschiede zwischen ihnen erkennen lassen. Die untere Hälfte enthält Symbole und Zeichen, während die Felder der oberen leer sind. Das könnte darauf verweisen, dass die Botschaften des Unbewussten nur über Symbole zu uns sprechen.

Das griechische Wort Symbol bedeutet jedoch auch generell „das Zusammengeworfene" und wird somit zu einem wichtigen Begriff für diese Karte. Nur im Zusammenwirken von Bewusstem und Unbewusstem kann sich ein vollständiges Selbst entwickeln. Und das Zusammenspiel von Person und Schicksal sorgt für Resonanzen und Synchronizitäten (Gleichzeitigkeiten) zwischen uns und dem Lauf der Welt.

Praxistipps: *Die Zusammenarbeit mit dem Schicksal beginnt und wächst mit der liebevollen und gleichsam kritischen Annahme von „Zufällen" und Zusammenhängen, die über das eigene Verständnis hinausgehen. Die Arbeit mit dem Zufall, wie sie gerade das Tarot-Kartenlegen er-laubt, ist ein ideales Training dafür. Ziehen Sie in den nächsten zehn Tagen jeweils eine Tageskarte!*

Grand tirage

En interaction avec le destin la vie individuelle s'enrichit des élément universels, elle se voit multipliée par deux : « On ne vit que deux fois ! » Ne gaspillez pas vos forces à assurer votre survie. Ni la simple survie ni une héroïque vie « au-dessus » ne constitue le summum des possibilités.

La carte présente un zodiaque qui ressemble à une « tablette parlante », à un witchboard. À l'extérieur du cercle évoluent cinq figures qui représentent une variation de célèbres portraits des quatre évangélistes et quatre éléments feu, eau, air et terre ; sur le bord en haut se trouve une silhouette orientale portant un cimeterre.

Au centre, le cercle est séparé en deux, allusion au conscient et à l'inconscient chez l'homme. Les deux moitiés se complètent tout en présentant des différences entre elles. La moitié inférieure contient des symboles et des signes alors que les cases de la moitié supérieure sont vides. Cela pourrait être l'indication que les messages de l'inconscient ne nous sont transmis que par symboles.

Néanmoins, le mot grec symbole signifie en général « mettre ensemble » et devient par là même riche de sens pour cette carte. Une personnalité complète ne peut se développer que par la concomitance du conscient et de l'inconscient. Et l'interaction de la personne et du destin crée des résonances et des simultanéités entre nous et le cours du monde.

Conseils pratiques : *La collaboration avec le destin débute et évolue grâce à l'acceptation à la fois bienveillante et critique des « hasards » et coïncidences qui surpassent notre entendement. À cet effet, le travail avec le destin, tel que le permet la lecture des cartes du tarot, est un entraînement idéal. Tirez quotidiennement une carte dans les dix prochains jours !*

Strength
Kraft
Force

The Art of Loving

This card is all about dealing deliberately with your vital energy and lust of life, the love all of creation.

The flowers on the card may be the flowers of love, but could also be Baudelaire's "flowers of evil." Dalí's signature integrates the swastika, an ancient Indo-Aryan symbol of the sun and of life.

The beastly creature on the left resembles a toad, at first sight, but under closer scrutiny, the body of a lion becomes apparent along with the teeth of a combat dog. These are all that kind of animal that longs to be released from a curse, like the bewitched prince of many fairy tales.

The key to discovering your own strength is a loving and determined handling of your id (libido, instinct, energy). The woman and the animal together evoke the archetypal story of "Beauty and the Beast." If the Beast is released from its curse, Beauty gains her freedom, too. This card is not just about strength, power, and lust, but also stands for the cultivation of your personality, which will enable you to minimize harmful influences on your life and which allows your own creative forces to blossom.

If you succeed, you will be able to grow beyond the limitations of your ego and you will learn where you have to draw the line.

Practical advice: *Beware of useless ideals and of violence in the name of love. Give your lust for life another chance. Living fully means always being totally in the present. This is the card of the high points and peak experiences in sexuality as well as in all other aspects of life.*

Die Kunst des Liebens

Hier geht es um den bewussten Umgang mit der Lebenskraft und die bewusste Lust, die Liebe zur Schöpfung.

Die abgebildeten Blumen können sowohl als die Blumen der Liebe, wie auch als die berühmten „Blumen des Bösen" im Sinne Baudelaires gedeutet werden. Dalís Signatur bildet eine Swastika, das alte Symbol für Sonne und Leben.

Die tierähnliche Gestalt erinnert auf den ersten Blick an eine Kröte, bei näherer Betrachtung zeigt sie einen Löwenkörper sowie das Gesicht und die Zähne eines Kampfhundes, allesamt Tiergestalten, die erlöst werden müssen – wie der verzauberte Prinz im Märchen.

Insgesamt liegt der Schlüssel zur Kraft hier im liebevollen und energischen Umgang mit dem „Es" (Libido, Trieb, Energie). Frau und Tier zusammen greifen den Archetyp von der Schönen und dem Biest auf. Die Erlösung der einen hängt mit der Erlösung des anderen zusammen. So steht diese Karte nicht nur für Kraft und Lust, sondern auch für eine persönliche Kultur, in der es uns gelingt, schädliche Einflüsse auf das eigene Leben zu minimieren und die schöpferischen Kräfte zum Blühen zu bringen.

Wir wachsen über die Grenzen des eigenen Ichs hinaus und erfahren, wo die richtigen Grenzen zu ziehen sind.

Praxistipps: *Hüten und schützen Sie sich vor falschen Idealen und vor Gewalt im Namen der Liebe. Geben Sie der Lebenslust eine neue Chance. Mit voller Kraft zu leben, heißt, vollständig im Augenblick anwesend zu sein. So ist dies auch die Karte der Höhepunkte und der Gipfelerlebnisse in der Sexualität und in allen anderen Bereichen des Lebens.*

L'art d'aimer

Ici le rapport conscient avec la vitalité et le plaisir, l'amour de la Création, est le thème central.

Les fleurs peuvent être interprétées comme les fleurs de l'amour mais aussi comme les fameuses « fleurs du mal » au sens baudelairien. La signature de Dalí représente une swastika, le symbole antique du soleil et de la vie.

L'animal représenté rappelle une tortue au premier abord, si l'on y regarde de plus près il a le corps d'un lion et le visage d'un chien de combat, animaux qui doivent être délivrés comme le prince ensorcelé d'un conte de fées.

En résumé, la clé de la FORCE réside ici dans le rapport énergique avec le « ça » (libido, instinct, énergie). La femme et l'animal évoquent ensemble l'archétype de la belle et de la bête. La délivrance de l'une dépend de la délivrance de l'autre. La carte ne se fonde pas seulement sur la force et le plaisir, mais aussi sur une culture personnelle grâce à laquelle nous parvenons à minimiser les effets néfastes sur notre vie et à faire s'épanouir les forces créatrices.

Nous grandissons au-delà des frontières du moi et apprenons à poser les vraies limites.

Conseils pratiques : *Détournez-vous et protégez-vous des faux idéaux et de la violence au nom de l'amour. Donnez une nouvelle chance à la joie de vivre. Vivre de toutes ses forces signifie être pleinement présent dans l'instant. Ainsi avons-nous ici la carte des orgasmes en sexualité et dans tous les autres domaines de la vie.*

The Hanged Man
Der Gehängte
Le Pendu

Passion

At a first glance, the upside-down position of THE HANGED MAN appears to be rather grotesque. No wonder that strangeness, rapture, and the absurd are all elements of this card. But there is another important element: THE HANGED MAN is at peace with the world, except that his point of reference is not worldly but transcendental. His essence is suspended in the heavenly, the transcendental, in a manner reminiscent of religious images. At the same time, the picture could be interpreted as an underwater world, a land of dreams, or an otherworld, in which THE HANGED MAN is immersed.

Saint Francis' motto was "Metanoeite," which can be translated as "Turn around and change." His symbol is the St. Anthony's Cross. Saul turned into Paul. Stories about shamans, sorcerers like Merlin, or gods like Odin abound, who all had to undergo severe trials, during which each experienced a transformation.

On the other hand, the picture hints at inappropriate passivity and at a person who simply "hangs on." THE HANGED MAN believes in the thing to which he is attached. And he is attached to what he believes. How tragic it would be if the belief turned out to be superstition.

So it is important to evaluate your own belief system, which may often involve turning everything upside down and completely changing your own point of view.

Practical advice: *Reassess your own beliefs and presumptions. If you have found your belief system to be valid, do not hesitate to place the utmost confidence in it. A meaningful faith and a purposeful passion are a great boon.*

Passion

Auf den ersten Blick erscheint die „Hängepartie" der Kartengestalt grotesk. Das Verrückte, Entrückte wie auch das Absurde gehören sicherlich zum Inhalt dieser Karte. Doch es geht noch um etwas anderes: DER GEHÄNGTE scheint in sich zu ruhen, nur dass sein Bezugspunkt eben nicht auf der Erde, nicht irdisch definiert ist. Seine „Basis" ruht im Himmlischen, im Transzendenten und erinnert an religiöse Bilder. Zugleich erinnert das Bild auch an eine Art Unterwasserwelt, ein Land der Träume, eine Anderswelt, in die der Gehängte hineinreicht.

„Metanoeite", zu deutsch „Kehret um und wandelt Euch", lautete der Wahlspruch des Franz von Assisi, dessen Symbol das Antoniuskreuz ist. Saulus wandelte sich zum Paulus, und es gibt zahlreiche Geschichten von Schamanen, von Zauberern wie Merlin oder Gottheiten wie Odin, die allesamt Prüfungen zu durchlaufen hatten, aus denen sie verändert hervorgingen.

Andererseits gibt das Bild natürlich auch einen Hinweis auf eine unangemessene Passivität, auf einen Menschen, der „sich hängen lässt". DER GEHÄNGTE glaubt an das, woran er hängt. Und er hängt an dem, woran er glaubt. Tragisch, wenn sich der Glaube als Aberglaube herausstellt.

Es kommt daher darauf an, den eigenen Glauben zu prüfen. Gerade dafür ist es manchmal notwendig, alles auf den Kopf zu stellen und den eigenen Standpunkt umzukehren.

Praxistipps: *Untersuchen Sie die Grundlagen ihres Glaubens und scheuen Sie sich nicht, sich ihm nach gründlicher Prüfung restlos anzuvertrauen: Ein sinnvoller Glaube und eine bewusste Passion sind ein hohes Gut!*

Passion

À première vue le personnage suspendu sur la carte est plutôt grotesque. Le thème véhiculé dans cette carte est la folie, l'isolement et aussi l'absurde. Mais il est question aussi d'autre chose : LE PENDU a l'air d'être bien avec lui-même, simplement son point d'attache n'est pas sur la terre, n'est pas de nature terrestre. Sa base est de nature céleste, transcendentale, et rappelle les images pieuses. L'image évoque aussi une sorte de monde sous-marin, un pays de rêves, un monde étranger que le pendu semble rejoindre.

« Metanoeite », en français « changez, transformez-vous », telle était la devise de François d'Assise dont l'emblème est la croix de saint-Antoine. Saul se métamorphosa en Paul, et il existe une multitude d'histoires de chamans, de magiciens comme Merlin ou de divinités comme Odin, qui tous durent traverser des épreuves dont ils ressortirent transformés.

D'autre part, l'image fournit aussi l'indication d'une passivité déplacée, d'un être qui se laisse aller. LE PENDU croit à ce à qui il est accroché. Et il est accroché à ce qu'il croit. Tragédie si la croyance s'avère une superstition.

Il est important d'examiner sa propre croyance. Pour ce faire, il est parfois nécessaire de tout renverser et de changer de point de vue.

Conseils pratiques : *Examinez les fondements de vos croyances et, après un examen approfondi, n'hésitez pas à vous confier à elles sans limite : une foi bien fondée et une passion vécue sont un bien précieux !*

Death
Tod
La Mort

Living Uniqueness

This card is all about something coming to an end. Depending on whether you consider this good or bad, you will experience joy or sorrow. The card also warns that there is something you must attend to. You have to let go of something and create some space, in which the rose may blossom. The wide-open landscape and the long lines emphasize the impression of great openness, perhaps even eternity. The high-flying swallow evokes a feeling of exuberance.

The branches growing out of the bent figure on the left may be interpreted as signs of new life. Note that this card is not the last of the 22 Major Arcana, but only number 13. Life goes on. The blooming rose reminds us that life and especially love are stronger than death. One can be dead while still alive. And one may live long after one has died. DEATH is not nothingness. It is the destroyer of illusions and of all that no longer fits into your life. It is a part of a process of metamorphosis.

The aim is for all of your desires and fears to be cleansed and clarified. Thus we become willing and ready again and serenely open. The question of what you want to experience, create, and harvest in this life becomes even more pressing.

This card can also imply that you feel threatened by violence and destruction, perhaps to the point of glorifying death. Brutality does not only hurt the other, but yourself as well. Learn to put your power to good uses on your own behalf, not to use it against others.

Practical advice: *If you want your life to be fruitful, you have to attend to what needs to be done at the right moment. Which one of your fruits is ripe? What is still missing? What is no longer fitting? How can you strive towards the fulfillment of your desires?*

Gelebte Einmaligkeit

Die Karte TOD steht für ein Ende. Je nachdem, ob etwas Schönes oder Schlimmes sein Ende erfährt, spüren Sie hier Trauer oder Freude. Das Bild besagt aber auch: Es gibt etwas zu erledigen. Hier heißt es, loslassen und Platz schaffen, damit die Rose erblühen kann. Das weite Land und die langen Linien unterstreichen den Eindruck von Offenheit, möglicherweise von Ewigkeit. Die hochfliegende Schwalbe drückt ein Gefühl der Hoch-Stimmung aus.

Die Zweige auf der gebückten Figur links im Bild lassen sich als Zeichen eines neuen Lebens deuten. Außerdem ist die Karte nicht die letzte der 22 großen Arkana, sondern die Nummer 13. Das Leben geht weiter, und die blühende Rose bedeutet, dass das Leben und die Liebe stärker sind als der Tod. Man kann tot sein, lange bevor man stirbt, und man kann leben, lange nachdem man gestorben ist. So oder so bedeutet der TOD nicht Nichts. Er bedeutet die Zerstörung von Illusionen, die Aufhebung von Überaltertem, ist Teil aller Wandlungsprozesse.

Ziel ist eine Reinigung und Klärung unserer Wünsche und Ängste. Wir gewinnen eine neue Bereitschaft und eine abgeklärte Offenheit. Unser Wirken geht über den Tod hinaus. Umso dringender stellt sich die Frage, was wir in diesem Leben ernten, erleben und gestalten wollen.

Die Karte kann allerdings auch bedeuten, dass man sich von Gestalt und Zerstörung bedroht fühlt oder den Tod gar verherrlicht. Mit brutaler Härte schadet man jedoch nicht nur anderen, sondern letztlich auch sich selbst. Man muss lernen, Kraft und Gewalt nicht gegen andere, sondern für sich einzusetzen.

Praxistipps: *Wenn ein Leben Früchte tragen soll, muss im passenden Rhythmus das Nötige für die gewünschte Ernte getan werden. Welche Früchte sind jetzt reif? Welche Ziele haben sie noch nicht erreicht? Was passt nicht mehr zu Ihnen? Wie können Sie Ihren Wünschen Nachdruck verleihen?*

Unicité vécue

La carte de LA MORT signifie la fin. Si quelque chose de beau ou de tragique finit, vous éprouvez de la joie ou de la tristesse. Mais l'image signale aussi : quelque chose doit être réglé. Il s'agit ici de lâcher prise et de faire de la place pour que la rose puisse fleurir. Le paysage étendu et les lignes allongées soulignent l'impression d'ouverture, peut-être d'éternité. L'hirondelle volant haut dans le ciel exprime un sentiment d'euphorie.

Les branches que tient la silhouette courbée à gauche de l'image peuvent être le signe d'un vie nouvelle. En outre la carte n'est pas la dernière des 22 grands arcanes, mais la carte n° 13. La vie continue et la rose en fleur témoigne que la vie et l'amour sont plus forts que la mort. On peut être mort longtemps avant de mourir et l'on peut vivre, longtemps après avoir trépassé. De toute façon la mort n'est pas vide de sens. Elle signifie la destruction d'illusions, l'anéantissement de ce qui est trop vieux, elle fait partie de tous les processus de changement.

Le but est un épurement et une clarification de nos désirs et de nos peurs. Nous gagnons une nouvelle disponibilité et une limpide ouverture d'esprit. Nos actions dépassent le stade de la mort. La question d'autant plus cruciale se pose sur ce que nous voulons récolter, vivre et construire dans cette vie.

Mais la carte peut aussi vouloir dire que l'on se sent menacé par la violence et la destruction ou que la mort est glorifiée Toutefois, la brutalité ne nuit pas seulement aux autres, elle se retourne finalement contre soi. Il faut apprendre à ne pas employer la force et la violence contre l'autre mais pour soi-même.

Conseils pratiques : *Si une vie doit porter des fruits, il faut faire le nécessaire à un rythme approprié pour avoir la récolte souhaitée. Quels fruits sont mûrs maintenant – quels résultats font encore défaut? Qu'est-ce qui ne vous convient plus? Comment pouvez-vous renforcer vos désirs?*

Temperance
Mäßigkeit
Tempérance

True Will

This image differs from all the others in Dalí's tarot deck. The colors are relatively pale, creating a somewhat over-exposed impression. The image is more like a sketch then a finished painting and it also seems to be less artful than the others. All these features have given rise to consider-able speculation. Rachel Pollack has called the picture a "crude comic"; others consider it to be a rather awkward homage to Dalí's lady friend Amanda Lear, while still oth-ers simply suspect that Dalí didn't know what to do with a card called TEMPERANCE.

In the upper left corner, we can see some letters painted over in blue, but these also fail to explain the true meaning of the card. Either it is just a blunder, a changeling among the 78 cards, or its meaning lies in a different realm alto-gether. Even in ancient Greece, long before the first tarot cards were created, temperance was considered to be one of the cardinal virtues. It has to do with the right measure of all things and with basic human creativity.

We will not find our own true measure, our art, and our own style of living by looking up to idols and masters. What seems to be a foundling among Dalí's tarot cards is really a provocation: the card urges us to become active and as an artist and a master of the art of life in designing our own lives.

Traditionally, TEMPERANCE is considered to be a fire card. Purification through fire sloughs off all dross, allowing true will to be reborn. This can only be recovered by giving up the position of commentator and spectator and becoming an active participant in life.

Practical advice: *Existing facts may be melted down and newly forged. Joyfully change the world and begin to play with new possibilities. Establish your own "creativity workshop." In your daily life, find a time and place to take a break and tarry awhile on a regular basis.*

Der wahre Wille

Dieses Bild unterscheidet sich grundlegend von den anderen des Dalí-Tarot. Die Farben sind relativ blass, es wirkt wie überbelichtet, ist eher skizzenhaft angelegt und scheinbar weniger kunstvoll als andere. Damit hat diese Karte Anlass zu Spekulationen gegeben. Rachel Pollack nannte sie einen „kruden Comic", andere vermuteten eine eher unbeholfene Huldigung von Salvador Dalí an seine Freundin Amanda Lear, und wieder andere schlossen schlicht, Dalí habe eben mit „Mäßigkeit" nichts anfangen können. Oben links erkennt man einige Buchstaben unter blauer Farbe, aber auch sie geben keinen Hinweis auf die Bedeutung dieses Bildes.

Entweder ist diese Karte gleichsam ein Missgriff, ein Wechselbalg unter den 78 Karten, oder ihre Bedeutung ist eine andere. Schon in der Antike, lange bevor es die ersten Tarot-Karten gab, war die Besonnenheit – und mit ihr der Aspekt des Maßhaltuns – eine der vier Kardinaltugenden. Es geht um das Maß der Dinge, um die elementare menschliche Schöpferkraft.

Dieses Maß, diese Kunst und Lebenskunst finden wir nicht, indem wir zu Idolen und Meistern aufblicken. Das scheinbare Findelkind unter Dalís Tarot-Karten ist eine Provokation: Die Karte fordert uns auf, selbst aktiv zu werden, als Künstler und Lebenskünstler einen eigenen Lebensentwurf zu skizzieren.

Traditionell gilt die MÄSSIGKEIT als eine Feuerkarte. In der Läuterung des Feuers werden Schlacken abgestoßen und der wahre Wille neu geboren. Der wahre Wille wird erst dann gefunden, wenn wir den Standpunkt des kommentierenden Betrachters aufgeben und selbst ins Bild und ins Geschehen eintreten.

Praxistipps: *Bestehendes kann eingeschmolzen und neu geschmiedet werden. Wenden Sie sich der lustvollen Verwandlung ihrer Welt, dem Spiel mit neuen Möglichkeiten zu. Richten Sie sich eine „Kreativitätswerkstatt" ein: einen Ort und eine Zeit im Tagesablauf, wo Sie regelmäßig verweilen.*

La vraie volonté

Ce portrait est différent des autres du Tarot de Dalí. Les couleurs sont relativement fades, il semble suréclairé et plutôt conçu comme une esquisse, avec moins de raffinement que les autres. La carte a donné lieu à maintes spéculations. Rachel Pollack l'a qualifiée de « grossière BD », d'autres y virent un hommage maladroit de Salvador Dalí à son amie Amanda Lear, et d'autres encore en concluent simplement que Dalí n'était guère inspiré par cette carte. En haut à gauche on peut voir quelques lettres teintées de bleu, mais elles n'apportent aucune indication sur le sens de cette image. Soit la carte est en quelque sorte une erreur, un changeling parmi les 78 cartes, soit sa signification est tout autre. Dès l'Antiquité, longtemps avant l'apparition des premières cartes de tarot, la tempérance était l'une des quatre vertus cardinales. Elle consiste en la mesure des choses, en la force élémentaire de création humaine.

Nous ne trouvons pas cette mesure, art et art de vivre, en admirant les idoles et les maîtres. Cet « enfant trouvé » parmi les cartes du tarot de Dalí est une provocation : la carte nous incite à être nous-mêmes actifs, à esquisser notre propre projet de vie en artiste et bon vivant.

La TEMPÉRANCE est traditionnellement une carte de feu. Dans la purification par le feu les toxines sont rejetées et la vraie volonté renaît. Nous ne retrouvons la vraie volonté qu'en quittant le point de vue de l'observateur et en entrant nous-mêmes dans l'action.

Conseils pratiques : *Tout ce qui existe déjà doit être fondu et reforgé. Tournez-vous vers la voluptueuse métamorphose de votre univers, le jeu des nouvelles chances. Aménagez-vous un « atelier de créativité » : un lieu et une heure de la journée où vous séjournez régulièrement.*

The Devil
Der Teufel
Le Diable

EL DIABLO XV

XV THE DEVIL ♂

Creative Tampering with Taboo

The card depicts a hermaphrodite figure with a wild mane, a horned head, and a further horn on one knee, holding a wand or a flute in its hand and bouncing off some kind of pedestal. Two black arms release the figure or try to grab at it. This card appears strange at first glance, but it cleverly avoids a stereotypical portrayal of the Devil. So we are able to ask, "What meaning does the Devil have for us today?" Each and every human being brings something new into the world, but we all have certain qualities and peculiarities that do not fit into the present framework. Every human being continues the story of creation—and therefore is bound eventually to enter the realm of taboo.

THE DEVIL card clearly indicates that some kind of taboo has been violated. What was implicit now becomes visible. This can be used to your advantage because you can now take on the task of openly dealing with taboos, affirming meaningful ones, and getting rid of others that are senseless.

Don't be put off by the bully. This is your chance to break some old horns. On the one hand, THE DEVIL represents a vampire and a real burden and vexation. No wonder we are afraid. Yet this is our opportunity to rid ourselves of the darkness that we have finally recognized for what it is. On the other hand, THE DEVIL represents the "prodigal son," that part of us that we have always tended to deny and neglect although we secretly and rightfully long for it. Now is the time to bring the prodigal son home.

Practical advice: *Once you have shed light onto the darkness, the vampire will turn to dust and the hidden will take on shape and color as it emerges. Dare to face the unknown and observe it closely until you can decide how much of it to use and what to discard.*

Tabuarbeit

Eine hermaphroditische Gestalt mit wilden Haaren, Hörnern am Kopf und einem Horn am Knie trägt einen Stab oder eine Flöte und verlässt einen Sockel. Zwei schwarze Arme lassen sie los oder greifen nach ihr. Das Bild mag befremdlich wirken, vermeidet jedoch eine klischeehafte Darstellung des Teufels. So lässt sich genauer fragen, was der Teufel für uns heute bedeutet. Jeder Mensch bringt etwas Neues in die Welt, darunter auch Eigenarten und Qualitäten, die nicht einfach in den Rahmen des Bestehenden hineinpassen. Jeder Mensch schreibt auf seine Art die Schöpfungsgeschichte weiter – und berührt damit irgendwann auch Tabubereiche.

Die Karte DER TEUFEL signalisiert, dass die Schwelle des Tabus überschritten ist. Was zuvor unterschwellig vorhanden war, wird nun sichtbar. Eben darin liegt der Vorteil, aber auch die Aufgabe; man muss sich mit Tabus auseinandersetzen, sinnvolle Tabus beachten oder sogar neue etablieren und sinnlose abbauen.

Lassen Sie sich nicht ins Bockshorn jagen: Hier bietet sich die Chance, ein paar alte „Hörner" abzustoßen. Auf der einen Seite stellt der Teufel einen Vampir, eine wirkliche Last und Bedrohung dar. Davor fürchten wir uns zu Recht, und diesen Teil der Finsternis können wir jetzt endlich loswerden, weil wir ihn erstmals erkennen. Andererseits verkörpert der Teufel ein „Kellerkind", den Teil von uns, den wir bisher stiefmütterlich oder stiefväterlich behandelt haben, obwohl wir insgeheim und mit Recht eine Sehnsucht nach ihm empfinden. Diesen können wir uns jetzt aneignen.

Praxistipps: *Wenn wir Licht ins Dunkel bringen, zerfällt der Vampir zu Staub, und das Verborgene gewinnt Form und Farbe. Stellen Sie sich dem Unbekannten, beobachten Sie es, bis Sie genau wissen, was Sie davon nutzen können und was nicht.*

Un travail tabou

Une silhouette hermaphrodite à la chevelure ébouriffée, avec des cornes sur la tête et une corne au genou, porte une étoile ou une flûte et quitte son piédestal. Deux bras noirs la lâchent, puis veulent la saisir. Si le tableau peut paraître étrange, il contourne une représentation convenue du diable. Ainsi se pose plus précisément la question de la signification du diable pour nous aujourd'hui. Chaque individu apporte quelque chose de nouveau dans le monde, ses particularités et ses qualités qui ne s'inscrivent pas forcément dans le cadre des choses déjà existantes. Chaque individu poursuit à sa façon l'histoire de la Création – et touche à un moment donné à des sujets tabous.

La carte du DIABLE signalise que le seuil du tabou est franchi. Ce qui auparavant était sous-jacent est désormais visible. Là réside l'atout mais aussi la mission, il faut se pencher sur les tabous, confirmer ou créer les tabous salutaires et démonter les tabous inutiles.

Ne vous laissez pas intimider : vous avez ici la chance de faire peau neuve. D'un côté, le diable est une sorte de vampire, un véritable gêneur et un importun. Nous le craignons à juste titre et nous ne pouvons enfin nous débarrasser de cette zone d'ombre qu'en la perçant à jour. D'un autre côté, le diable incarne un « parent pauvre », cette part de nous que nous avons négligée, bien que nous éprouvions pour lui une grande attirance. Nous pouvons maintenant nous l'approprier.

Conseils pratiques : *Si nous apportons la lumière dans l'obscurité, le vampire retombe en poussière et ce qui est caché reprend forme et couleur. Regardez en face l'inconnu, examinez avec précision ce que vous pouvez utiliser ou non.*

The Tower
Der Turm
La Maison Dieu

Encounter with the Absolute

Two archetypes determine the meaning of this card: the Tower of Babel and Pentecost. The building of the Tower of Babel is a symbol of human megalomania, culminating not only in the destruction of the tower but also in the Babylonian confusion of tongues. Pentecost is the opposite of the building of the tower. The Holy Ghost descends upon the disciples in the form of a storm and tongues of fire. As they start to talk, everyone hears themselves speaking in their own language. Instead of a confusion of tongues, this event symbolizes the tearing down of all language barriers.

Babel and Pentecost are two opposite poles. Violence destroys and results in speechlessness and confusion. In contrast, love tears down all language barriers and makes true communication possible without limits.

The card cautions you to beware of megalomania and lack of steadfastness. There might be rocky times ahead. You are urged to leave your ivory tower and your personal objections and pretences behind when the time is ripe. This card also involves jumping out of the clouds and turning the free fall into flying.

Practical advice: *Go ahead and give it your all! You will gain more love and protect yourself better from danger if you learn consciously to deal with your energy. Risk being more direct! Make a leap into the unknown—even if the consequences are unfathomable.*

Begegnung mit dem Absoluten

Zwei Archetypen bestimmen die Bedeutung dieser Karte:
der Turmbau zu Babel und das Pfingstereignis. Der Turmbau zu Babel steht für den menschlichen Größenwahn,
dessen Ergebnis nicht nur die Zerstörung des Turms,
sondern auch die „babylonische Sprachverwirrung" war:
Die Menschen verstehen einander nicht mehr. Das
Pfingstereignis steht für das Gegenteil: Der „Heilige
Geist" kommt in Gestalt von Sturm und Feuerzungen auf
die Jünger herab, diese beginnen zu reden, und jeder hört
sie in der eigenen Muttersprache. Statt Sprachverwirrung
findet eine Aufhebung der Sprach- und Verständigungs-
grenzen statt.

Babel und Pfingsten als entgegengesetzte Pole. Gewalt
zerstört und führt zu Sprachlosigkeit und Verwirrung.
Liebe dagegen hebt die Sprachbarrieren auf, sie ermög-
licht eine Verständigung über alle Grenzen hinweg.

Die Karte warnt vor Größenwahn und mangelnder
Standhaftigkeit. Es kann zu Erschütterungen kommen,
doch da ist auch die Aufforderung, persönliche Einwände
und Vorwände – den eigenen Elfenbeinturm – aufzuge-
ben, wenn die Zeit dafür reif ist! Die Karte steht auch
für den Sprung aus den Wolken, für die Verwandlung des
Fallens in ein Fliegen.

Praxistipps: *Setzen Sie Ihre ganze Energie ein! Sie gewinnen mehr Liebe und schützen sich um so besser vor gewaltsamen Zumutungen, je bewusster Sie mit diesen Energien
umgehen. Riskieren Sie mehr Direktheit und wagen Sie den
Sprung in Neues, auch wenn das Ergebnis offen bleibt.*

Rencontre de l'absolu

Deux archétypes donnent à cette carte tout son sens : la
tour de Babel et le message de la Pentecôte. La tour de
Babel symbolise la mégalomanie des hommes qui aboutit
non seulement à la destruction de la tour, mais aussi à la
« cacophonie babylonienne ». Les humains ne se com-
prennent plus entre eux. Le message de la Pentecôte
transmet l'inverse : le « Saint Esprit » descend sous forme
de tempête et de langues de feu sur les apôtres, ces der-
niers se mettent à parler et chacun(e) les entend dans sa
langue maternelle. À un chaos de langues succède l'aboli-
tion des barrières de langage et de compréhension.

Babel et la Pentecôte, deux pôles radicalement opposés.
La violence est destructrice, elle entraîne le mutisme et la
confusion. En revanche, l'amour supprime les barrières de
langage, permet la compréhension par-delà les frontières.

Cette carte met en garde contre la folie des grandeurs et
le manque de ténacité. Des secousses peuvent se produire,
mais l'appel est bien présent de renoncer à ses objections
et prétextes – la tour d'ivoire individuelle – quand l'heure
est venue ! La carte symbolise le saut du haut des nuages et
la transformation de la chute en vol.

Conseils pratiques : *Mobilisez toute votre énergie ! Vous
obtiendrez plus d'amour et vous vous protégerez d'autant
mieux contre les agressions brutales que vous gérerez en
toute conscience vos énergies. Risquez plus de contact direct
et oser le saut dans la nouveauté, même si le résultat se fait
attendre.*

The Star
Der Stern
L'Étoile

Personal Truth

Personal truth often seems to be like a distant star. It takes a long time to attain. But all our dreams are focused upon that star; our personal truth is the fount of all our dreams. This source will never dry up. You only have to find it and, as the figure on the card shows, take it into your own hands and raise it up high (hold in high esteem, cherish and venerate). Once the star lightens up your day as well as your night, then the truth will be revealed in all its beauty.

Sometimes, the card warns you of inappropriate brazenness or compromise. The great blue serpent in the sky represents the wonders of creation that you yourself experience. But the card also reminds you to be aware of the pitfalls of THE STAR, namely the "star cult." Be careful not to use your own light to put others in the shade. Be equally careful not to neglect your own light by becoming mesmerized by other distant stars.

Pitchers and chalices represent emotional needs, desires, and fears. In this sense, the figure holds her emotional needs in her hands. We carry the vessel that we are! An old idea claims that man as a whole is but a vessel in the hands of God—a receptacle that is filled and emptied out during the course of a lifetime. This vessel symbolizes the individual's part in the great stream of life.

Practical advice: *"Each life follows its own star." (Hermann Hesse) Reveal yourself, do your part. Do not hide your own beauty nor be shy about revealing your own truth. Give generously. Do not hide your light under a bushel. However, remember that your star is only a small point in a much larger galaxy of stars.*

Persönliche Wahrheit

Die persönliche Wahrheit erscheint oft wie ein ferner Stern, ein langer Weg ist manchmal erforderlich, um zu ihm zu gelangen. Doch all unsere Träume drehen sich um diesen Stern, die persönliche Wahrheit ist die Quelle unserer Träume. Diese Quelle kann nie versiegen; man muss sie nur finden und, wie die Bildfigur, in die Hand nehmen und hochhalten (ehren, schätzen, sich bewusstmachen). Wenn dann der Stern nicht nur die Nacht, sondern auch den Tag erhellt, zeigt sich diese Wahrheit in ihrer ganzen Schönheit.

Manchmal warnt die Karte jedoch vor einer unangebrachten Schamlosigkeit oder Bloßstellung. Die große blaue Himmelsschlange steht für die Wunder der Schöpfung, die Sie selbst erleben. Aber sie warnt auch vor den Tücken des Sterns: vor allem vor dem „Star-Kult", davor, mit dem eigenen Licht andere in den Schatten zu stellen oder in der blinden Bewunderung für ein Idol das eigene Licht zu missachten. Krüge und Kelche symbolisieren seelische Bedürfnisse, Wünsche und Ängste. So verstanden trägt, erfasst und begreift die Bildfigur eben ihre seelischen Bedürfnisse. Wir tragen das Gefäß, das wir selbst sind! Gleichzeitig sind wir als Menschen letztlich als Ganzes ein Gefäß in der Hand Gottes – ein Gefäß, das sich im Laufe des Lebens füllt und leert, ein Gefäß, das den Anteil des Einzelnen am großen Strom des Lebens symbolisiert.

Praxistipps: *„Jedes Leben steht unter seinem eigenen Stern" (Hermann Hesse). Offenbaren Sie sich, leisten Sie Ihren Beitrag, halten Sie mit Ihrer Schönheit und Ihrer Wahrheit nicht hinter dem Berg. Geben Sie großzügig. Stellen Sie Ihr Licht nicht unter den Scheffel, aber vergessen Sie dabei nicht, dass Sie nur ein kleiner Teil des großen Ganzen sind.*

Vérité personnelle

La vérité personnelle apparaît souvent comme une lointaine étoile, parfois une longue distance est à parcourir pour l'atteindre. Toutefois, tous nos rêves tournent autour de cette étoile, la vérité personnelle est la source de nos rêves. Cette source ne peut jamais tarir ; il suffit de la trouver, comme cette femme, de la prendre dans sa main et de la soulever (respecter, estimer, apprécier). Si alors l'étoile éclaire non seulement la nuit mais aussi le jour, cette vérité resplendit dans toute sa beauté.

Cependant la carte met en garde contre un manque de pudeur ou une mise à nu déplacés. Le long serpent bleu incarne le miracle de la Création, que vous vivez vous-même. Mais il avertit contre les défauts de l'étoile : surtout contre le culte de la star, contre la tentation de faire ombrage aux autres par sa propre lumière ou la vénération aveugle d'une idole au mépris de son propre rayonnement. Chopes et coupes symbolisent les besoins de l'âme, les désirs et les peurs. Vu sous cet angle, le personnage saisit et comprend ses besoins spirituels. Nous portons la cruche que nous sommes nous-mêmes ! Parallèlement, nous, êtres humains, sommes un récipient dans la main de Dieu – un récipient qui se remplit et se vide, un récipient qui symbolise la contribution de l'individu au grand fleuve de la vie.

Conseils pratiques : *« Chaque vie est sous le signe de son étoile » (Hermann Hesse). Confiez-vous, apportez votre participation, ne cachez pas votre beauté et votre vérité. Soyez généreux dans vos dons. Ne mettez pas votre lumière sous le boisseau, mais dites-vous bien aussi que vous n'êtes qu'une petite partie du Grand Tout.*

The Moon
Der Mond
La Lune

Deliverance

THE MOON represents the collective unconscious and "oceanic feelings." The full moon will lure hidden instincts into the open, with the potential to shake us up emotionally. Do not lose courage! Perhaps we are gripped by emotional tension that we can't quite fathom.

There is a danger of getting too absorbed in our vacillating moods. Instead of putting ourselves in the picture, we hide in the big city jungle, howl at the moon like the dogs or wolves—to be seen at the bottom left of the card—or become petrified like the big towers. This is an opportunity for empathy to deepen. We feel at one with all living beings, as we are equally at home in the past, the present, and the future. This card conveys the promise of integrating that which has been formerly suppressed and transmuting the spiritual distress into the uplifting artful realms of the soul. The tedium of the everyday will be transformed into real fulfillment.

Practical advice: *Accept your intense emotions as a reality that wants to be lived, just like any other aspect of your being. Then you may safely swim about in the deep waters of your psyche. Be at peace with yourself and the world, open up your heart and cease to be self-absorbed.*

Erlösung

Der Mond steht für das kollektive Unbewusste, für die „ozeanischen Gefühle". Insbesondere der Vollmond weckt verborgene Instinkte und besitzt die Fähigkeit, uns emotional aufzuwühlen. Hier ist Mut zu großen Gefühlen gefordert! Vielleicht erfasst uns eine emotionale Unruhe, die wir nur schwer einzuschätzen wissen.

Die Gefahr besteht dann darin, dass wir uns von diesen seelischen Wechsellagen absorbieren lassen. Anstatt persönlich ins Bild zu treten, tauchen wir womöglich im Dschungel der Großstadt unter, heulen den Mond an wie die Hunde (oder Wölfe), die links unten im Bild zu sehen sind oder stehen versteinert da wie die großen Türme. Gleichzeitig ergibt sich aber auch eine große Chance, ein gesteigertes Einfühlungsvermögen. Nichts Menschliches bleibt uns fremd, und wir sind in Vergangenheit, Gegenwart und Zukunft gleichermaßen zu Hause. Die große Verheißung dieser Karte ist das Wiedererlangen des vormals Verdrängten – die Verwandlung einer seelischen Unruhe in eine kunstvoll-erhebende Kultur der Seelenkräfte, die Verwandlung des Alltags in ein erfüllteres Leben.

Praxistipps: *Berücksichtigen Sie ihre „großen Gefühle" als eine Realität, die gelebt sein will. So gelingt es Ihnen, sich auch in großen Gewässern zu bewegen, ja, freizuschwimmen. Machen Sie Ihren Frieden mit sich und ihrer Umwelt, öffnen Sie ihr Herz und legen Sie jede Selbstbefangenheit ab.*

Délivrance

La lune est le symbole de l'inconscient collectif, des « sentiments océaniques ».

La peine lune en particulier éveille les instincts cachés et possède la faculté de secouer nos émotions. Le courage des grands sentiments est ici exigé ! Peut-être sommes-nous pris d'une agitation émotionnelle que nous ne pouvons que difficilement évaluer. Le danger consiste à ce que nous nous laissions absorber par ces sautes d'humeur. Au lieu d'occuper la scène nous nous immergeons peut-être dans la jungle de la grande ville, hurlons à la lune avec les chiens (ou les loups) qui ornent le bas de l'image à gauche ou nous restons debout, figés comme les hautes tours. Mais en même temps une grande chance s'offre, une plus grande empathie. Rien de ce qui est humain ne nous reste étranger, et nous nous sentons à l'aise dans le passé, le présent et le futur. La grande promesse de cette carte est le recouvrement des refoulements anciens – la métamorphose de l'instabilité intérieure en une culture raffinée des forces spirituelles, la transformation du quotidien en une vie plus épanouie.

Conseils pratiques : *Considérez les « grands sentiments » comme une réalité qui demande à être vécue. Ainsi réussirez-vous à vous mouvoir, à nager librement dans des eaux plus profondes. Faites la paix avec vous-même et votre entourage, ouvrez votre cœur et débarrassez-vous de toutes vos inhibitions.*

The Sun
Die Sonne
Le Soleil

Enlightenment

The lion is a typical sun symbol while the Greco-Roman Apollo appears here as the god of light. Yet the card is rendered in darker tones: most versions of this card depict twins, mostly shown as children, which discreetly hints at the second birth! The second birth is a metaphor, which means that you as an adult have to be reborn, and moreover give birth to yourself this time around. Your first birth brought you into this world. Your "second birth" is nothing less than deliberately choosing your own life's path, no longer restricted by habitual behavior and fixed routines but informed by free choice and by exercising your own free will. Traditional behavior and thought patterns are replaced by a consciously chosen lifestyle. The "second birth" may be followed by a third, a fourth birth, and more, in a progressive path of renewal. But the "second birth" is decisive, as the first one to be undertaken deliberately.

This theme is common to the Buddhist goal of enlightenment or the Christian maxim "If you do not become like the little children, you will not enter the kingdom of heaven."

This second birth is possible only as the result of a process of becoming. As long as you are lacking a true understanding of yourself, you will remain in an in-between state, in a period of "being on the road." The subdued colors of the picture are in keeping with the tribulations on the way to the sun, the very center of yourself. This card is about finding your way towards the sun, which is located at the heart of the matter.

Practical advice: *Beware of all delusions. Surrender to the stream of life energy within and without yourself. "Love God and do what you want to do." (St. Augustine)*

Erleuchtung

Der Löwe ist ein typisches Sonnensymbol, und auch der griechisch-römische Apoll erscheint hier als der Gott des Lichts. Dennoch wirkt die Karte insgesamt eher dunkel: Fast alle bekannten Varianten dieser Karte zeigen ein Zwillingspaar, meist in der Gestalt von Kindern, und deuten damit diskret das Thema der zweiten Geburt an! Die „zweite Geburt" bedeutet, dass Sie sich als Erwachsener ein zweites Mal und diesmal selbst gebären. Nach der ersten Geburt, die ihr jetziges Leben eröffnete, stellt die zweite Geburt eine selbstgewählte Lebensgestaltung dar, die nicht durch Gewohnheit und Routine, sondern durch freie Wahl und freien Willen geprägt ist. An die Stelle eines erlernten Verhaltens tritt das selbstgewählte Denken und Handeln. An die zweite Geburt kann sich natürlich auch eine dritte, eine vierte etc. anschließen, ein anhaltender Prozess der Erneuerung. Aber die „zweite Geburt" ist die entscheidende, weil sie die erste bewusste Neugeburt ist.

Diese Idee findet sich auch in dem buddhistischen Streben nach Erleuchtung und der christlichen Maxime „Wenn ihr nicht werdet wie die Kinder, werdet ihr nicht eingehen ins Himmelreich". Die zweite Geburt setzt aber ein Werden voraus. Solange ein geeignetes Selbstverständnis fehlt, befindet man sich in einer Übergangssituation, einer Zeit der Wanderschaft. Die dunklen Farben stehen hier für die Mühsal auf dem Weg zur Sonne, zur eigenen Mitte. Hier geht es um die Verarbeitung von Erfahrungen und den Weg zur Sonne, die in der eigenen Mitte sitzt.

Praxistipps: *Hüten und schützen Sie sich vor Blendwerk. Vertrauen Sie sich dem Strom der Lebensenergie an. „Liebe Gott und tu, was du willst" (Augustinus).*

Illumination

Le lion est un symbole typique du soleil et Apollon, le dieu gréco-romain de la lumière, est également présent. Pourtant la carte apparaît sombre dans l'ensemble : presque toutes les variations connues de cette carte en présentant un couple de jumeaux, le plus souvent des enfants, font discrètement allusion au thème de la deuxième naissance ! La « deuxième naissance » signifie que vous vous mettez au monde vous-même une deuxième fois. Après la première naissance qui fut le début de votre vie actuelle, la deuxième naissance signifie une forme de vie délibérément choisie, qui n'est pas imprégnée d'habitude et de routine, mais de choix libre et de volonté souveraine. Au comportement transmis par l'éducation succèdent la pensée et l'action indépendantes. La deuxième naissance peut naturellement être suivie d'une troisième, d'une quatrième, etc., un processus permanent de renouvellement. Mais la « deuxième naissance » est décisive, parce qu'elle constitue la première naissance consciente.

Cette idée se trouve aussi dans la recherche bouddhiste de l'illumination et dans la maxime chrétienne « Si vous ne redevenez pas comme des enfants, vous n'entrerez pas dans le royaume des cieux ». Mais la deuxième naissance suppose une évolution. Tant que l'assurance personnelle fait défaut, on se trouve dans une situation transitoire, une période de cheminement. Les couleurs sombres traduisent ici l'effort fourni sur la route du soleil, vers le centre de la personnalité. Le thème majeur ici est la confrontation avec ses expériences et le chemin vers le soleil, qui brille au centre de l'individu.

Conseils pratiques : *Détournez-vous et protégez-vous de la poudre aux yeux. Fiez-vous au courant de l'énergie vitale. « Aime Dieu et fais ce que tu veux » (Saint Augustin).*

Judgment
Gericht
Le Jugement

The Day of Judgment is Today

The image on the card is a traditional depiction of the Day of JUDGMENT, somewhat modified by the butterflies and the two faces in profile. An angel is sounding the trumpet, the graves are opening up, and the dead are being brought back to life. In the foreground, we see an open shell sketched in black ink, revealing its pearl. This detail represents the message of the card.

Powerful forces are being set in motion; latent energies are being awakened. Processes of change and transformation are immanent.

This card challenges you to take a closer look at and come to terms with those extreme aspects of your life. Desires and fears, as well as the habit of putting the blame on yourself and others, will have to be dealt with over and again, until the mistakes of your past have been put to rights and your future path freed from old obstacles. . Only then will rebirth be more than a mere repetition of the old.

The story of JUDGMENT Day is not just a religious myth: it is to be taken literally. The Day of JUDGMENT is today! Each and every morning we are faced with the task of becoming wide awake and gathering all of our energy, so that we can really bury all that is dead and gone and prepare ourselves for the birth of what is yet to come.

If we can accept every single day as a gift, we will gain in confidence and be able to welcome life's challenges. Desires and fears will always exist, but we can learn to deal with them appropriately. We will become receptive to the colorful spectacle that is life, which is inviting our participation.

Practical advice: *Let go of what has been. Say your goodbyes and make your peace with the past. Learn to forgive without forgetting. Everything is important. You have made your choices in the past and now you are free to choose anew and to decide which road you want to take.*

Der Jüngste Tag ist heute

Etwas verfremdet durch die Schmetterlinge und durch
die beiden Gesichter im Profil stellt das Bild die traditi-
onelle Szene des Jüngsten Gerichts dar: Ein Engel bläst
die Posaune, Gräber tun sich auf, und Tote werden wieder
zum Leben erweckt. Im Vordergrund sehen wir in schwar-
zer Tusche die Andeutung einer geöffneten Muschel,
die ihre Perle darbietet. Dieses Detail steht für die ganze
Karte.

Starke Energien werden freigesetzt, schlafende Energien geweckt, es ist Zeit für den Prozess der Umformung
und des Wandels. Diese Karte fordert Sie auf, auch die
extremen Seiten des Lebens in den Blick zu nehmen
und sich ihnen zu stellen. Wünsche, Ängste, Schuldzu-
weisungen und Selbstvorwürfe müssen immer wieder
vergegenwärtigt werden, bis die Fehler der Vergangenheit
geklärt und der Weg in eine neue Zukunft freigemacht ist.
Erst dann bedeutet Wiedergeburt neues Leben und keine
Wiederholung.

Die Überlieferung vom Jüngsten Tag ist nicht nur ein
religiöses Märchen. Wir dürfen die Geschichte wörtlich
nehmen: Der Jüngste Tag ist heute! Jeden Tag aufs Neue
geht es darum, wach zu werden und alle Energien anzunehmen, Totes zu beerdigen und sich für die Geburt des
noch Ungeborenen zu öffnen. Wenn wir jeden Tag als
Geschenk nehmen können, schöpfen wir täglich neues
Vertrauen und neue Bereitschaft für unser Leben. Verlangen und Ängste werden uns immer begleiten, aber wir
können lernen, mit ihnen umzugehen. Der Schatten, der
Druck, die Enge lösen und öffnen sich. Wir öffnen uns für
das farbenprächtige Schauspiel des Lebens, das zum Mit-
machen aufruft. Jeder Tag ist gleichzeitig Abschied und
Neuanfang.

Praxistipps: *Ziehen Sie einen Strich unter das, was war.
Versöhnen oder verabschieden Sie sich. Lernen Sie verzeihen, ohne zu vergessen. Alles ist wichtig. Sie haben in der
Vergangenheit gewählt und sind auch jetzt frei, sich neu zu
entscheiden.*

Le Jugement dernier c'est aujourd'hui

Avec ses papillons et ses deux visages de profil, l'image
représente la scène traditionnelle du Jugement dernier
de manière un peu insolite. Un ange joue du trombone, la
terre s'ouvre et les morts renaissent à la vie. Au premier
plan un coquillage ouvert qui offre sa perle apparaît,
esquissé à l'encre noire. Ce détail est significatif pour la
carte tout entière.

De puissantes énergies semblent libérées, les énergies
endormies réveillées, l'heure d'un processus de transformation et de changement a sonné. Cette carte exhorte à
différencier les faces extrêmes de la vie et à les utiliser.
Désirs et craintes, accusations et remords doivent être
sans cesse réenvisagés jusqu'à ce que les erreurs du passé
soient éclaircies et le chemin vers un nouvel avenir sans
obstacle. Alors seulement la re-naissance est synonyme
de vie nouvelle et non de répétition.

Le récit du Jugement dernier n'est pas seulement un
conte religieux. Nous pouvons prendre l'histoire au pied
de la lettre : le Jugement dernier c'est aujourd'hui. Jour
après jour il faut se réveiller et prendre sur soi toute l'énergie d'enterrer ce qui est mort et d'être ouvert pour la naissance de ce qui n'a pas encore vu le jour. Si nous acceptons
chaque jour comme un cadeau, nous en tirons une nouvelle confiance et sommes prêts pour une vie nouvelle.
Désir et peurs seront toujours nos compagnons, mais nous
pouvons apprendre à les apprivoiser. L'ombre, la tension,
la mesquinerie s'évanouissent. Nous ouvrons notre être au
spectacle multicolore de la vie qui nous invite à entrer
dans le jeu. Chaque jour est à la fois fin et recommence-
ment.

Conseils pratiques : *Tirez un trait sur le passé. Récon-
ciliez-vous et mettez un point final. Apprenez à pardonner
sans oublier. Tout est important. Vous avez choisi par le
passé et vous êtes aussi désormais libre de vous réorienter.*

The World
Die Welt
Le Monde

Resolution of Contradictions

This card is linked to the image of THE CHARIOT: the frame at the center of the composition is reused as a motif indicative of a kind of cage. Furthermore, THE WORLD also refers to the content of THE DEVIL card: the vampire or bogeyman and the prodigal son as symbols of the taboos that can be rediscovered in the big black being, which is imprisoned and seems to be weeping.

This card seems to convey the pessimistic message that evil always puts the righteous in chains and will eventually triumph. But an alternative reading is possible: the Three Graces—and with them faith, love, and hope—will help the world to advance. On long leashes, they pull up this dark and fiery creature from the depths of the earth to emerge at the surface. Humanity has not just descended from heaven to earth like angels, but is also a product of a long evolution. On every level of our development as humans, we are called upon to deal with our heritage. Although we never cease to discover dangerous traits in ourselves and others, we also constantly discover new, hitherto unknown areas of growth. In a positive sense, the ropes or chains represent our dependency on time and space. Our individual existence is bound to the existence of all others. We have inherited the earth from our parents and merely borrowed it from our children. We should not jeopardize this inheritance.

Practical advice: *It is your task and your strength to step forward and show yourself. The way you live in this world determines what the world is in a reciprocal relationship. Use your time on earth wisely and enjoy your stay here.*

Aufhebung der Widersprüche

Diese Karte knüpft an das Bild des WAGENS an; das Motiv des Rahmens im Zentrum seiner Bildfigur wird hier als eine Art Käfigrahmen wieder aufgegriffen. Darüber hinaus verweist DIE WELT aber auch auf den Inhalt der Karte DER TEUFEL: Der Vampir/Quälgeist und das Kellerkind als Sinnbilder von Tabus, finden sich in dem großen schwarzen, eingesperrten und offenbar weinenden Wesen wieder.

Man könnte dieses Bild sicher als eine pessimistische Botschaft, als ein Abbild der Herrschaft des Bösen lesen. Eine andere Lesart lässt aber auch die Möglichkeit zu, dass die drei Grazien – und mit ihnen Glaube, Liebe und Hoffnung – die Welt voranbringen und an langen Zügeln auch dieses dunkle feurige Wesen aus der Tiefe allmählich an die Oberfläche ziehen. Die Menschen sind eben nicht nur als Engel vom Himmel auf die Erde gekommen, sondern stehen am Ende einer langen Entwicklung. Jeder weitere Schritt auf dem Weg unserer menschlichen Entwicklung bedeutet erneut, sich mit unserem Erbe auseinanderzusetzen. Immer wieder entdecken wir so bedrohliche, gefährliche Züge in uns selbst und bei unseren Mitmenschen; immer wieder stoßen wir aber auch auf bisher unentdeckte Entfaltungsmöglichkeiten. Die Stricke oder Ketten bedeuten im positiven Sinne auch die Gebundenheit an Raum und Zeit: Unsere Existenz ist untrennbar mit der anderer Menschen verknüpft. Wir haben die Erde von unseren Eltern geerbt und von unseren Kindern nur geliehen. Setzen wir sie nicht aufs Spiel.

Praxistipps: *Ihre Stärke und Ihre Aufgabe ist es jetzt, selbst in die Mitte zu treten. Wie Sie die Welt leben, so ist sie auch für Sie! Nutzen Sie Ihre Zeit auf der Erde und genießen Sie sie!*

Abolition des contradictions

Cette carte rappelle l'image du CHARIOT, le motif du cadre au centre de son personnage est repris comme une sorte de cage. En outre, LE MONDE est aussi à rapprocher de la carte du DIABLE : le vampire/mauvais esprit et le « parent pauvre », symboles de tabous refoulés, se trouvent réunis dans le grand personnage noir, enfermé et visiblement en larmes.

On pourrait interpréter cette gravure comme un message pessimiste, comme l'image du règne du mal. Mais une autre interprétation permet aussi de voir les trois Grâces – à savoir la foi, l'amour et l'espoir – faire progresser le monde et ramener peu à peu à la surface ce sombre personnage enfoui dans les profondeurs. Les hommes ne sont pas descendus du ciel sur la terre comme des anges, ils sont le produit final d'une longue évolution. Chaque nouveau pas sur le chemin de l'évolution humaine signifie toujours de se pencher sur notre ascendance. Sans cesse nous découvrons en nous et chez nos contemporains des traits menaçants, dangereux ; mais sans cesse aussi nous atteignons des chances d'épanouissement jusqu'alors insoupçonnées. Les cordes et chaînes symbolisent dans un sens positif le lien avec l'espace et le temps : notre existence est indissociable de celle des autres. De nos parents nous avons hérité la Terre et nous ne l'avons que prêtée à nos enfants. Ne la mettons pas en jeu.

Conseils pratiques : *Votre force et votre mission sont désormais de vous placer vous-même au centre. Le monde est aussi pour vous tel que vous le ressentez ! Profitez de votre temps sur terre et jouissez de votre séjour !*

The Fool
Der Narr
Le Fou

The Zero as Role Model

Zero (or the missing number) stands for nothing. It warns you against living a meaningless life. Seen from another angle, the zero point defines your personal starting point, the site of unity within yourself, at the very core of your being. Like the initial point of a coordinate system, this card represents the beginning of everything that makes up an individual.

To look into the future with courage implies charting your own course, not least when all role models have failed you and you are forced to act into the blue without any prior support. The more unusual your path, the more panic you will experience if you have to go down it. Pan in Greek means "all." Therefore, panic means "all-at-once." The more room you give THE FOOL in your life, the easier it will be to get used to accepting yourself, God, and the world as they are, as the supplicant saint in the picture demonstrates. In this way, everything you know takes on a special importance in your life—when the time is right.

Look at the shadowy figure by the wayside. It could represent your second self that you desperately feel the need and long for. Do not take lightly the feeling that you are missing out on something. The fulfillment of these desires and the banishment of deep-seated fears are a priority. THE FOOL represents a state of unadulterated bliss.

Practical advice: *As a fool, you are open to experiment and free to learn from all experience. You are entitled to lack answers and to change your point of view at will. Put your faith in your own originality and trust the world. Do not let others drive you crazy. It is foolish to concern yourself with things or events that cannot be appropriately judged at the present time.*

Null als Vorbild

Die Null (oder schlichtweg die fehlende Zahl) ist ein Nichts, und sie warnt Sie vor einem Leben ohne Sinn. Der „Nullpunkt" bezeichnet aber auch den innerpersönlichen Schnittpunkt, die Stelle des inneren Zusammenhalts, den inneren Kern des Selbst. Wie der Nullpunkt eines Koordinatensystems, so bedeutet diese Karte auch den Anfang von allem, was die eigene Person ausmacht.

Der Mut zur Zukunft bedeutet Mut zum eigenen Weg, gerade wenn der Nutzen aller Vorbilder gegen Null geht, man gleichsam offen und ohne Rückendeckung handelt. Je ungewohnter der eigenständige Weg ist, umso mehr kommt Panik auf, falls dieser doch einmal beschritten werden muss. Das griechische Wort „pan" bedeutet „Alles", Pan-ik ist demnach „Alles auf einmal". Je mehr Spiel-Raum DER NARR in unserem Leben erhält, umso mehr haben wir akzepiert, „Gott", die Welt und uns selbst so zu nehmen, wie wir sind, so wie der dargestellte betende Heilige. Alles, was man weiß und kennt, bekommt so einen Stellenwert im eigenen Leben – alles zu seiner Zeit.

Beachten Sie die Schattengestalt am Wegesrand, sie könnte Ihr zweites Ich darstellen, etwas, das Sie schmerzlich vermissen und ersehnen. Wenn Sie das Gefühl haben, etwas zu versäumen, nehmen Sie es nicht auf die leichte Schulter. Die Erfüllung dieser Wünsche und die Aufhebung grundlegender Ängste werden dann zur Hauptaufgabe. DER NARR steht für einen Zustand wunschlosen Glücks.

Praxistipps: *Als Narr sind Sie offen für Experimente und frei, aus ihnen zu lernen und Ihre Ansichten zu ändern. Frei, keine Antworten zu haben, Ihrer eigenen Originalität und der Welt zu vertrauen. Lassen Sie sich nicht verrückt machen. Nur ein Narr macht sich Gedanken zu Ereignissen und deren Konsequenzen, die zum jetzigen Zeitpunkt nicht beurteilt werden können.*

Le zéro comme modèle

Le zéro (ou tout simplement le chiffre manquant) est un néant et il vous vous met en garde contre une vie dénuée de sens. Mais le « point zéro » désigne aussi la césure personnelle intérieure, l'endroit de la cohérence intérieure, le noyau central de la personnalité. Comme le point zéro d'un système de coordonnées, cette carte est le début de tout ce qui constitue la personne.

Le courage d'aller vers l'avenir signifie le courage de suivre son chemin, en particulier quand l'utilité des modèles avoisinent le chiffre zéro, on agit alors ouvertement et sans recours. Plus le chemin individuel est inhabituel, plus la panique s'installe, s'il faut pourtant le suivre. Le mot grec « pan » signifie « tout », pan-ique veut donc dire « tout d'un seul coup ». Plus LE FOU prend de place dans notre vie, plus nous avons accepté de prendre « Dieu », le monde et nous-mêmes tels que nous sommes, comme le saint en prière de l'image. Tout ce que nous savons et connaissons a une place spécifique dans notre vie – chaque chose en son temps.

Observez la silhouette sur le bord du chemin, elle pourrait figurer votre deuxième « moi », quelque chose qui vous manque terriblement et que vous recherchez. Si vous avez le sentiment de rater quelque chose, ne le prenez pas à la légère. L'accomplissement de ces désirs et l'anéantissement de peurs profondes deviennent alors la tâche majeure. LE FOU correspond à un état de bonheur parfait.

Conseils pratiques : *Tel un fou, vous êtes ouvert aux expériences et libre d'apprendre par elles et de modifier vos pensées. Libre de n'avoir aucune réponse, de faire confiance à votre originalité et au monde. Ne vous affolez pas. Seul un fou réfléchit aux événements et à leurs conséquences qui ne peuvent pas encore être mesurées sur le moment.*

MINOR
ARCANA

KLEINE
ARKANA

PETITS
ARCANES

Queen of Wands
Königin der Stäbe
Reine de Bâton

QUEEN OF WANDS

The Joy of Living and Self-Determination

All court cards represent an ideal. They stand for the confident handling of the respective element, in this case, the fire element (wands). This is especially true of the figure depicted on this card, which portrays the French queen Marie Antoinette from a painting by Marie Louise Élisabeth Vigée-Lebrun.

If you draw this card, not just the mastery of a single aspect of your will and vigor is being addressed but your confident handling of all forces of fire, your mastery as an energetic being. Many versions of this card show a cat, but here, a tail-wagging dog leaps towards the queen. Play, movement, and hunting instinct are just as important for this queen as living in and with nature, as signified by the tree and the sketchily drawn birds sitting on its branches.

It is important to note that the tree and the dog are located outside the queen's frame of reference. The success of your actions is critically dependant upon recognizing the existence of subliminal and unconscious, mainly vegetative processes. Instinctive drives, energetic action, and will, the forces of growth represented by the wands, are of utmost importance to this end.

The QUEEN OF WANDS is the mistress of basic instincts, which include sexuality, self-preservation, and reproduction. Likewise, a belief in your creative powers enables you to face seemingly insurmountable obstacles and to create new life out of nothing.

Pactical advice: *Rely on your ability to take charge at the right moment and to get things moving. In order to appreciate enemies and obstacles as nothing but challenges and new chances, you might have to modify your way of thinking. Recognize your abilities and decide upon your own goals.*

Lebensfreude und Selbstbestimmung

Alle „Hofkarten" stellen einen Idealtyp dar – Souveränität im Umgang mit dem betreffenden Element, hier mit dem Element Feuer (Stäbe). Das gilt in besonderer Weise auch für diese Bildfigur, eine Darstellung von Königin Marie Antoinette aus einem Gemälde von Marie Louise Elisabeth Vigée-Lebrun.

Wenn Sie diese Karte ziehen, ist nicht nur ein einzelner Aspekt im Bereich von Willen und Tatkraft gefragt, sondern der souveräne Umgang mit den Feuerkräften insgesamt, Ihre ganze Meisterschaft als Energiewesen. Viele Versionen dieser Karte zeigen eine Katze – hier springt ein schweifwedelndes Hündchen der Königin entgegen.

Spiel, Bewegung und Jagd sind für diese Königin ebenso wichtig wie das Leben in und mit der Natur, verdeutlicht durch den Baum und die darin angedeuteten Vögel. Zu beachten ist allerdings, dass sich Hund und Baum außerhalb ihres Lebensrahmens befinden. Der Erfolg des Handelns hängt daher entscheidend davon ab, diese unbewussten, unterschwelligen, eher vegetativ ablaufenden Vorgänge, Neigungen und Interessen zu erkennen. Trieb, Tatkraft und Wille, die Wachstumskraft der Stäbe, sind hier entscheidend. Die KÖNIGIN DER STÄBE ist die Meisterin der „Grundtriebe": Sexualität, Selbsterhaltung und Fortpflanzung. Durch Vertrauen in diese schöpferische Kraft, erwächst die Fähigkeit, auch in scheinbar ausweglosen Situationen aus dem vermeintlichen Nichts neues Leben zu schaffen.

Praxistipps: *Verlassen Sie sich auf Ihre Fähigkeit, zur richtigen Zeit einzugreifen und die Dinge in Bewegung zu setzen. Begreifen Sie Gegner und Hindernisse als Herausforderungen und neue Chancen, auch wenn Sie dabei umdenken müssen. Erkennen Sie, was in Ihnen steckt, und setzen Sie sich Ihre eigenen Ziele.*

Joie de vivre et autonomie

Toutes les cartes dites de cour représentent un type idéal – souveraineté avec l'élément en question, ici avec l'élément du feu (bâton). Ceci vaut en particulier pour ce personnage, une reproduction de la reine Marie-Antoinette d'après un tableau de Marie-Louise-Élisabeth Vigée-Lebrun.

Si vous tirez cette carte, ce n'est pas un seul aspect dans le domaine de la volonté et de l'activité qui est interpelé, mais la domination souveraine des forces du feu en général, tout votre potentiel d'énergie. Sur de nombreuses versions de cette carte apparaît un chat. Ici, c'est un petit chien frétillant qui bondit vers la reine.

Jeu, mouvement, instinct de chasse sont pour la reine aussi importants que la vie dans et avec la nature, concrétisée par l'arbre et les oiseaux qui y sont suggérés. Il convient toutefois de noter que le chien et l'arbre se trouvent à l'extérieur de son cadre de vie. Le succès de l'action dépend donc essentiellement du discernement de ces processus, penchants et tendances inconscients, sousjacents, d'ordre plutôt végétatif. L'instinct, la force d'action et la volonté, la poussée des bâtons sont ici déterminants. La REINE DE BÂTON est la maîtresse des « instincts profonds » : sexualité, auto-conservation et reproduction. À travers la confiance en cette force créatrice grandit l'aptitude à engendrer à partir de rien une vie nouvelle même dans des situations apparemment sans issue.

Conseils pratiques : *Fiez-vous à votre capacité d'intervenir au bon moment et de faire bouger les choses. Considérez vos adversaires et obstacles comme des défis et de nouvelles chances, même s'il vous faut changer de cap. Reconnaissez ce qui est en vous et fixez-vous vos propres objectifs.*

King of Wands
König der Stäbe
Roi de Bâton

KING OF WANDS

Ordeals of Fire

In order to depict THE SUN, which is traditionally associated with the KING OF WANDS, it is not unusual to
portray a child. However, the choice of a child-king (Louis
XV by Hyacinthe Rigaud) is most unusual for the KING
OF WANDS card.

The meaning of this symbol is not quite as innocent
as one might suppose. As an adult, you have to become a
child again in order to confidently handle the fire within
you (instinctive drives, actions, and will). The giant wand
represents a phallus as well as a witch's broom. It is a symbol of motivation, growth, and vitality as well as of power
and the strength to succeed.

Underneath the throne, we see a small animal, which
could be an ermine or a stoat. It warns you to beware of
nagging doubts, intrigues, and beastliness, but also represents the ability to grit your teeth and carry on, purposefully, perhaps putting aggression to good use, in order to
reach your goal. The fur of the ermine can also indicate
royal dignity.

As in many other tarot decks, the back of the throne is
emphasized, rising up like a mighty red flame surrounded
by a blue silhouette. This apparition conveys an air of
coolness or stiffness in its shadowy face, seen in profile.
The visage looks amused as well as stern. As a child, we
are usually uninhibited. But once we grow up, we lose contact with the world of the child and are often haunted by
nagging doubts. Or we refuse to grow up and are suddenly
and unexpectedly shocked by the power within us, for
good and ill.

Practical advice: *Recognize your tasks and needs as what
they really are: opportunities. Be willing to walk through
fire to fulfill your heart's desire—skillfully and without fear.*

Feuerproben

Für die Darstellung DIE SONNE, die traditionell in engem Zusammenhang mit der Karte KÖNIG DER STÄBE gesehen wird, ist es üblich, eine Kindergestalt zu verwenden. Das Bildnis eines Kindkönigs (Louis XV. von Hyacinthe Rigaud) ist für die Darstellung des KÖNIGS DER STÄBE hingegen ungewöhnlich.

Die Bedeutung dieser Symbolik ist nicht so kindlich-harmlos, wie man vielleicht vermutet. Man muss als Erwachsener wieder zum Kind werden, wenn man souverän mit seinem Feuer (Triebe, Taten, Wille) umgehen möchte. Der riesige Stab ist Phallus-Symbol und Hexenbesen, Zeichen von Triebkraft, Wachstum und Lebendigkeit, von Stärke und Durchsetzungsvermögen.

Unter dem Thron ist ein Tier zu sehen: vielleicht ein Hermelin oder Marder. Es warnt vor beißenden Zweifeln, vor Intrigen und Bösartigkeiten, steht zugleich aber auch für die Fähigkeit, sich durchzubeißen, zielstrebig, gegebenenfalls unter Einsatz von Aggression, sein Ziel zu verfolgen. Der Pelz des Hermelins ist zudem auch ein Symbol königlicher Würde.

Die Rückwand des Throns ist, wie in vielen Tarot-Karten, besonders betont. Wie eine mächtige rote Flamme ist sie anzusehen, umgeben von einer blauen Silhouette, die Erstarrung oder Coolness anzeigt, in ihr erkennbar ein schattenhaftes Gesicht im Profil, lustig oder böse schauend. Als Kind gehen wir meist unbefangen damit um. Als Erwachsene verlieren wir entweder den Kontakt zur Kinderwelt – nagende Zweifel stellen sich immer wieder ein –, oder wir weigern uns, erwachsen zu werden, und erleben im Nachhinein oft mit Erschrecken, wieviel Kraft tatsächlich in uns steckt, im Guten wie im Schlechten.

Praxistipps: *Begreifen Sie Ihre Aufgaben und Notwendigkeiten als Chancen. Gehen Sie für Ihre Herzenswünsche durchs Feuer – mit Geschick und ohne Sorgen.*

Épreuves du feu

Pour la représentation du SOLEIL que l'on considère traditionnellement en relation avec la carte ROI DE BÂTON, la coutume veut qu'on reproduise une figure enfantine. En revanche, le portrait d'un roi encore enfant (Louis XV peint par Hyacinthe Rigaud) pour incarner le ROI DE BÂTON est inhabituel.

Le sens de ce symbolisme n'est pas aussi innocent qu'on pourrait le supposer. L'adulte doit redevenir enfant s'il veut souverainement maîtriser son feu (instinct, actions, volonté). Le bâton géant est symbole phallique et balai de sorcière, signe de dynamisme, de croissance, et de vivacité, de force et de capacité à s'imposer. Sous le trône on aperçoit un animal, peut-être une hermine ou une martre. L'animal à fourrure symbolise la mort et la renaissance de la volonté, elle rappelle l'épreuve du feu et le progrès personnel. L'animal à fourrure met en garde contre les doutes mordants, les intrigues et les bassesses, mais incarne aussi la capacité de foncer tous crocs dehors avec persévérance en utilisant au besoin l'agression pour atteindre son objectif. Quant à l'hermine, la fourrure peut aussi être symbole de la majesté royale.

Le dos du trône est, comme dans tous les types de tarot, particulièrement mis en relief. Il apparaît, tel une puissante flamme rouge, entouré d'une silhouette bleue qui est comme figée ou très froide, d'où émerge un visage de profil plein d'ombre au regard amusé ou furieux. Enfants, nous sommes le plus souvent spontanés. Une fois adultes, soit nous perdons le contact avec le monde des enfants et des doutes mordants nous poursuivent sans cesse. Soit nous refusons de devenir adultes et constatons plus tard, souvent avec horreur, combien de force sommeille en nous, en bien comme en mal.

Conseils pratiques : *Considérez vos tâches et devoirs comme autant de chances. Traversez le feu pour réaliser vos désirs profonds – avec habileté et sans craintes.*

Knight of Wands
Ritter der Stäbe
Cavalier de Bâton

KNIGHT OF WANDS

Your Life's Purpose

Since the horse and its rider are relatively small and rather sketchily drawn, one might assume that this card is not that important. But this is far from being the case. Violet-red lines surround the figure like an enormous flame. In relationship to the horseman, the wand is more than life-size. A blue toad adorned with stars or diamonds squats underneath the horse. All these symbols have one common denominator: "Become who you are!" For this is the card of your life's mission. When we start out on our journey, we are small, just like the horse and rider, more an outline than a finished picture. The details have to be augmented and colored in. Our aim in life and our potential is self-realization and the full development of our personality. The violet-red lines delineate this huge task. The gigantic wand hints at strong drives and a sustainable energy supply. Our life's tasks are the greatest and best that we will ever encounter. They require and focus all our strength; their completion lasts a lifetime. Often on this journey, high ideals and toad-like instincts have to be overcome. If you possess a lot of fire, you are not only very courageous, but often also extremely tired, retiring, or irritable. "Once burned, twice shy." The blue ornate toad functions as a point of reference in two ways: the knight appears to flee from it and yet the creature also exerts an attractive force.

Practical advice: *You possess an incredible amount of energy. Bring light into the darkness. Help those who are weaker than yourself. Commit yourself to meaningful projects that will benefit many people. Where the darkness is greatest, your light is most needed. It is here that you will discover your life's purpose, a mission so great that it will take a whole lifetime to accomplish. Start your journey now!*

Lebensaufgaben

Weil Ross und Reiter relativ klein und nur in Umrissen gezeichnet sind, könnte man dieses Bild für unscheinbar halten. Doch dem ist keineswegs so. Wie eine riesige Flamme umgeben die violettroten Linien die Bildfiguren. Der Stab ist im Verhältnis zur menschlichen Gestalt überdimensioniert. Im Untergrund hockt eine blaue Kröte, mit Sternen oder Diamanten geschmückt. Diese Symbole besitzen einen gemeinsamen Nenner: „Werde, der du bist!" Denn dies ist die Karte der Lebensaufgaben: Wir beginnen unseren Lebensweg klein, so wie Pferd und Reiter im Bild, mehr ein Umriss als ein fertiges Bild – der Inhalt muss noch gefüllt und ausgemalt werden. Unser Ziel, unsere Möglichkeit ist die volle persönliche Entfaltung und Selbstverwirklichung; die große Bedeutung wird durch die violettroten Linien angezeigt. Der riesige Stab weist auf einen ausgeprägten Trieb, eine lang andauernde Energie. Lebensaufgaben sind die besten und größten Aufgaben, die wir uns stellen können. Sie dauern ein ganzes Leben, bündeln und fordern all unsere Kräfte. Hehre Ideale oder krötenhafte Instinkte mögen auf diesem Weg zu überwinden sein. Wer viel Feuer hat, ist nicht nur besonders mutig, er oder sie ist möglicherweise auch besonders müde, schüchtern oder irritierbar. „Gebranntes Kind scheut das Feuer." Die blaue, geschmückte Kröte drängt sich als Fluchtpunkt im doppelten Sinne auf: Der Reiter scheint vor ihr zu fliehen und gleichzeitig von ihr angezogen zu werden.

Praxistipps: *In Ihnen stecken enorme Energien. Bringen Sie Licht ins Dunkel, helfen Sie Schwächeren, und machen Sie sich stark für sinnvolle Projekte, die vielen Menschen großen Nutzen bringen. Wo es am dunkelsten ist, wird Ihr Licht am meisten gebraucht. Dort finden Sie geeignete Lebensaufgaben, die so groß sind, dass sie für ein ganzes Leben reichen. Machen Sie sich jetzt auf den Weg!*

Des tâches pour la vie

Comme le cavalier et sa monture sont relativement petits et dessinés seulement en contours, l'image pourrait paraître insignifiante. Cependant, il n'en est rien. Telle une flamme géante, les lignes rouge-violet enveloppent les figures. Le bâton est surdimensionné en comparaison du personnage humain. Sous lui est accroupi un crapaud bleu, orné d'étoiles et de diamants. Ces symboles possèdent un dénominateur commun : « Deviens qui tu es ! » Car ceci est la carte des tâches de la vie : nous commençons le chemin de notre vie en petit, comme le cheval et le cavalier de l'image, davantage esquisse que portrait fini – le contenu doit être encore rempli et peint en entier. Notre but, notre chance est le plein épanouissement personnel ; l'importance en est soulignée par les lignes rouge-violet. Le bâton géant signale un dynamisme prononcé, une énergie de longue haleine. Les tâches pour la vie sont les meilleures et les plus grandes tâches que nous puissions nous donner. Elles nous occupent toute une vie, focalisent et stimulent toutes nos forces. Idéaux nobles et instincts amphibiens seront peut-être à surmonter sur cette route. Qui a beaucoup de feu n'est pas seulement particulièrement courageux, il ou elle est peut-être particulièrement fatigué(e), timide ou irritable. « Un enfant brûlé craint le feu. » Le crapaud bleu couvert de bijoux s'impose comme point de fuite à double titre. Le cavalier semble le fuir et en même temps être attiré par lui.

Conseils pratiques : *Vous recelez un énorme potentiel d'énergie. Apportez de la lumière dans l'obscurité, aidez les plus faibles et engagez-vous dans des projets intelligents qui sont d'une grande utilité pour beaucoup d'êtres humains. La lumière est le plus nécessaire là où l'obscurité est la plus profonde. Là vous trouverez des missions à votre mesure, si grandes qu'elles suffisent pour une vie entière. Mettez-vous en route dès maintenant !*

Page of Wands
Page der Stäbe
Valet de Bâton

PAGE OF WANDS

Renewed Strength

Only on this card is the central figure totally enveloped in his own aura, from head to foot! This has a double meaning: the PAGE OF WANDS (in other decks also KNAVE or PRINCESS) is totally immersed in his own concerns. He surrenders to his flame and his passion unconditionally and is always full of enthusiasm. At the same time, the card counsels us to be aware of the limitations of our perceptions, because we are absorbed in our own world. The snake-like or butterfly-like drawings around the central figure alert us to our much greater potential. Our zest for action and desire to develop urge us on to reach beyond our own boundaries now.

In relation to our motivational forces (wands, fire, energy) the scope of our actual experience is relatively small. This is a danger, but also an opportunity. Beware of naive inactivity as well as of effusive zeal. We once entered this life full of the will to survive, to grow, and to express ourselves. We can harness this zeal now to explore the world thoroughly, greeting each success or failure as a new experience. If we welcome ordeals of fire and recognize them as a form of inner purification, we will find ourselves enriched by these lessons. Our ability always to go beyond ourselves gives us renewed strength and replenishes our youthful vitality.

Practical advice: *Learn to understand energies that are larger than you are. Beware of narrow-mindedness. Hold onto that which makes your heart sing and your spirit soar!*

Frische Kräfte

Nur bei dieser Karte ist die Bildfigur von ihrer eigenen Aura von Kopf bis Fuß ganz umgeben! Die Karte ist mehrdeutig: Zu den Besonderheiten des PAGEN (in anderen Tarot-Decks auch BUBE, PRINZESSIN) DER STÄBE gehört das völlige Eintauchen in die eigene Betroffenheit, man ist ganz Feuer und Flamme, man gibt sich seinem Schwarm und seiner Begeisterung ohne Einschränkung hin. Gleichzeitig warnt die Karte damit vor der begrenzten Reichweite des Bewusstseins: Man erfasst eben nur die eigene Welt. Die eigenen Möglichkeiten sind jedoch größer, was durch die schlangen- und falterartigen Farblinien außerhalb der zentralen Bildfigur dargestellt wird. Tatendrang und Wachstumslust stellen uns jetzt vor die Aufgabe, über uns selbst hinauszuwachsen.

Im Vergleich zu dem, was uns bewegt und umtreibt (Stäbe, Feuerenergie), ist die Erfahrung, die wir mitbringen, gering. Das ist Gefahr und Chance zugleich. Wir müssen uns hüten vor ahnungsloser Untätigkeit und vor schwärmerischem Eifer. Wie wir einst die Welt betreten haben, voller Lebenswillen, instinktivem Wachstumsdrang und selbstverständlicher Triebkraft, so können wir auch unser jetziges Leben hingebungsvoll entdecken und jeden Erfolg oder Misserfolg, jedes Ereignis als neue Erfahrung begrüßen. Wenn wir Feuerproben bejahen und als innere Reinigung erleben, werden wir diese Erfahrungen als Bereicherung empfinden. Die Fähigkeit, über uns hinauszuwachsen, schenkt uns immer wieder neue Kraft und erhält so unsere Jugendlichkeit.

Praxistipps: *Begreifen Sie Energien, die größer sind als Sie selbst. Hüten und schützen Sie sich vor Engherzigkeiten. Halten Sie sich an das, was Ihr Herz in Schwung hält!*

Forces nouvelles

Sur cette carte seulement le personnage est entièrement enveloppé de sa propre aura de la tête aux pieds! Cette carte transmet donc plusieurs messages: une des particularités du VALET (dans d'autres jeux de tarot également PAGE, PRINCESSE) DE BÂTON est son immersion totale dans sa propre exaltation, on est absolument tout feu tout flamme, on s'adonne sans réserve à son idole et à son enthousiasme. La carte met ainsi en garde contre une portée limitée de la conscience: on ne peut en effet cerner que son univers individuel. Néanmoins, les chances personnelles sont plus grandes, ce dont témoignent les lignes de couleur aux allures de serpent et de papillons qui entourent la figure centrale. Dynamisme et désir de progression nous imposent désormais la tâche de nous surpasser.

En comparaison de ce qui nous fait bouger et nous anime (bâtons, énergie du feu) l'expérience que nous accumulons ne pèse pas lourd. Ceci constitue à la fois un danger et une chance. Nous devons éviter la passivité naïve et le zèle idolâtre. Comme lorsque nous sommes venus au monde, pleins de vitalité, de désir de croissance et de dynamisme inné, nous pouvons aussi explorer notre vie actuelle avec émerveillement et saluer chaque succès et chaque échec comme une expérience nouvelle. Si nous acceptons les épreuves du feu, nous les vivons comme une purification intérieure. La capacité de nous dépasser nous procure sans cesse une vigueur nouvelle et conserve ainsi notre juvénilité.

Conseils pratiques: *Saisissez les énergies qui sont plus grandes que vous-même. Gardez-vous et protégez-vous des mesquineries. Attachez-vous à ce qui donne de l'élan à votre cœur!*

Ace of Wands
Ass der Stäbe
As de Bâton

Instinctive Drive

The growing flower on the right symbolizes personal drives, motivating forces, and the endeavors of each individual. Human beings possess basic instincts such as self-preservation and reproduction as well as "cultural instincts" such as love and aggression.

Our instincts determine our behavior and actions, as the symbolic hands on this and other cards of the wands show. We can only succeed in all our endeavors and put out green shoots if we are in constant contact with our inner fire.

Yet sometimes, we fail. We have to go through many ordeals of fire, sometimes even burning to cinders like the mythical phoenix, if we want to be born again, as symbolized by the sickle in the upper right-hand corner and the flower.

The positive result of all such transformational processes is a cleansing and purification of our instincts and behavior. Therefore, wands and the fire element in general are symbols of the human will. If all goes well, we will discover our true will.

This card is all about finding our real identity and true home. To be centered within ourselves and at the same time at home in the world often entails two conflicting issues or two ends of a wand that need to be united.

Practical advice: *This card challenges you to do something active and yet also to have the courage to let something happen. You will learn the answer by doing. Follow your energy and keep moving. Closely observe your fellow human beings and pay attention to relevant forces.*

Triebkraft

Die Pflanzentriebe symbolisieren die persönlichen Triebe eines Menschen, seine Impulse und Bestrebungen. Neben den „Grundtrieben" wie Selbsterhaltung und Fortpflanzung prägen das menschliche Verhalten auch „Kulturtriebe" wie Liebe und Hass.

Unsere Triebe bestimmen unsere Handlungen, ausgedrückt durch das Symbol der Hände, die wir im vorliegenden Bild und einigen anderen Stab-Karten wiederfinden. Wenn wir in gutem Kontakt mit unserem inneren Feuer sind, dann „kommen wir auf einen grünen Zweig", unsere Vorhaben gelingen uns.

Mitunter aber scheitern unsere Vorhaben. Wir haben Feuerproben zu bewältigen, und manchmal müssen wir wie der Vogel Phönix innerlich verbrennen, um dann neu zu erstehen. (Dies drücken im vorliegenden Bild die Sichel ganz oben und die Blume aus.)

Das positive Ergebnis solcher Läuterungs- und Wandlungsprozesse ist eine Reinigung, eine Läuterung unserer Triebe und Taten. So gelten die Stäbe und das Element Feuer auch als Symbole des menschlichen Willens. Wenn es gut geht, finden wir unseren wahren Willen. Nicht zuletzt geht es um die eigene Identität und die Heimat, die wir in dieser Welt finden. Bei sich und in der Welt zu Hause zu sein, stellt oftmals zwei gegensätzliche Aufgaben dar, quasi die beiden Enden des einen Stabes, die es miteinander zu vereinen gilt.

Praxistipps: *Stab-Karten sind einerseits die Aufforderung zum aktiven Handeln, fordern andererseits aber auch den Mut, etwas geschehen zu lassen. Im Handeln finden Sie die gesuchte Antwort oder Lösung. Folgen Sie Ihrer Energie, bleiben Sie in Bewegung. Beachten Sie die Entwicklung Ihrer Mitmenschen, und berücksichtigen Sie alle wirksamen Kräfte.*

Énergie

Les pousses végétales symbolisent les instincts profonds de l'homme, ses impulsions et ses efforts. En plus des « instincts primitifs » comme les instincts de conservation et de reproduction, les instincts « civilisé » tels l'amour et la haine déterminent le comportement humain.

Nos instincts influent sur nos actes, exprimés ici par le symbole des mains, que nous retrouvons aussi dans plusieurs autres cartes de bâton. Si nous avons un bon contact avec notre feu intérieur, alors nous sommes bien branchés et notre projet réussit.

Mais parfois nos entreprises échouent. Nous devons surmonter des épreuves du feu et quelquefois brûler intérieurement comme le phénix, pour renaître à nouveau. (La faucille en haut de l'image ainsi que la fleur en sont l'expression imagée.)

Le résultat positif de tels processus d'amélioration et d'évolution est une purification, une transformation de nos instincts et de nos actes. Aussi, les bâtons et le feu font figure de symboles de la volonté humaine. Si cela fonctionne, nous trouvons notre volonté réelle. Il s'agit de notre propre identité et de la patrie que nous trouvons en ce monde. Être chez soi en soi-même et dans le monde, voilà deux objectifs bien souvent contradictoires, en somme les deux extrémités d'un seul bâton qu'il convient d'associer.

Conseils pratiques : *Les cartes de bâton sont d'une part l'encouragement à une action concrète, mais exigent d'autre part le courage de laisser les événements se produire. Dans l'action vous trouverez la réponse désirée ou la solution. Suivez votre énergie, restez en mouvement. Observez l'évolution des personnes de votre entourage et stimulez toutes les forces actives.*

Two of Wands
Zwei der Stäbe
Deux de Bâton

Primal Forces

Two wands or two flames represent primal energies or basic instincts that are hard to handle. This conflict might pertain to short-term interests and intentions, such as having to accomplish two different things at the same time or wanting to do so. More fundamental conflicts may be at stake, such as loving two people at the same time or co-ordinating family and career. The message of this card is that a solution is always to hand! It is possible to overcome even the greatest of difficulties. Turn emotional conflicts into practical tasks and find the solution that fits the problem.

This solution always has to do with an alchemical transformation of the coarse into the subtle. Break up the seemingly insurmountable problem into smaller portions that are easier to deal with. This approach is much more useful than "staring the snake in the eye" (note the green something at the foot of the figure) and much better than false compromises.

It is necessary to have a model and a vision of the cho-sen objective — like the miniature castle with swans de-picted on the silver platter or mirror that the woman is carrying. It may be necessary to go through the fires of hell to achieve these goals. The bird on the right could be a cock, the symbol of alertness and of pride. With a little imagination, a phoenix can be identified, the bird of fire, the legendary bird that has to burn up periodically to be reborn from the ashes and regain its beauty. Rather than a martial rendering of this card, Dalí emphasizes the aspect of beauty.

Practical advice: *Great tasks lie before you. Do not allow yourself to be pushed into a corner. You will succeed only if your will and your enthusiasm are unbroken. Rely on your own strength. Have confidence in your determination and your self-discipline. Wait until your vision has become clear and your mind is made up. Then do not hesitate any longer. Act with all your might.*

Urkräfte

Zwei Stäbe, zwei Flammen stehen für Grundenergien, für grundlegende Triebe, deren richtige Handhabung Mühe macht. Dieser Widerspruch kann sich auf eher kurzfristige Interessen und Absichten beziehen, so wie man im Alltag zwei Aufgaben gleichzeitig erfüllen muss oder möchte. Es können aber auch stärkere Grundkonflikte gemeint sein, etwa wenn man zwei Menschen gleichzeitig liebt oder einen Konflikt zwischen Familie und Karriere verspürt.

Die Botschaft dieser Karte lautet: Es gibt eine sinnvolle Lösung. Es ist möglich, auch übergroße Konflikte zu meistern. Wandeln Sie emotionale Konflikte in praktische Aufgaben und Lösungswege um.

Die Lösung hat mit einer „alchemistischen Wandlung" vom Groben zum Feinen zu tun: Das zunächst riesige Problem gilt es, in kleine handliche Stücke aufzuteilen. Das ist besser, als „auf die Schlange zu starren" (symbolisiert durch das grüne Etwas zu Füßen der Bildfigur) und besser als jeder faule Kompromiss!

Man braucht ein Modell – wie es die Bildfigur in Gestalt des Schlosses mit Schwänen auf einem Spiegel oder Silbertablett vor sich trägt –, eine Vision der eigenen Ziele. Und man braucht die Bereitschaft, für seine Ziele durchs Feuer zu gehen. Der Vogel am Bildrand könnte ein Hahn sein, Symbol für Aufgeweckheit und Stolz, oder – mit mehr Phantasie – auch ein Feuervogel, ein Phönix. Der Vogel Phönix verbrennt sich in gewissen Abständen und entsteht hernach aus seiner Asche in neuer Schönheit. Diese Schönheit, und nicht das Martialische beschreibt Dalí in diesem Bild.

Praxistipps: *Große Aufgaben fordern Sie heraus. Lassen Sie sich nicht in die Enge treiben. Der Erfolg hängt von Ihrem ungebrochenem Willen und Ihrer Begeisterung ab. Daher zählen Vertrauen in die eigene Kraft, Entschlossenheit und Beherrschtheit. Warten Sie, bis Ihre Vision sich deutlich herauskristallisiert und Ihr Entschluss feststeht. Dann zögern Sie nicht länger. Handeln Sie und setzen Sie all Ihre Energien ein.*

Forces primitives

Deux bâtons ou deux flammes symbolisent les énergies profondes, les instincts élémentaires qui sont bien difficiles à manier. Ce paradoxe peut s'appliquer à des désirs et intentions à court terme, comme on doit ou voudrait remplir simultanément deux tâches. Mais il peut être aussi question de deux conflits plus profonds, comme lorsqu'on aime deux personnes à la fois ou qu'on ressent par exemple un conflit entre famille et carrière.

Le message de cette carte est le suivant : une solution adéquate existe. Il est possible de régler d'immenses conflits. Transformez les conflits émotionnels en tâches pratiques et en dénouements heureux.

La solution n'est pas sans rappeler une « transformation alchimique » de la grossièreté à la finesse : il faut diviser le problème apparemment géant en petits morceaux. Cela vaut mieux que « de fixer du regard le serpent » (symbolisé par la chose informe aux pieds du personnage) et cela est préférable à tout compromis tordu !

On a besoin d'un modèle – comme la figure en porte un sur un miroir ou un plateau sous forme d'un château où apparaissent des cygnes –, d'une vision de ses propres objectifs. Et il faut être disposé à traverser le feu pour atteindre ses objectifs. L'oiseau au bord de l'image pourrait être un coq, symbole de l'éveil et de l'orgueil, ou encore – avec plus d'imagination – un oiseau de feu, un phénix. Le phénix se brûle plusieurs fois et renaît de ses cendres encore plus beau qu'avant. C'est la beauté, et non l'aspect martial, que Dalí souligne dans cette image.

Conseils pratiques : *De grandes tâches sont là pour vous défier. Ne vous laissez pas enfermer dans la petitesse. Le succès dépend de votre volonté intacte et de votre enthousiasme. La confiance en votre propre force, la détermination et la maîtrise sont donc indispensables. Attendez que votre vision se soit cristallisée et que votre décision soit irrévocable. Alors n'hésitez pas plus longtemps. Agissez et engagez toutes vos énergies.*

Three of Wands
Drei der Stäbe
Trois de Bâton

Prudence

The human longing for distant shores shows up on this card in several forms. The big ship symbolizes wanderlust, the spirit of adventure, and the yearning for faraway places. The female silhouette does not represent any particular woman, but women in general, the mother archetype, or the feminine principle. Many philosophers have described the ocean as the "eternally feminine," the source and aim of all our striving.

The female silhouette and the ship hint at opposing desires: the longing for closeness and the desire for remoteness, for home and abroad, arrival and departure. It requires a lot of practical experience and individual metamorphoses. Personal advances (represented by the butterflies) unite instincts and actions (symbolized by wands and ship) patiently and serenely (the shadowy woman and the ocean), in such a way that one does not take precedence over the other.

What's so special about this image is the way that the woman and the ship are connected. Even the greatest of undertakings are based on aspects close to hand, namely in personal relationships. It is contact with others that gives us the energy and the fuel to go forth into the farthest corners of the earth.

Practical advice: *Acting half-heartedly is a waste of time. If you put all your effort and all your power into something, you will succeed. Become clear what it is that you want to achieve and which personal and emotional needs are related to your most important goals! Deliberate action is the key to passion as distinguished from mere enthusiasm. Be aware of what you are doing.*

Besonnenheit

Die Sehnsucht nach neuen Ufern zeigt sich in diesem Bild gleich mehrfach. Das große Schiff symbolisiert Fernweh, Unternehmungsgeist und Abenteuerlust. Die Frauen-Silhouette stellt in dieser abstrakten Form nicht so sehr eine bestimmte Frau dar, sondern die Frau im Allgemeinen, die Mutter, das Weibliche. Auch das Meer wird vielfach beschrieben als das „Ewig-Weibliche", Urgrund und Ziel allen Strebens. Die Silhouette und das Schiff stehen möglicherweise für Gegensätze: den Wunsch nach Weite und die Suche nach Nähe; für Heimat und Fremde; für Ankunft und Abschied.

Es braucht Erfahrung und persönliche Metamorphosen (Entwicklungsschritte, die durch die Schmetterlinge betont werden), bis wir unsere Trieb- und Tatkraft (dargestellt durch die Stäbe und das Schiff) mit Hingabe, Geduld und Gleichmut (dargestellt durch Schattenfrau und Meer) so vereinen können, dass nicht das eine auf Kosten des anderen geht. Das Besondere dieser Darstellung besteht darin, dass es das Schiff und die Frauengestalt in einen Zusammenhang stellt. Auch abenteuerliche Großunternehmungen haben demnach ganz naheliegende Gründe – eben in den persönlichen Beziehungen. Und in diesen Verbindungen zu anderen liegt, im guten wie im schlechten Sinn, der Treibstoff, die Energie, die uns bis in die entlegensten Winkel der Erde bringt!

Praxistipps: *Halbherziges Agieren bringt Sie nicht weiter. Es gibt bessere Lösungen, die Ihren ungeteilten Einsatz und Ihre ganze Kraft erfordern. Machen Sie sich bewusst, was Sie erreichen wollen und welche persönlichen, emotionalen Bedürfnisse mit Ihren wichtigsten Zielen im Grunde verbunden sind! Bewusstes Handeln ist die entscheidende Basis für eine Begeisterung, die sich vom bloßen Enthusiasmus dadurch unterscheidet, dass sie weiß, was sie tut.*

Modération

L'aspiration à de nouveaux rivages est présente à plusieurs égards sur cette image.

Le grand bateau symbolise le désir de voyages, l'esprit d'entreprise et le goût de l'aventure. La silhouette féminine sous cette forme abstraite ne représente pas tant une femme particulière que la femme en général, la mère, la féminité. La mer est souvent également décrite comme l'« éternel féminin », cause profonde et but de toute ambition. La silhouette et le bateau représentent peut-être des contrastes: la nostalgie de pays lointains et la recherche de la proximité ; la patrie et l'étranger ; l'arrivée et le départ.

L'expérience et les métamorphoses personnelles (stades d'évolution que matérialisent les papillons) sont nécessaires afin que nous puissions unir notre dynamisme et notre énergie (représentés par les bâtons et le bateau) à notre ardeur, notre patience et notre constance (représentées par l'ombre féminine et la mer), que l'un ne se fasse pas aux dépens de l'autre. La particularité de cette création consiste en la liaison établie entre le bateau et la figure féminine. De fait, même de grandes entreprises ont des mobiles très naturels – à savoir les relations personnelles. Et dans ces relations avec l'autre, dans le bon comme dans le mauvais sens, réside le carburant, l'énergie qui nous entraîne jusqu'au bout du monde !

Conseils pratiques : *Agir sans conviction ne vous avance à rien. Il existe de meilleures solutions qui exigent votre engagement sans partage et toute votre force. Soyez conscient de ce que vous voulez atteindre et quels besoins personnels et émotionnels sont au fond liés à vos objectifs majeurs ! Une action consciente est la base déterminante pour un engouement qui se différencie du simple enthousiasme par le fait qu'il est conscient de ce qu'il fait.*

Four of Wands
Vier der Stäbe
Quatre de Bâton

The Wonders of Creation

Dance, music, and play are united in this picture. Blue-green garlands can be seen above the figures and blue flowers below. The four wands are framed by two typical Dalí crutches and a red ribbon (cloth or ornament).

The sheet music reminds us of a heavenly score or a divine instruction book. One might assume that it is God's will for us to dance, sing, and be merry. But also that our human merriments are small and go around in circles unless we take the higher dimension of our being into consideration. In many cultural traditions, a blue flower represents the mysteries of life and the wonders of creation.

The term "wonders of creation" pertains to our most intimate, our most difficult, and most beautiful experiences. Birth, marriage, and death (which may be represented by the three figures) always take us to the very limits of our understanding. Through being confronted with these sometimes frightening, sometimes wonderful, but always amazing limits to our comprehension, we develop a hunger for culture, a yearning to express that which really moves us through play, music, and dance! All truly creative endeavors are born out of testing our limits in some way.

Parties and cultural events may either inspire us or divert us to the extent that we almost lose track of ourselves. This card is all about rediscovering what really moves you, deepening your understanding of yourself, as you climb up the ladder of life.

Practical advice: *Avoid petty solutions and false compromises. Neither forget nor hide your true motives and authentic feelings. They are the true source of your motivation and will guarantee your greatest successes.*

Wunder der Schöpfung

Tanz, Musik und Spiel finden sich im Bild vereint. In der Höhe sieht man blaugrüne Girlanden und in der Tiefe eine blaue Blume, die vier Stäbe werden von zwei typischen Dalí-Krücken und einem roten Band (Tuch, Ornament) eingerahmt.

Das aufgeschlagene Notenbuch lässt an eine himmlische Partitur, eine „göttliche" Spielanleitung denken. „Gott" will, dass wir singen, tanzen und uns vergnügen, so könnte man schlussfolgern. Und: Unsere Vergnügen sind klein und drehen sich im Kreise, solange wir die höheren und tieferen Dimensionen nicht beachten. Die blaue Blume ist in vielen Kulturen ein Inbegriff der Geheimnisse des Lebens, der Wunder der Schöpfung.

Die Wunder der Schöpfung betreffen unsere intimsten – schwierigsten und schönsten – Erfahrungen. Geburt, Hochzeit und Tod (ein Dreiklang, der sich möglicherweise in den drei Bildfiguren wiederfindet) führen uns immer wieder an die Grenzen unserer Erkenntnis. Und an diesen manchmal erschreckenden, oft wunderbaren, immer aber erstaunlichen Grenzen der Erkenntnis erwächst das Bedürfnis nach Kultur – der Wunsch, in Spiel, Musik und Tanz das auszudrücken und zu verarbeiten, was uns bewegt! Alle wirklich kreativen Prozesse berühren in irgendeiner Weise diese intimen Grenzerfahrungen.

Feiern und kulturelle Veranstaltungen können uns beflügeln oder so „zerstreuen", dass wir uns kaum noch wiederfinden. Es kommt darauf an, (wieder) zu spüren, was uns innerlich bewegt, das eigene Selbstverständnis zu vertiefen, je höher wir im Leben steigen.

Praxistipps: *Meiden Sie halbherzige Lösungen und faule Kompromisse. Ihre wahren Beweggründe und Ihre echten Gefühle sollten Sie nicht verbergen oder vergessen. Sie liefern Ihnen die beste Motivation und garantieren Ihnen die schönsten Erfolge.*

Miracle de la Création

Danse, musique et jeu se trouvent réunis dans cette image. Dans le haut on voit des guirlandes vert-bleu et dans le bas une fleur bleue, les quatre bâtons sont encadrés des fameuses béquilles de Dalí et d'un ruban rouge (tissu, ornement). Le cahier de notes ouvert fait penser à une partition céleste, une composition musicale « divine ». « Dieu » veut que nous chantions, dansions et nous amusions, semble-t-il. Et nos plaisirs sont petits et tournent en rond tant que nous ignorons les dimensions plus profondes et supérieures. Pour de nombreuses civilisations la fleur bleue est le symbole des mystères de la vie, des miracles de la Création.

Les miracles de la Création touchent nos expériences les plus intimes – les plus pénibles et les plus belles. Naissance, mariage et mort (une trinité qui se retrouve peut-être dans les trois personnages) nous entraînent sans cesse aux limites de notre connaissance. Et aux limites parfois effrayantes, souvent merveilleuses, toujours étonnantes de la connaissance grandit le besoin de culture – le désir d'exprimer et d'assimiler par le jeu, la musique et la danse tout ce qui nous émeut.

Tous les processus vraiment créatifs touchent nos expériences les plus intimes.

Les fêtes et manifestations culturelles peuvent nous élever ou nous « distraire » si bien que nous nous retrouvons à peine. Il importe de sentir (à nouveau) ce qui nous touche intérieurement, d'approfondir la connaissance de notre personnalité, plus nous nous élevons dans la vie.

Conseils pratiques : *Évitez les solutions bancales et les compromis tordus. Vous ne devriez pas cacher vos mobiles réels et vos sentiments véritables. Ils vous apportent la meilleure motivation et vous garantissent les plus belles réussites.*

Five of Wands
Fünf der Stäbe
Cinq de Bâton

Shaping Your Will

Wands stand for instinctive drives and initiative and represent the fire element. Five wands are the essence of the fire element: the human will. Our will is made up of our deeds and intentions, our consciously chosen actions, and our unconscious motives.

As long as the fire of life burns, your will is constantly being reshaped. In the background, seven or eight helmets of lance-bearers and twelve lances can be seen on the card. Each one of the twelve lances and of the five green wands represents a certain type of energy. As if participating in a huge game of pick-up sticks, it is your task to gather up this energy, to sort through it, and to focus it on something worthwhile.

Different interests and tendencies are always pulling in different directions. What has first priority? How can several goals be attained at the same time?

An integral part of this process of shaping the will is for existing role models to become obsolete. The red area in the middle of the card stands for your personal fire, your power and vivacity, creating new facts that go way beyond traditional experiences, thus dismissing those redundant conceptions.

Do not spread your energies too thin. Center yourself. See your current tasks as tests of your determination, your willpower—and your playfulness. Find out which aspects of your will are in harmony with your desires and so able to get something moving. Find out which acts of will are superfluous, because you are still trying to force something to happen that is actually no longer relevant, or has not yet become so.

Practical advice: *Create space in your daily routine. This might include taking some time out or establishing your own room. New alternatives are waiting to be explored and tested in your personal relationships and in your career. Go for it!*

Willensbildung

Stäbe stehen für Triebe und Tatkraft, sie symbolisieren das Element Feuer. Fünf Stäbe verkörpern die Quintessenz des Feuerelements – den Willen. Er setzt sich aus unseren Taten und Absichten, aus bewussten Aktionen und unbewussten Ereignissen zusammen.

Solange das Lebensfeuer brennt, bildet sich auch der persönliche Wille permanent neu. Im Hintergrund sind Lanzen und Helme von Lanzenträgern zu erkennen. Jede dieser Lanzen und jeder der fünf grünen Stäbe im Bild stellen ein Stück Energie dar. Wie in einem überdimensionalen Mikado gilt es nun, diese Energien zu sammeln, zu sortieren und zu bündeln. Unterschiedliche Interessen und Neigungen müssen immer wieder miteinander ringen: Was hat Priorität? Wie können mehrere Ziele gleichzeitig erreicht werden?

Zu diesem Prozess der Willensbildung gehört auch, überkommene Leitbilder zu überwinden. Die rote Farbfläche in der Bildmitte steht für das persönliche Feuer, für Kraft und Lebendigkeit, die neue Fakten schaffen, die sich nicht mehr an Vorbildern orientieren, weil sie über bisherige Erfahrungen hinausgehen.

Verzetteln Sie sich nicht im Spiel der Kräfte. Achten Sie auf Ihre Mitte. Nehmen Sie Ihre aktuellen Aufgaben als Bewährungsproben für Ihre Entschlossenheit, Ihre Willensstärke und – Ihre Spielfreude! Testen Sie: Welche Bestrebungen des Willens entsprechen wirklichen Wünschen und können deshalb etwas bewegen? Welche Willens- oder Kraftakte sind überflüssig, weil Sie etwas erzwingen wollen, das nicht mehr oder noch nicht aktuell ist?

Praxistipps: *Sorgen Sie für Spielraum in Ihrem Alltag: Dazu können Mußestunden oder etwa die Einrichtung eines eigenen Zimmers verhelfen. Aber auch in Ihren privaten Beziehungen und Ihren beruflichen Aufgaben warten neue Alternativen darauf, dass Sie sie entdecken und erkunden. Tun Sie es!*

Formation de la volonté

Les bâtons représentent les instincts et le dynamisme, ils symbolisent l'élément du feu. Cinq bâtons incarnent la quintessence du feu – la volonté. Celle-ci se compose de nos actes et intentions, des actions conscientes et des événements conscients.

Tant que le feu de la vie flambe, la volonté personnelle se reforme en permanence.

En arrière-plan apparaissent les lances et les casques de hallebardiers. Chacune de ces lances et chacun des cinq bâtons verts de l'image représentent une part d'énergie. Comme dans un jeu de mikado surdimensionné il s'agit à présent de rassembler ces énergies, de les trier et de les réunir. Intérêts et penchants divers doivent sans cesse s'affronter : Où est la priorité ? Comment atteindre plusieurs objectifs simultanément ?

Surmonter les clichés transmis fait aussi partie de ce processus de formation de la volonté. La surface rouge au centre de l'image figure le feu personnel, la force et la vivacité, qui créent les faits nouveaux et ne s'orientent plus sur les modèles parce qu'ils surpassent les expériences vécues jusqu'alors.

Ne vous dispersez pas dans le jeu des forces ! Ne négligez pas votre milieu. Considérez vos défis actuels comme des épreuves de vérité pour votre détermination, votre force de caractère et – votre amour du jeu ! Faites le test : Quels efforts de la volonté correspondent aux désirs véritables et que peuvent-ils provoquer ? Quels actes de volonté ou de force sont superflus parce qu'ils veulent obtenir de force quelque chose qui n'est plus ou pas encore actuel ?

Conseils pratiques : *Créez-vous un espace de liberté dans votre quotidien : sous forme d'heures de détente ou en aménageant une pièce rien que pour vous. Mais dans vos relations privées et dans vos tâches professionnelles de nouvelles alternatives attendent que vous les découvriez et les exploitiez. Alors agissez !*

Six of Wands
Sechs der Stäbe
Six de Bâton

Gaining Strength

At first glance, the picture seems to show a proud and strong horseman. At second glance, however, we discover that he is holding only one of the six wands in his hand. Five wands remain in the background.

On the left, we see a small, faceless figure. It represents man's proverbial inner child. We may rightfully assume that this aspect of the rider is underdeveloped as the figure is drawn so sketchily and with no face. As long as the rider fails to accept his inner child, and as long as he exploits only a fraction of the powers at his disposal (only one of six wands), he will be driven by childish motives and fears—without even being aware of it.

We often assume that we have to suppress our weaknesses in order to become proud and strong. The picture shows us that in reality, the opposite is true. If you acknowledge strengths as well as weaknesses, you will become much stronger. (See the horse and the energy of the five additional wands.) The five wands represent influences and events that are beyond your control. If you know your strengths and your weaknesses, you will become much more flexible. Thus you enhance your ability to cooperate with your destiny.

You need to reconcile yourself with your inner child and with your own animalistic aspects. You must make peace with your own imperfections and say good-bye to many immature habits. This process of growing up is represented by the ring and the single wand, which symbolize the differences between as well as the unification of the feminine and the masculine. A mature sexuality makes demands on your personal power and enhances it, vitalizing your self-confidence. It is important to recognize the feminine and the masculine as two aspects of your own personality.

Practical advice: *Do not be intimidated and don't intimidate others. Stand up for what moves you and go for it wholeheartedly.*

Kraftzuwachs

Auf den ersten Blick zeigt die Karte einen stolzen, starken Reiter. Bei genauerer Betrachtung sehen wir, dass er nur einen der sechs Stäbe in der Hand hält; fünf Stäbe stehen im Hintergrund.

Vorn im Bild ist eine kleine, gesichtslose Gestalt zu erkennen. Diese Figur verkörpert das sprichwörtliche Kind im Mann. Seine schemenhafte Gestalt deutet an, dass diese Seite im Leben des Reiters wenig ausgebildet ist. Solange der Reiter das „innere Kind" nicht annimmt und verleugnet, solange treiben ihn kindlicher Eifer oder kindliche Ängste an, ohne dass er sich dessen besonders bewusst ist; und solange bewegt er sich auch nur mit einem Bruchteil der zur Verfügung stehenden Kräfte (nur mit einem von sechs Stäben).

Häufig meinen wir, man müsse Schwächen unterdrücken, um Stolz und Stärke zu demonstrieren. Das Bild kann zeigen, dass es sich in Wahrheit gerade umgekehrt verhält. Wer zu seinen Stärken und Schwächen steht, gewinnt zusätzliche Kräfte, dargestellt durch das Pferd und die Energie der fünf zusätzlichen Stäbe. Diese stehen für Einflüsse und Ereignisse, die nicht in unserer Hand liegen. Wer seine Stärken und Schwächen kennt, wird flexibler. So erweitern wir unsere Fähigkeit, „mit dem Schicksal zusammenzuarbeiten".

Dazu gehört die Versöhnung mit dem „inneren Kind" und mit den eigenen animalischen Anteilen, eine Versöhnung mit der eigenen Unvollkommenheit – und ein Abschied von manchen „grünen", das heißt noch unreifen Gewohnheiten. Dieser Prozess des Erwachsenwerdens findet sich im Bild auch in Gestalt von Ring und Stab, als Zeichen für die Vereinigung des Weiblichen und des Männlichen, wieder. Eine lebendige erwachsene Sexualität fordert und fördert die persönliche Kraft und ein vitales Selbstbewusstsein. Männlich und weiblich gilt es dabei, auch als zwei Seiten der eigenen Person zu sehen.

Praxistipps: *Lassen Sie sich nicht einschüchtern und setzen Sie auch andere nicht unter Druck. Vertreten Sie, was Sie innerlich bewegt, und setzen Sie sich ganz dafür ein.*

Amplification des forces

À première vue la carte montre un fort et fier cavalier. En y regardant de plus près nous voyons qu'il ne tient qu'un seul des six bâtons ; les cinq autres apparaissent à l'arrière-plan.

Sur le devant de l'image est dessinée une petite silhouette sans visage. Ce petit personnage incarne l'enfant proverbial enfoui dans l'homme. Sa forme schématique signalise que cette face est peu développée dans la vie du cavalier. Tant que le cavalier n'accepte pas ou renie l'« enfant intérieur », un zèle puéril ou des peurs enfantines l'animeront sans qu'il en soit particulièrement conscient ; et il n'utilisera qu'une fraction des forces dont il dispose (seulement l'un des six bâtons).

Souvent nous croyons qu'il faut absolument vaincre nos faiblesses pour faire démonstration d'orgueil et de force. L'image peut prouver qu'en réalité le contraire est le cas. Qui admet ses forces et ses faiblesses acquiert des forces supplémentaires, représentées par le cheval et l'énergie des cinq autres bâtons. Ceux-ci symbolisent les influences et les événements qui ne sont pas sous notre contrôle. Qui connaît ses forces et ses faiblesses devient plus flexible. Ainsi nous amplifions notre faculté à « collaborer avec le destin ».

Il ne faut pas oublier la réconciliation avec l'« enfant intérieur » et nos propres parts d'animalité, une réconciliation avec nos propres imperfections – et de quelques habitudes « vertes », c'est-à-dire encore immatures. Ce processus consistant à devenir adulte se retrouve sur l'image sous forme de cerceau et de bâton, signes de l'union du féminin et du masculin. Une sexualité vivante et adulte exige et favorise la force personnelle et une assurance personnelle vitale. Il faut considérer ici le masculin et le féminin comme les deux facettes d'une même personne.

Conseils pratiques : *Ne vous laissez pas intimider et ne mettez pas non plus les autres sous pression. Soutenez ce qui vous touche intérieurement et investissez-vous à fond.*

Seven of Wands
Sieben der Stäbe
Sept de Bâton

A New Level

This card often appears to be rather puzzling. It is all about the power of our actions. In the background, we see scenes from rural life in the olden days. They represent our life's journey with its many stages that sometimes repeat themselves at a higher level. Articulated at an angle against this background, seven wands and four arms and hands can be seen.

Hands and arms symbolize what and how we appreciate and handle things. This card indicates openness and reserve, the palms of our hands as well as the outside, and similarly of our actions. Our handicaps (that word hand again!) can be identified in the image as the hand with the protuberance and the fingerless hand (the first and second hands from the top). When arms and wands lie across our life's journey, they indicate that we do not have to accept what is being handed to us. We are being encouraged to march to the sound of our own tune, and shine our own light. Yet we are warned not to put up any unnecessary resistance towards life.

The thin blue figure on the right shows that we all possess roots that reach deep into the earth (see the spiral at the foot of the blue figure). We possess tools that enable us to reach for the stars (see the crutch or pincers that elongate the right hand of the figure).

We are always on an evolutionary journey. We constantly learn to deal with complex tasks and handle our energies. The seven wands arranged one above the other represent a ladder with seven rungs: a Jacob's ladder, which bridges the gap between heaven and earth, between our wishes and reality.

Practical advice: *All existing facts can be changed by your actions. But doing just for the sake of doing and morbid ambition will only harm you. It is of utmost importance to reach a new level and to use your power wisely and in a relaxed manner.*

Neues Niveau

Mitunter wirkt dieses Bild zunächst unverständlich. Es geht um die Macht unserer Handlungen. Im Hintergrund der Karte sind Szenen aus dem bäuerlichen Leben früherer Tage zu sehen. Diese stehen für unseren Lebensweg mit seinen Stationen, die sich manchmal wiederholen und zugleich weiterentwickeln. Quer zu diesen Szenen im Hintergrund liegen die sieben Stäbe sowie vier Arme und Hände.

Hände und Arme stellen symbolisch dar, was und wie wir etwas begreifen und bewegen. Hier zeigen sich Offenheit und Verschlossenheit, Außen- und Innenseiten unserer Hände/Handlungen. Auch unsere Handicaps (darin wieder das Wort Hand) sind im Bild als fingerlose Hand und Hand mit Geschwulst (zweite und erste Hand von oben) zu erkennen. Wenn nun Arme und Stäbe quer über den Szenen des Lebensweges liegen, bedeutet dies: Wir können uns dem Gang der Ereignisse entgegenstellen. Das ist eine Ermutigung, „aus der Reihe zu tanzen" und das eigene Licht zur Geltung zu bringen. Aber es ist auch eine Warnung vor Blockaden und unnötigen Widerständen.

Wie die kleine blaue Figur am rechten Rand illustriert, besitzen wir Wurzeln, die uns in der Erde verankern (die Spirale unter den Füßen), und uns stehen Werkzeuge zur Verfügung, die uns bis in den Himmel reichen lassen (die Krücke oder Zange als verlängerte rechte Hand der kleinen Figur).

Wir befinden uns auf einem Entwicklungsweg; wir lernen, mit unseren Aufgaben und Energien umzugehen. In diesem Sinne bedeuten die sieben übereinanderliegenden Stäbe eine Stufenleiter – eine Jakobsleiter, die die Kluft zwischen Himmel und Erde, zwischen Wunsch und Wirklichkeit überbrückt.

Praxistipps: *Sie haben die Möglichkeit, Bestehendes zu verändern. Aktionismus und Ehrgeiz schaden dabei eher. Entscheidend ist vielmehr ein neues Niveau, ein unverkrampfter, wacher Einsatz der Kräfte.*

Nouveau niveau

Cette image peut paraître incompréhensible au premier abord. Il s'agit du pouvoir de nos actions. À l'arrière-plan de la carte sont évoquées des scènes de la vie rurale d'antan. Celles-ci représentent notre chemin de vie avec ses stations qui parfois se répètent et simultanément évoluent. Les sept bâtons, ainsi que quatre bras et mains, entrecoupent ces scènes de fond.

Les mains et bras symbolisent ce que nous saisissons et agitons et comment nous le faisons. Ici apparaissent ouverture et herméticité, les faces et revers de nos mains/actions. Nos handicaps (dérivé du mot « hand in cap » en anglais) sont aussi présents dans l'image sous forme d'une main sans doigt et d'une main recouverte d'une tumeur (deuxième et première main à partir du haut). Si les bras et bâtons traversent les scènes de notre vie, cela signifie : nous pouvons nous dresser contre le cours des événements. C'est un encouragement à « sortir des rangs » et à mettre en valeur notre propre lumière. Mais c'est aussi un avertissement contre les blocages et résistances inutiles.

Comme la petite figure bleue sur le rebord droit l'illustre, nous avons des racines qui nous relient à la terre (la spirale sous les pieds de la silhouette bleue) et nous disposons d'instruments qui nous permettent de toucher le ciel (la béquille ou tenaille, prolongement de la main droite du petit personnage).

Nous nous trouvons sur une voie de transition ; nous apprenons à accepter nos tâches et à répartir nos énergies. Dans ce contexte les sept bâtons tracés les uns au-dessus des autres symbolisent une échelle – une échelle de Jacob, qui surmonte le vide entre ciel et terre, entre désir et réalité.

Conseils pratiques : *Vous avez la possibilité de transfomer ce qui existe. L'excès de zèle est ici plutôt néfaste. Ce qui importe beaucoup plus est un nouveau niveau, un investissement décomplexé et vigilant de vos forces.*

Eight of Wands
Acht der Stäbe
Huit de Bâton

Greater Responsibility

Wands represent vital energies—drives and aims ensure that the inner fire keeps on burning. Eight wands form a pattern of manifold and diverse energies. This is the card of multifarious energy transfer. As in the superimposition of several magnetic fields, the forces involved may either neutralize or enhance each other.

Dalí's version of this card is unusual as it shows a scene from *The Oath of the Horatii* by Jacques-Louis David. The Horatii secured the power of Rome around 660 BC by using subterfuge in a struggle against the Curiatii. Oath and treason, ideals and idols become topical whenever we encounter strong powers and have to learn to face them. Dalí rightfully puts the power of enthusiasm at the center of his picture.

The book in front of the two wands emphasizes the moving power of the human spirit and of the written word! Great undertakings require motivation and enthusiasm. The right word at the right time can work miracles and heal wounds. But false ideals can also make the blood boil. They open up old wounds and create new ones by being overly zealous or by exercising blind obedience. The insect on the left shows that this all happens on a subconscious, vegetative, or automatic level. The card counsels you to become aware of your own motivating forces and your goals, and to take full responsibility for your own actions. You are challenged to grow in understanding and stature!

Practical advice: *Make sure that good vibrations exist between you and other people. Learn to understand what moves you and others. Become more sensitive to the needs of all parties involved. Then you will be able to harmonize many different types of energy and accomplish many things without having to resort to manipulation.*

Größere Verantwortung

Stäbe verkörpern Lebensenergien – Trieb und Ziel lassen das innere Feuer brennen. Acht Stäbe stellen ein Muster recht zahlreicher, vielfältiger Energien dar. Es ist eine Karte der mannigfachen „Energieübertragung". Wie in der Überlagerung mehrerer Magnetfelder können sich unterschiedliche Kräfte verstärken oder gegenseitig aufheben.

Zu den Besonderheiten dieser Version Dalís gehört zunächst die Wahl des Ausschnitts aus dem Bild „Der Schwur der Horatier" von Jacques-Louis David. Die Horatier sicherten um 660 v. Chr. durch eine List im Kampf gegen die Curatier die Vorherrschaft Roms. Schwur und Verschwörung, Ideale und Idole werden immer dann zum Thema, wenn wir großen Energien begegnen und lernen müssen, mit diesen Kräften umzugehen. Dalí stellt mit Recht die Macht der Begeisterung in den Mittelpunkt des Bildes.

Das Motiv des Buches mit den zwei Stäben betont die bewegende Kraft des Geistes und des Wortes! Große Aufgaben erfordern Motivation und Enthusiasmus. Ein gutes Wort zur rechten Zeit kann Wunder wirken und Wunden heilen. Aber auch falsche Ideale bringen das Blut in Wallung – sie reißen neue Wunden, schaffen neue Verletzungen durch blinden Gehorsam oder Eifer. Das Insekt links im Bild zeigt, dass sich dies alles eher auf einer vegetativen, unbewussten oder automatischen Ebene abspielt. So ist diese Karte in der Praxis eine Aufforderung, sich seiner Antriebe und Ziele bewusster zu werden und insgesamt eine größere Verantwortung für das eigene Handeln zu übernehmen. Aufgabe und Lösung bestehen gleichermaßen darin, zu wachsen: an Einsicht und an persönlicher Größe!

Praxistipps: *Sorgen Sie für einen guten Energiefluss und für gute „Schwingungen", im Umgang mit sich selbst und mit anderen. Machen Sie sich bewusst, was Sie und andere wirklich bewegt. Verfeinern Sie die Wahrnehmung der Interessen aller Beteiligten. Dann werden Sie ohne jede Manipulation viele Energien vereinen und viele Anliegen voranbringen!*

Une plus grande responsabilité

Les bâtons incarnent les énergies vitales – instinct et finalité font brûler le feu intérieur. Huit bâtons représentent un modèle d'énergies nombreuses et variées. Ceci est une carte de « transmission d'énergie » multiple. Comme dans la superposition de plusieurs champs magnétiques diverses forces peuvent se renforcer ou s'annuler réciproquement.

Le choix d'un fragment du tableau « Le Serment des Horaces » de David compte parmi les particularités de cette version de Dalí. Vers 660 avant J.-C., les Horaces assurèrent la supériorité de Rome grâce à une ruse dans un combat contre les Curiaces.

Serment et conjuration, idéaux et idoles sont toujours un thème central lorsque nous devons faire face à de puissantes énergies et apprendre à les approcher. Dalí place à juste titre la force de l'enthousiasme au centre de l'image. Le motif du livre aux deux bâtons souligne la force mobilisante de l'esprit et de la parole ! Les grandes tâches exigent motivation et ardeur. Un mot juste au bon moment peut faire des miracles et guérir des blessures. Mais les faux idéaux peuvent échauffer le sang – ils ouvrent de nouvelles plaies, créent de nouvelles blessures par l'obéissance aveugle ou l'excès de zèle. L'insecte à gauche de l'image montre que tout cela se joue sur un plan végétatif, inconscient ou automatique. Ainsi cette carte est-elle pratiquement une invitation à prendre conscience de ses instincts et motifs et d'assumer en général une plus grande responsabilité face à ses propres actes. La tâche et la solution consistent, l'une comme l'autre, à grandir : en perspicacité et en valeur personnelle !

Conseils pratiques : *Assurez-vous d'un bon flux d'énergie et de bonnes « vibrations » dans vos rapports avec vous-même et avec autrui. Prenez conscience de ce qui vous touche vraiment, vous et les autres. Soyez perceptifs aux intérêts de tous les participants. Alors vous pourrez sans aucune manipulation unir beaucoup d'énergies et faire progresser beaucoup de désirs !*

Nine of Wands
Neun der Stäbe
Neuf de Bâton

Stalking

This card is a symbol of searching, of awareness, and of intuitive perception. Many things are growing (see the nine wands) and changing (the autumn scene). Like a hunter stalking his prey or a scout exploring the way, you need to be intuitively alert and vigilant. Naturally, this card is not about the actual hunter or scout as a profession, it is a symbol of heightened awareness as a personal way of being.

If your perception has been heightened, you will be better able to understand the motives and hidden interests behind certain actions. Thus you will be able to discover the "green man" in the woods. This figure appears in many traditions. He symbolizes nature around us and within. Dalí depicts his green man with frog's feet, thus making him an amphibious creature living between water and earth. He reaches out to the stalking hunter.

On the one hand, this card shows us the final goal of all our searching. Intuition and awareness are the path as well as the destination, the journey as well as the reward. Sometimes, we get lost in routine and repetition. We fail to perceive the great mystery that is awaiting us.

On the other hand, this card encourages us to say good-bye to the uncivilized life of a semi-barbarian. Intuition and awareness serve to overcome certain primal fears. Let go of redundant instincts and presumptions. Trust your actual perceptions and learn from all your experiences.

Practical advice: *Your actual situation challenges you to become more vital and to live life to the fullest. Abandon your old fears and fulfill your most important wishes! Activate your senses! Learn to recognize outdated habits.*

Auf der Pirsch

Ein Bild der Suche, der Achtsamkeit und der intuitiven Wahrnehmung: Vieles ist im Wachstum (Stäbe) und im Wandel (Herbst) begriffen. Wie ein Jäger auf der Pirsch oder ein Kundschafter auf seinem Pfad brauchen wir eine verstärkte Aufmerksamkeit, eine intuitive Wachheit. Natürlich geht es nicht um das Jagen und Kundschaften als konkrete Tätigkeit, sondern um ein Sinnbild für eine gesteigerte Aufmerksamkeit als einem persönlichen Normalzustand.

Unsere verfeinerte Wahrnehmung lässt uns auch die Interessen und Motive hinter den Aktionen besser verstehen. Und so finden wir den Weg zu dem „grünen Mann" im Wald. Der „grüne Mann" tritt in alten Überlieferungen auf; er symbolisiert die Natur um und in uns. Bei Dalí hat er Froschfüße – ein Amphibienwesen, also an der Grenze von Wasser und Erde beheimatet. Er neigt sich dem Menschen auf der Pirsch, auf der Suche zu.

Einerseits zeigt sich hier das Ziel der persönlichen Suche. Intuition und Achtsamkeit sind Weg und Ziel zugleich: Sie ermöglichen es uns, auf die Suche zu gehen und in der Suche zu uns selbst zu finden. Manchmal allerdings verlieren wir uns, dann regieren Routine und Wiederholung und wir übersehen das große Geheimnis, das dort draußen auf uns wartet.

Auf der anderen Seite bedeutet die Karte aber auch, Abschied zu nehmen vom unzivilisierten Leben eines „Halbwilden". Mit Intuition und Aufmerksamkeit gelingt es uns, überholte Ur-Ängste hinter uns zu lassen. Es gilt, sich von seinen alten Verhaltensmustern und bloßen Vermutungen bewusst zu lösen, den wirklichen Wahrnehmungen zu trauen und alle zugänglichen Erfahrungen zu nutzen.

Praxistipps: *Ihre aktuelle Suche verlangt nach einem lebendigeren und bewussteren Leben. Bauen Sie Ängste ab und erfüllen Sie wichtige Wünsche! Aktivieren Sie Ihre Sinne! Und erkennen Sie überlebte Gewohnheiten.*

À la chasse

Une image de quête, de méditation et de perception intuitive. Beaucoup d'éléments sont présents dans la croissance (bâtons) et le changement (automne). Comme un chasseur à l'affût ou un éclaireur sur son sentier, il nous faut une attention accrue, une vigilance intuitive.

Naturellement, il ne s'agit pas du chasseur ou de l'éclaireur comme d'une profession concrète, mais du symbole d'une vigilance renforcée comme état normal personnel. Notre perception sensibilisée nous fait aussi mieux comprendre les intérêts et motifs derrière les actes. Et ainsi trouvons-nous le chemin qui nous conduit à l'« homme vert » de la forêt. L'« homme vert » apparaît dans les vieux récits traditionnels ; il symbolise la nature autour de nous et en nous. Pour Dalí il a des pattes de grenouille – une créature amphibie, vivant à la fois dans l'eau et sur la terre. Elle se penche vers l'homme à l'affût, qui bat la campagne.

D'une part transparaît ici le but de la quête personnelle. Intuition et vigilance sont à la fois chemin et but : ils nous permettent de partir à la recherche et, dans cette recherche, de nous trouver nous-mêmes. Parfois cependant, nous nous perdons, alors règnent la routine et la répétition et nous omettons de voir le grand mystère qui nous attend, là dehors.

Mais d'autre part, la carte signifie aussi de se détacher de la vie primitive d'un « demi-sauvage ». Grâce à l'intuition et à la vigilance nous réussissons à laisser nos vieilles peurs profondes derrière nous. Il s'agit de nous débarasser de nos vieux instincts et doutes, de nous fier aux véritables perceptions et d'utiliser toutes les expériences possibles.

Conseils pratiques : *Votre quête actuelle exige une vie plus excitante et plus consciente. Rejetez vos craintes et réalisez vos désirs profonds ! Activez vos sens ! Et reconnaissez vos habitudes périmées.*

Ten of Wands
Zehn der Stäbe
Dix de Bâton

A Fulfilled Life

This card shows a heavily burdened figure, warning not to become too weighed down by life. The ghostly face in the left upper corner represents in this context a bad conscience or the always demanding superego.

But the card can also be interpreted in a totally different way. Dalí, who often made fun of the Catholic Church, demonstrates in this picture the positive meaning of the Christian symbol of the cross. The burdened figure at the center represents Jesus, who carries the cross and the ten wands on his shoulder all at the same time.

To carry ten wands means to accept all available energies, all instincts, purposes, and motives. To make a bundle of the ten wands means nothing less than to accept life with all its energies and tasks unconditionally and in its totality. This is also the true meaning of the cross. The cross as a symbol is much older than Christianity. Like the circle or the square, it stands for the division and integration of all forces (for example, the four points of the compass). The Christian maxim "Those who love Jesus should take up his cross and follow him" has the positive meaning of accepting life unconditionally and committing oneself wholeheartedly.

Dalí shows this absolute devotion to life in a remarkable manner. The butterflies symbolize transformational power, and viewed this way, the face represents a clear conscience and the vision of a meaningful purpose in life.

Practical advice: *Throw off your old burdens and wake up to what is actually going on. Only by giving your undivided attention and affection to someone or something will you be able to completely understand him, her, or it. You have to go forward and commit yourself. This way, you will always be a step ahead.*

Erfülltes Leben

Die Karte zeigt eine beladene Gestalt – eine Warnung davor, das Leben unnötig schwerzunehmen. Das geisterhafte Gesicht in der linken oberen Bildecke ist dann das „schlechte Gewissen", ein forderndes Über-Ich.

Aber die Karte lässt auch eine andere Deutung zu. Ausgerechnet Salvador Dalí, der oftmals die (katholische) Kirche verspottete, macht mit diesem Bild deutlich, welch positive Bedeutung das christliche Kreuzzeichen haben kann. Die beladene Figur in der Bildmitte zeigt Jesus, und er trägt auf seiner Schulter gleichzeitig das Kreuz und die zehn Stäbe.

Die zehn Stäbe zu tragen, heißt, alle verfügbaren Lebensenergien, alle greifbaren Triebe, Ziele und Motive anzunehmen. Die Bündelung der zehn Stäbe bedeutet daher, das Leben mit all seinen Kräften und Aufgaben ohne Vorbehalte anzunehmen. In nichts Anderem aber besteht auch die allgemeine Bedeutung des Kreuzes: Das Kreuz als Symbol ist älter als das Christentum und ist – vergleichbar dem Kreis oder dem Quadrat – ein Zeichen der Unterscheidung und der Integration aller Kräfte (etwa aller Himmelsrichtungen). Die christliche Maxime „Wer Jesus liebt, der nehme sein Kreuz auf sich und folge ihm nach" bedeutet im positiven Sinn auch die bedingungslose Annahme des Lebens, ein hundertprozentiges Engagement.

Diese vollständige Hingabe an das Leben zeigt Dalí in beeindruckender Weise. Die Schmetterlinge stehen für die Möglichkeiten zur Transformation, das große Gesicht für ein gutes Gewissen und die Vision einer sinnvollen persönlichen Lebensaufgabe.

Praxistipps: *Werfen Sie Ballast ab und begreifen Sie die Dinge neu! Erst wenn Sie einem Menschen oder einer Sache Ihre ungeteilte Zuneigung schenken, verstehen Sie ihn oder sie ganz. Sie müssen sich nach vorne neigen, sich vorwagen und hineingeben. So haben Sie die Nase vorn.*

Une vie accomplie

La carte représente un personnage ployant sous la charge qu'il porte – un conseil de ne pas prendre la vie trop au tragique. Le visage fantomatique, en haut à gauche de l'image, symbolise la « mauvaise conscience », un sur-moi exigeant.

Mais la carte autorise également une autre interprétation. Salvador Dalí, qui a pourtant souvent tourné l'Église (catholique) en dérision, souligne par cette allégorie le message positif que la croix au sens chrétien peut transporter. La figure surchargée au centre de l'image montre Jésus portant sur ses épaules la croix et aussi les dix bâtons.

Porter les dix bâtons signifie accepter toutes les énergies de la vie, tous les intincts, buts et motifs disponibles. L'assemblage des dix bâtons signifie donc accepter la vie sans réserve, de toutes ses forces, face à tous les défis. Mais la signification véritable de la croix est qu'elle est un symbole plus ancien que la chrétienté – comparable au cercle ou au carré –, un signe de la différenciation et de l'intégration de toutes les forces (par exemple tous les points cardinaux). La sentence chrétienne « Que celui qui aime Jésus porte sa croix et le suive » est synonyme au sens positif de l'acceptation absolue de la vie, d'un engagement total. Dalí dépeint ce don entier à la vie de manière impressionnante. Les papillons incarnent les chances de transformation, le grand visage la bonne conscience et la vision d'une tâche de vie personnelle enrichissante.

Conseils pratiques : *Rejetez les charges inutiles et reconsidérez les choses ! Vous ne comprenez une personne ou un objet que si vous lui accordez une empathie sans partage. Vous devez vous pencher en avant, oser aller de l'avant, vous donner à fond. Ainsi aurez-vous une longueur d'avance.*

Queen of Cups
Königin der Kelche
Reine de Coupe

QUEEN OF CUPS

The Voice of the Heart

A rather idiosyncratic, yet truly apt composition. In the upper right corner, we see a little heart or a rose, which symbolizes the shadow as well as the product of exuberant imagination—similar to the phantom shown in the PAGE OF CUPS. What at a first glance appear to be dishevelled hair and two crutches become arteries and veins on closer inspection. The central figure represents the heart itself, which is being nourished by the great blood vessels and from which all smaller arteries emerge.

The QUEEN OF CUPS is really a queen of shells. Her head is graced with a crown that boasts a peak reminiscent of the dome of St. Peter's Basilica in Rome. In this card, Dalí has used elements of at least two famous paintings. The central figure was taken from the painting of Elizabeth of Austria by François Clouet whereas her thin moustache was inspired by Marcel Duchamp's well-known persiflage of the *Mona Lisa*. With his unique composition, Dalí underscored the intended double-entendre.

Many—even modern—interpretations accept only one aspect of the QUEEN OF CUPS and reject the other. Some praise her sensitivity, her emotional and psychic abilities, while others are critical of her reserve, toughness, and introspection. In fact, all these attributes are equally fitting. It is our task to find the common denominator in all these conflicting emotions and eschew one-sided perspectives. Openness and coherence, softness and hardness, female and male qualities are the poles that make for an intact inner life. The result will be spiritual autonomy and personal independence.

Practical advice: *Take a walk along a river or lake. Meditate near the water. Embellish yourself and your surroundings. Show the beauty and costliness of your feelings. Open up your heart.*

Die Stimme des Herzens

Eine eigenwillige und vielsagende Bildkomposition: Der rechte Bildrand zeigt ein kleines Herz oder eine Rose, zugleich Schatten und Produkt überbordender Phantasie wie jenes Phantom im Bild des PAGEN DER KELCHE. Was auf den ersten Blick wie zerzauste Haare und zwei Krücken erscheint, erweist sich bei näherer Betrachtung als Blutgefäße. Die Figur in der Bildmitte markiert das Herz selbst, das durch die großen Adern versorgt wird und von dem alle Blutgefäße ausgehen.

Die KÖNIGIN DER KELCHE ist eine Muschelkönigin, und ihren Kopf krönt eine Kuppel, die an die Spitze des Petersdoms in Rom erinnert. Dalí hat hier mehrere Bildzitate verarbeitet. Die Bildfigur ist dem Gemälde „Elisabeth von Österreich" von François Clouet entnommen, der dünne Schnurrbart entstammt der bekannten Persiflage auf die Mona Lisa von Marcel Duchamp. Mit dieser einzigartigen Komposition gibt Dalí entscheidende Hinweise für die Interpretation dieser Karte.

Viele Kommentare zur KÖNIGIN DER KELCHE sind zu einseitig; entweder wird sie ausschließlich gelobt – für ihre einfühlsamen, emotionalen und medialen Fähigkeiten. Oder sie wird mit Skepsis beschrieben – wegen ihrer Verschlossenheit, ihrer Herbheit, ihrer Nabelschau. Tatsächlich treffen all diese Aspekte zu, doch kommt es darauf an, diese widersprüchlichen Eigenschaften zu vereinen. Zur Bedeutung dieser Karte gehört gerade die Überwindung der einseitigen Sichtweisen! Offenheit und Geschlossenheit, Gefühl und Härte, weibliche und männliche Aspekte sind die Pole, die Basis eines intakten Seelenlebens. Ergebnis dieses Prozesses ist seelische Eigenständigkeit und persönliche Selbstständigkeit!

Praxistipps: *Gehen Sie an einem Fluss oder an einem See spazieren. Meditieren Sie dort. Schmücken Sie sich und Ihre Umgebung. Zeigen Sie die Schönheit und die Kostbarkeit Ihrer Gefühle. Öffnen Sie Ihr Herz.*

La voix du cœur

Une composition picturale originale et riche de sens : le bord droit de l'image montre un petit cœur ou une rose, à la fois ombre et produit d'une imagination débordante comme le fantôme du VALET DE COUPE. Ce qui apparaît à première vue comme une chevelure ébouriffée et deux béquilles représente, quand on y regarde de plus près, des vaisseaux sanguins avec artère et veine. Le personnage au centre de l'image est en quelque sorte le cœur approvisionné par les grandes veines et d'où partent tous les vaisseaux sanguins.

La REINE DE COUPE est une reine toute en coquillages, sa tête est couronnée d'une coupole qui rappelle le dôme de la Basilique Saint-Pierre de Rome. Dalí a confondu ici plusieurs fragments de tableaux. La figure centrale est tirée du portrait d'« Élisabeth d'Autriche » de François Clouet, la fine moustache est inspirée de la fameuse parodie de Mona Lisa par Marcel Duchamp. Par cette composition picturale unique Dalí donne des indications précieuses quant à l'interprétation ambivalente de cette carte.

Jusqu'à présent, le fait que les commentaires n'aillent que dans un sens ou dans l'autre constitue un problème. Soit la REINE DE COUPE ne reçoit que des éloges – pour ses facultés sentimentales, émotionnelles et médiales. Soit elle est décrite avec scepticisme – à cause de son repli sur soi, de son âpreté, de sa vanité. Certes, tous ces aspects la caractérisent, toutefois l'important est de concilier ces qualités contradictoires. Surmonter les points de vue sectaires est, sans nul doute, une des significations de cette carte ! Ouverture d'esprit et hermétisme, sentiment et dureté, aspects féminins et masculins sont les pôles, la base d'une vie spirituelle intacte. Le résultat de ce processus est l'indépendance de l'âme et l'autonomie personnelle !

Conseils pratiques : *Allez vous promener au bord d'un fleuve ou d'un lac. Méditez-y. Embellissez-vous et ce qui vous entoure. Laissez-voir la beauté et la qualité de vos sentiments. Ouvrez votre cœur.*

King of Cups
König der Kelche
Roi de Coupe

KING OF CUPS

Your Heart's True Desire

Strong emotions and intense desire are the essential features of the KING OF CUPS. A big glass vessel surrounds the central figure, which has been taken from a 1585-90 painting by El Greco portraying the French king Louis IX.

The glass symbolizes a test tube or an amniotic sac. On the one hand, it is a positive symbol of transformation, like the alchemistic crucible, and of growing life, like the womb. On the other hand, it is a negative symbol reminding us of unpredictably dangerous scientific experiments. The glass vessel also stands for an invisible wall and shield such as a negative spell or a curse. If this king doesn't want to become a prisoner of his own needs and emotions, he will have to learn to successfully deal with the highest emotional heights as well as the pits. This lesson is symbolized by the lily scepter (see THE EMPRESS and THE EMPEROR) while the wand in his right hand, with a fist or Devil's head at the end, indicates a person with focused energy who is not afraid of any taboos (devils) and who walks his path with a clear conscience and free of sin (lily).

Instincts and presentiments, temptations and often confusing needs have to be dealt with firmly. The fulfillment of your dominant desires and the dissolution of basic fears will lead to personal maturity and to the surmounting of all vain longing—leading to a blessed state of perfect contentment.

It is through change that we grow and the more we grow, the better we can deal with change. If we are careful not to neglect our true nature in the process, our personal dignity will be augmented.

Practical advice: *Be true to your desires. If you walk through a dark tunnel, take a light with you. Do not be afraid of confronting taboos and the dark side—but do not become too fascinated by them either! As you learn to deal with your dominant emotions, your true desires will become clear.*

Wahres Verlangen

Starke Gefühle und ein intensives Verlangen bestimmen den KÖNIG DER KELCHE. Ein großes Glas umgibt die Bildfigur, die auf ein Porträt des französischen Königs und Heiligen Ludwig IX. von El Greco (1585-1590) zurückgeht.

Das Glas ist zugleich Retorte, Reagenzglas und Fruchtblase. Im positiven Sinn ein Symbol der Wandlung wie ein alchemistischer Tiegel und Inbegriff werdenden Lebens wie eine Gebärmutter, beinhaltet es im negativen Sinn auch die bedrohliche Andeutung unberechenbar gefährlicher Laborversuche. Außerdem stellt das gläserne Gefäß zunächst eine fast unsichtbare Mauer und Abschirmung dar, wie ein Bann oder ein Fluch. Wenn er nicht ein Gefangener von Bedürfnissen und Affekten sein will, wird dieser König lernen müssen, zum Souverän im Umgang mit Seelentiefen und Himmelshöhen zu werden. Dies drücken auch das Lilienzepter (vgl. DIE HERRSCHERIN und DER HERRSCHER) und – am Stab in seiner Rechten – die geballte Faust oder der kleine Teufelskopf aus: eine geballte Energie, die auch vor Tabus (Teufeln) nicht haltmacht und die mit reinem Gewissen ohne Schuld (Lilie) ihren Weg findet.

Instinkte und Ahnungen, verlockende Reize und mitunter verwirrende Bedürfnisse warten auf Klärung. Die Erfüllung wichtiger Wünsche und der Abbau tiefer Ängste führen zu persönlicher Reife und zur Überwindung des Verlangens – in jenen wünschenswerten Zustand wunschlosen Glücks.

An Wandlungsprozessen können wir reifen und durch Reife Wandlungen aushalten und gestalten. Wenn wir dabei die (eigene) Natur nicht vergessen, kann die Würde des Menschen wachsen!

Praxistipps: *Verfolgen Sie konsequent die Befriedigung ihrer Wünsche. Nehmen Sie ein Licht mit, wenn Sie durch einen „Tunnel" schreiten. Lassen Sie sich von Tabus und Abgründen weder erschrecken noch verzaubern! Je besser Sie verstehen, Ihre Gefühle wahrzunehmen, umso klarer kristallisiert sich Ihr Verlangen.*

Désir véritable

De forts sentiments et un désir intense définissent le ROI DE COUPE. Un verre géant encadre la figure centrale qui est issue d'un portrait du roi de France saint Louis par El Greco (1585-1590).

Le verre est à la fois cornue, éprouvette et membranes fœtales. Au sens positif un symbole de l'évolution tel un creuset d'alchimiste et incarnation de la vie à naître, il contient dans un sens négatif aussi l'allusion menaçante à des expériences dangereuses et imprévisibles en laboratoire. En outre, le récipient de verre symbolise d'abord un mur presque invisible et un écran protecteur, comme un sortilège ou une malédiction. S'il ne veut pas être prisonnier de ses besoins et de ses impulsions, ce roi deviendra souverain de ses dépressions et de ses euphories. Le sceptre à fleur de lys (voir L'EMPEREUR et L'IMPÉRATRICE) et – sur la baguette dans sa main droite – le poing tendu ou la petite tête de diable en sont l'expression : une énergie intense, qui ne recule pas devant les tabous (diables) et trouve sa voie, la conscience tranquille et sans péché (lys).

Instincts et intuitions, charmes envoûtants et besoins parfois dérangeants attendent une explication. L'accomplissement de désirs essentiels et le rejet de peurs profondes mènent à la maturité personnelle et aident à surmonter l'attente passionnée – dans l'état enviable du bonheur parfait.

Grâce aux processus d'évolution nous pouvons mûrir et, par la maturité, supporter les changements et les influencer. Si nous n'oublions pas sur cette voie notre (propre) nature, la dignité de l'homme ne peut que grandir !

Conseils pratiques : *Soyez conséquent dans votre désir. Prenez une lampe si vous traversez un « tunnel ». Ne vous laissez ni effrayer ni envoûter par les tabous et abîmes ! Mieux vous savez percevoir vos sentiments et plus votre désir se cristallise.*

Knight of Cups
Ritter der Kelche
Cavalier de Coupe

KNIGHT OF CUPS

Living Faith

Great feelings and passions, your dreams and your personal goals are always a matter of faith. Past experiences can neither prove nor disprove future possibilities. But any reasonable and rational belief system will make use of all information gathered—and take into account the feelings of all in a positive as well as a negative sense.

Beliefs are like an ever-present cloak that we wrap ourselves up in and take with us wherever we go. Inappropriate beliefs hinder and stultify, making every step hard and sluggish. Appropriate beliefs, in contrast, are supportive, inspirational, and uplifting, helping us overcome any difficulties.

Dalí uses the 1800-01 painting by Jacques-Louis David of Napoleon charging to exemplify human willpower and passion. A (female) head with a very pronounced chin observes the horseman. This indicates that the KNIGHT OF CUPS is enveloped, fulfilled, or imprisoned by the lady (or more generally, person) of his heart.

The whole spectrum of passion, ranging from courtly love to frenzied infatuation, from loving devotion to woeful obsession, is contained within this card. The difference in scale of the small horseman in relation to the big female head hints at oedipal bonding (a mother complex). Or it might indicate the direction of evolution—from small to big, from internal drive to the external aim to grow and develop.

What personal meaning does this card have for you? Faith can move mountains. Big emotions move us the most and enable us to move the most. We are equipped with heart and mind so that we can experience and live out our deeply felt passions. What are your mental, emotional, and spiritual goals?

Practical advice: *Avoid naivety as well as superstition. Question and examine. Identify what moves and supports you in the long term. Do your sums and update your bookkeeping. Find a trustworthy conversation partner.*

Lebendiger Glaube

Große Gefühle und Leidenschaften, Lebensträume und wichtige persönliche Ziele sind stets auch eine Sache des Glaubens. Bisherige Erfahrungen sind nicht zwingend aussagekräftig hinsichtlich dessen, was die Zukunft an Möglichkeiten bereithält. Ein vernünftiger oder bewusster Glaube stützt sich aber auf alle verfügbaren Erfahrungen – und traut den Gefühlen aller Beteiligten im guten wie im schlechten Sinn vieles zu!

Glaubenssätze sind wie ein Mantel, der uns umhüllt und überall begleitet. Ein ungeeigneter Glaube hemmt und lähmt, macht jeden Schritt schwer und träge. Ein stimmiger Glaube dagegen trägt, beflügelt und begeistert. Er überwindet viele Schwierigkeiten.

Mit dem vorwärts stürmenden Napoleon – aus dem bekannten Gemälde von Jacques-Louis David (1800/01) – zitiert Dalí ein Paradebeispiel menschlicher Willenskraft und Leidenschaft. Der Reiter ist umgeben von einem (Frauen-)Kopf mit energischem Kinn. Der RITTER DER KELCHE ist gleichsam umhüllt, ganz erfüllt oder aber ganz gefangen von der Dame (oder allgemeiner: dem Menschen) seines Herzens.

Die ganze Vielfalt der Leidenschaft von Minne bis Obsession, von liebevoller Hingabe bis zu leidvoller Besessenheit wird damit angedeutet. Das Größenverhältnis vom kleinen Ritter zum großen (Frauen-)Kopf lässt an eine ödipale Bindung (Mutterkomplex) denken. Oder aber es symbolisiert die Entwicklung von klein nach groß, von innerer Triebkraft zu äußeren Wachstumszielen.

Was bedeutet das für die eigene Person? Der Glaube versetzt Berge. Es sind die großen Emotionen, die uns am meisten bewegen und die uns am meisten bewegen lassen. Wir besitzen Herz und Verstand, um tiefe und erhabene Leidenschaften wahrzunehmen und auszuleben. Welche seelischen, emotionalen und spirituellen Ziele verfolgen Sie?

Praxistipps: *Vermeiden Sie Gutgläubigkeit und Aberglauben. Untersuchen Sie und fragen Sie nach. Finden Sie heraus, was Sie langfristig bewegt und trägt. Rechnen Sie nach. Aktualisieren Sie Ihre Buchhaltung. Finden Sie einen vertrauenswürdigen Gesprächspartner.*

Foi vivante

Grands sentiments et passions, rêves d'une vie et buts personnels essentiels sont aussi en permanence une affaire de foi. Les expériences vécues jusqu'alors ne peuvent présumer de ce que l'avenir lointain réserve. Mais une foi solide ou consciente s'appuie sur toutes les expériences disponibles – et renforce les sentiments de tous les participants, dans le bon comme dans le mauvais sens !

Les dogmes de foi sont comme un manteau qui nous enveloppe et nous accompagne partout. Une croyance inadaptée freine et paralyse, rend chaque pas difficile et lourd. En revanche, une foi cohérente nous porte, nous stimule et transporte. Elle surmonte maintes difficultés.

Avec un Napoléon conquérant – extrait du célèbre tableau de Jacques-Louis David (1800/01) – Dalí trace un portrait exemplaire de la volonté humaine et de la passion.

Dans l'image le cavalier est entièrement entouré d'une tête (de femme) au menton énergique. Le CAVALIER DE COUPE est en quelque sorte enveloppé, empli ou encore prisonnier de la dame (ou de manière plus générale : de la personne) de son cœur.

Toute la diversité de la passion, de l'amour courtois à l'obsession en passant par le don plein d'amour et la déchirante folie, est ici suggérée. Le rapport de taille entre le petit cavalier et la grande tête (de femme) n'est pas sans rappeler une relation œdipienne (complexe de la mère). Ou bien il symbolise le passage du petit au grand, de l'énergie intérieure aux objectifs extérieurs de progrès.

Que signifie ceci pour soi-même ? La foi transporte les montagnes. Ce sont les grandes émotions qui nous touchent le plus et qui nous font le plus avancer. Nous possédons cœur et raison afin de percevoir et de vivre les passions profondes et élevées. Quels objectifs psychiques, émotionels et spirituels voulez-vous atteindre ?

Conseils pratiques : *Évitez la naïveté et la superstition. Examinez et interrogez. Trouvez ce qui vous touche et vous porte. Faites vos comptes. Actualisez votre comptabilité. Trouvez un interlocuteur digne de votre confiance.*

Page of Cups
Page der Kelche
Valet de Coupe

PAGE OF CUPS

Lightness of Heart

The figure in the picture raises a cup on high, "wearing his heart on his sleeve". The fish—normally hidden underwater—is clearly visible. The emotional content of the water element (psychic depths) is presented light-heartedly and light-handedly. Our emotions help us to discover something new.

This is the card of playfully mastering your emotions and emotional needs. It encourages you to leave the ghosts of the past behind (symbolized by the sketchily drawn figure on the left, which could be a light heart, a heart with eyes, a spectacled cobra, or a phantom of your imagination). This card is all about clearly identifying your desires and fears and acting accordingly.

If your own emotional state and that of others is not clear, this card counsels you to be cautious. Dalí uses the painting *The Indifferent Man* by Jean-Antoine Watteau (ca. 1717) for a reason. If you are overly careless in dealing with your emotional needs, you might end up even more unhappy and frightened. You might confuse your own inner mechanisms with outer influences or mysterious phantoms.

Do not play with your own emotions or those of others. But retain your carefree spirit. Do not be afraid to stand up for your feelings and to be as tough as you deem necessary. You will gain new insights through meditation, increased sensitivity, and understanding. This will be a constant source of joy for you. You will be able to help others emotionally and spiritually.

Practical advice: *Cleanse your psyche and evaluate your emotions. But do not dwell extensively on past mistakes, weaknesses, and fears. Balance your emotional account. Settle your own debts and ask others to settle theirs—financially, but more importantly, emotionally and spiritually.*

Leichtigkeit des Herzens

Die Bildfigur hebt den Kelch in die Höhe, sie trägt das „Herz auf der Hand". Der Fisch, sonst unter der Wasseroberfläche verborgen, ist deutlich sichtbar. Die Inhalte des Wasserelements (des Seelenlebens) werden mit leichter Hand dargeboten. Durch unsere Gefühle entdecken wir Neues.

Ein Bild der spielerischen Beherrschung von Gefühlen und Bedürfnissen! Die Karte ermuntert dazu, Geister und Gespenster hinter sich zu lassen (siehe die schemenhafte Bildfigur, die ein leichtes Herz, ein Herz mit Augen wie auch eine „Brillenschlange" oder ein Phantom der Einbildung darstellen kann). Es geht darum, Wünsche und Ängste klar zu benennen und entsprechend zu handeln.

Solange die Emotionen aller Beteiligten jedoch nicht klar sind, stellt die Karte eine Warnung dar: „L'Indifferent" (Der Unentschiedene) heißt das hier zitierte Gemälde von Jean-Antoine Watteau (ca. 1717). Ein leichtfertiger Umgang mit persönlichen Bedürfnissen produziert glücklose Leidenschaften und unnötige Ängste. Unbewusste Affekte treten uns wie eine höhere Gewalt oder wie ein geheimnisvolles Phantom scheinbar von außen entgegen.

Spielen Sie nicht mit Gefühlen, ob es nun die eigenen oder die anderer sind. Bewahren Sie sich Ihre innere Unbeschwertheit. Scheuen Sie sich nicht, sich für Ihre Gefühle zu engagieren und, wo nötig, die erforderliche Härte zu zeigen. Mit Einfühlung, Meditation und Verständnis gewinnen Sie neue Einsichten. Das ist für Sie selbst eine Quelle aufgeklärter Lebensfreude. Und für andere werden Sie so zu einer wichtigen Hilfe auf psychischem und spirituellem Gebiet.

Praxistipps: *Sorgen Sie für eine seelische Reinigung, prüfen Sie Ihre Gefühle. Vermeiden Sie es, „schmutzige Wäsche" zu waschen, in Fehlern, Schwächen und Ängsten zu wühlen. Reinigen Sie Ihr „emotionales Konto", begleichen Sie Schulden und holen Sie Außenstände herein – zwar auch finanziell, aber vor allem emotional und spirituell.*

Légèreté du cœur

Le personnage de la carte lève la coupe, il porte « le cœur sur la main ». Le poisson, d'habitude caché sous la surface de l'eau, est bien visible. Les composantes de l'élément aquatique (vie psychique) sont présentées d'une main légère. Nos sentiments nous font découvrir la nouveauté.

Un tableau du contrôle ludique des sentiments et besoins ! La carte nous encourage à laisser esprits et fantômes derrière nous (voir la silhouette schématique qui peut représenter un cœur léger, un cœur muni d'yeux aussi bien qu'un « serpent à lunettes » ou un fantôme de l'imagination). Il faut nommer clairement ses désirs et peurs et agir en conséquence.

Mais tant que les émotions de tous les participants ne sont pas claires, la carte est synonyme d'avertissement : « L'Indifférent », tel est le titre du tableau de Watteau (vers 1717) évoqué ici. Une approche irréfléchie de nos besoins personnels entraîne des passions malheureuses et des peurs infondées. Comme venues d'ailleurs, les impulsions inconscientes nous font face telle une force majeure ou comme un fantôme mystérieux.

Ne jouez pas avec vos sentiments, les vôtres comme ceux d'autrui. Conservez votre insouciance. N'hésitez pas à vous engager pour vos sentiments, et à faire montre de la dureté nécessaire, si besoin est. Par l'intuition, la méditation et la compréhension vous obtenez de nouvelles perspectives. C'est pour vous-même une source de joie de vivre limpide. Et pour les autres vous devenez ainsi un soutien important sur le plan psychique et spirituel.

Conseils pratiques : *Procédez à une purification spirituelle, analysez vos sentiments. Évitez de laver votre « linge sale », de fouiller dans les fautes, faiblesses et autres peurs. Assainissez votre « compte émotionnel », payez vos dettes et recouvrez vos créances – sur le plan financier bien sûr, mais surtout sur le plan émotionnel et spirituel.*

Ace of Cups
Ass der Kelche
As de Coupe

Inner Life

This card features two double images. Two faces are shown in profile, facing each other on the left and right side of a single cup. But the same visages could also be interpreted as two wings, raising the cup into the air. This image hints that the cup as a symbol is rather ambiguous concerning fullness as well as emptiness, good emotions as well as bad, exalted as well as pompous (arrogant) modes of your psyche.

Another contradiction of this card is the contrast between the vastness of the sea and the limited capacity of a single cup. Oceanic feelings enable us to experience connectedness with all. The single cup stands for the individual's inner life, the soul. Here, our place in the community is as important as our distinctiveness as an individual. If we manage to attain harmony of the individuality within the great flow of life, we will experience a very special baptism and drink deep from the fountain of youth. The secret of the ACE OF CUPS lies in purification of the psyche. If you can learn to delve deep into your feelings—through reconciliation or by letting go—thus ensuring that no bad feelings or compromises dull the clear mirror of your soul, you will stay young, regardless of your age.

The pictured seascape is more than just a personal tribute to Dalí's homeland, it is a general representation of the idea that we all are in need of a place we consider our true home, which we will find wherever we can purify our psyche and recharge our batteries, in short: wherever our soul takes wing.

Practical advice: *This is not the time for great promises or expectations but for personal integrity. Settle all problems that dull your feelings. Clear your emotions and take your own cup into your own hands.*

Seelisches Eigenleben

Die Karte zeigt ein Doppelgesicht. Zwei Gesichter stehen sich, links und rechts vom erhobenen Kelch, im Profil gegenüber. Gleichzeitig könnte man die zwei Gebilde als Flügel betrachten, die den Kelch in die Lüfte erheben. Damit wird schon bei diesem einzelnen Kelch auf die Doppeldeutigkeit des Symbols hingewiesen: Es geht um Fülle und Leere, gute und schlechte Gefühle, erhebende, aber auch hochtrabende Seelenklänge.

Ein weiterer Widerspruch besteht zwischen der Weite des Meeres und dem begrenzten Fassungsvermögen des einzelnen Kelchs. Die ozeanischen Gefühle lassen uns unsere Verbundenheit mit allem erleben.

Der einzelne Kelch steht für geistige Individualität, für unsere Seele, die für unseren Platz in der Gemeinschaft ebenso wichtig ist wie für unsere Besonderheit als Einzelwesen. Wo der persönliche Ausgleich zwischen der eigenen Person und dem großen Strom des Lebens gelingt, erleben wir eine Art Taufe, einen echten Jungbrunnen.

Das Geheimnis des ASSES DER KELCHE ist die seelische Reinigung: immer wieder eintauchen in die großen Gefühle – sich versöhnen oder verabschieden – und so dafür sorgen, dass keine negativen Gefühle oder faulen Kompromisse die Seele trüben. Das hält uns jung, unabhängig von unserem Lebensalter.

Die dargestellte Meereslandschaft ist nicht nur ein persönlicher Tribut Dalís an seine Heimat. Sie ist ein genereller Hinweis: Wir brauchen eine seelische Heimat, und wir finden sie dort, wo wir die Seele reinigen und erneut laden können – kurz, wo der Seele Flügel wachsen!

Praxistipps: *Jetzt ist nicht die Stunde großer Versprechen oder Verheißungen, sondern der persönlichen Aufrichtigkeit. Bereinigen Sie, was Ihre Gefühle trübt. Klären Sie Ihre Emotionen und nehmen Sie Ihren Kelch neu in die Hand.*

Vie autonome de l'âme

Cette carte présente d'emblée un double visage. Deux têtes de profil se font face à gauche et à droite de la coupe. On pourrait également voir dans ces reflets deux ailes qui soulèvent le calice. Le double sens du symbole est déjà dans manifeste dans ce récipient : il s'agit ici de plein et de vide, de bons et mauvais sentiments, de musique de l'âme exaltante mais aussi emphatique.

Une autre contradiction apparaît entre l'immensité de la mer et la capacité limitée du calice. Les sentiments océaniques nous font ressentir nos liens avec toute chose.

La coupe symbolise l'individualité spirituelle, notre âme qui est tout aussi essentielle pour notre place dans la communauté que pour notre singularité comme individu. Là où l'équilibre personnel s'opère entre la personne et le grand courant de la vie, nous assistons à une sorte de baptême, à une vraie source de jouvence.

Le secret de l'AS DE COUPE est la purification de l'âme : s'immerger sans cesse dans les grands sentiments – se réconcilier ou se séparer – et ainsi veiller à ce qu'aucun sentiment négatif ou compromis tordu ne trouble l'âme. Cela nous maintient jeune, quel que soit notre âge.

Le paysage marin représenté n'est pas seulement un hommage personnel de Dalí à son pays natal. C'est un message d'ordre général : nous avons besoin d'un chez-soi mental et nous le trouvons là où nous pouvons purifier l'âme et la régénérer – bref, là où l'âme se sent des ailes !

Conseils pratiques : *Ce n'est pas maintenant le temps des grandes promesses ou révélations, mais de la droiture personnelle. Assainissez ce qui pertube vos sentiments. Épurez vos émotions et reprenez la coupe en main.*

Two of Cups
Zwei der Kelche
Deux de Coupe

Your Emotional Range

This card shows a scene from the painting of *Cupid and Psyche* (1817) by François-Édouard Picot. The Greek myth as related by the Roman Apuleius in his work *The Golden Ass* tells the story of how the human Psyche and the divine Cupid longed for each other and how, after many trials, they were finally united.

That love can indeed give wings to the lovers is symbolized by the yellow caduceus of Hermes (two intertwined serpents) and the winged lion's head. The caduceus and winged lion were inspired by the TWO OF CUPS tarot card by A. E. Waite and P. C. Smith. These images represent both the happy uniting of two people in love, and their fatal entanglement.

On the abdomen of the prostrate Psyche, we recognize a big, wide-open eye. This is part of a face, which has been drawn around the scene in silhouette. On the left, the lips and the hairy chin of this head can be seen, which is reminiscent of a well-known portrait by Rembrandt. The unkempt hair on the chin and on the back of the head also point to certain characters from the story of *The Golden Ass*. All in all, this is a thoroughly ambiguous and complex picture.

The TWO OF CUPS card represents the polarities of our emotional life—sympathy and antipathy, affection and repulsion. Each of us has to learn to deal with the "two souls dwelling in our breast." As long as emotional matters are disturbed, you will not find your true identity. Our spiritual growth depends on the clarification of ambiguous feelings, leading to emotional maturity.

Practical advice: *The validity of your feelings should not depend on the approval or disapproval of others. Avoid false compromises in emotional and intimate matters. It is of utmost importance that you learn to deal purposefully with your emotional needs and feelings.*

Spannweite der Seele

Die Karte zeigt Amor und Psyche aus dem gleichnamigen Bild von François-Edouard Picot (1817). Der griechische Mythos, den auch der Römer Apuleus in seinem Werk „Der goldene Esel" aufgegriffen hat, erzählt die Liebesgeschichte zwischen der menschlichen Königstochter Psyche und dem göttliche Amor, die erst nach vielen Prüfungen zueinander finden. Die beflügelte Energie zweier Liebender zeigt sich auch in dem gelben Hermes-Stab (zwei Schlangen) mit dem geflügelten Löwenkopf. Hermesstab und geflügelter Löwe sind der Karte ZWEI DER KELCHE aus dem Tarot von A. E. Waite und P. C. Smith entlehnt. Sie bedeuten sowohl die glückliche Verbindung als auch die unselige Verquickung zweier Menschen.

Auf dem Unterleib der liegenden Psyche erkennen wir ein großes geöffnetes Auge. Dieses gehört zu einem Gesicht, das als Silhouette um die Bildszene gezeichnet ist. Links sind die Lippen und das zottelige Kinn dieser Kopfform zu erkennen. Dieser Kopf spielt auf ein bekanntes Rembrandt-Porträt an. Die zotteligen Haare am Kinn und am Hinterkopf des in Umrissen gezeichneten Kopfes erinnern zudem an Figuren aus „Der goldene Esel". Insgesamt also ein vieldeutiges, anspruchsvolles Bild.

Die Karte ZWEI DER KELCHE betont die Polarität des Seelenlebens – Sympathie und Antipathie, Zuneigung und Abneigung. Es gilt, das berühmte „zwei Seelen wohnen, ach! in meiner Brust" zu erkennen und in sich zu vereinen. Solange man seelisch zerrissen ist, findet man nicht zu seiner geistigen Identität. Die Klärung ungeklärter Emotionen, der geistige Reifungsprozess ist die Basis für unsere seelische Entwicklung.

Praxistipps: *Machen Sie Ihre Gefühle nicht von fremder Zustimmung oder Ablehnung abhängig. Meiden Sie faule Kompromisse in emotionalen und intimen Fragen. Der Umgang mit Gefühlen und Bedürfnissen ist in jeder Hinsicht entscheidend.*

Envergure de l'âme

La carte évoque l'Amour et Psyché d'après le tableau éponyme de François-Édouard Picot (1817). Le mythe grec, que le Romain Apulée a également repris dans son œuvre « L'Âne d'or », retrace l'histoire d'amour entre la princesse Psyché et le dieu Amour qui ne seront réunis qu'après de nombreuses épreuves. L'énergie ailée des deux amants est aussi symbolisée par le caducée jaune (à deux serpents) surmonté d'une tête de lion ailée. Le caducée et la tête de lion ailée sont inspirés de la carte DEUX DE COUPE du tarot de A. E. Waite et P. C. Smith. Ils expriment l'union heureuse tout comme la maléfique réunion de deux êtres.

Sur le ventre de Psyché allongée rayonne un œil grand ouvert. Celui-ci est partie d'un visage dessiné sous forme de silhouette autour de la scène. À gauche les lèvres et le menton hirsute de cette tête sont bien reconnaissables. Cette tête est d'une part un emprunt à un célèbre portrait de Rembrandt. D'autre part, les poils du menton et de la nuque de l'esquisse rappellent des personnages de « L'Âne d'or ». Dans son ensemble une image raffinée et riche de sens.

La carte DEUX DE COUPE souligne le dualisme de la vie mentale – sympathie et antipathie, attirance et rejet. Il convient ici de discerner « les deux âmes qui habitent dans notre sein » et de les unir. Tant que l'âme est déchirée, il est impossible de trouver son identité spirituelle. La clarification d'émotions insondées, le processus de maturation spirituel sont la base de notre évolution psychique.

Conseils pratiques : *N'aliénez pas l'authenticité de vos sentiments à l'acceptation ou au refus des autres. Fuyez les compromis boiteux pour ce qui touche les émotions et l'intimité. L'approche des sentiments et des désirs est déterminante en tout point.*

Three of Cups
Drei der Kelche
Trois de Coupe

Understanding Your Own Emotions

The depicted image evokes cosmic wisdom with its rendering of the Three Graces, the Three Fates, or the three wishes of many fairy tales: "All good things come in threes." The blue palm trees and the blue grotto impression point towards bliss, enchantment, and great joy. Life will become a feast if we venture beyond ourselves and learn to retain our emotional independence even in the company of others.

This card is all about the quality of feelings. The nudity of the figures does not only represent beauty and naturalness. Symbolically, it encourages honesty and at the same time warns of insolence (shamelessness and lack of culture). The red forms in the upper corners can be interpreted as a curtain, but are also reminiscent of the jellyfish seen in the SIX OF CUPS or some phantom figures on other cards. To the left and right, two springs gush forth, representing the inconsistencies and disharmonies of one's emotional life.

Overall, this is a lucky and auspicious card, if interpreted as a symbol of emotional intelligence. Conscious emotions are fruitful emotions. The magic of feeling needs to be enhanced by the magic of thoughts, words, and deeds to allow your personal means of expression to come alive. Integrate your feelings to become one in body, mind, and spirit. This inner unity constitutes the basis of happy and lasting relationships.

Practical advice: *Develop your emotional vocabulary. Learn to appreciate the feelings of others. Express your own feelings with gusto. Don't be afraid of emotional reactions. Approach others, or keep them at a distance, defining your own boundaries — even if you may be unaccustomed to this. The right word at the right time can make miracles come true.*

Begriffene Emotionen

Das vorliegende Bild erinnert an die drei Grazien, an die drei Nornen (Schicksalsgöttinnen), an die drei Wünsche eines Märchens und führt uns so zu einem kosmischen Reigen: Aller guten Dinge sind drei. Auch die blauen Palmen und das angedeutete Motiv der Blauen Grotte sind Hinweise auf Glückseligkeit, Bezauberung und große Freude. Das Leben wird zum Fest, wenn wir über uns hinauswachsen und auch in der Gemeinschaft unsere seelische Eigenständigkeit zu behaupten wissen.

Alles hängt von der Art, von der Qualität der Gefühle ab. Die Nacktheit der Bildfiguren bedeutet nicht nur Schönheit und Natürlichkeit. Symbolisch ermuntert sie zur Wahrheit und warnt zugleich vor Unverschämtheiten (vor Aufdringlichkeiten und mangelndem Schamempfinden). Die roten Gebilde in den oberen Kartenecken können als Vorhang gesehen werden, erinnern aber auch an die Qualle aus dem Bild SECHS DER KELCHE sowie an manches Schattengespenst auf anderen Karten. Es fließen zwei Quellen, links und rechts im Bild, sie stehen für die Unterschiede, die Widersprüche im Seelenleben.

Alles in allem eine glückliche und glückverheißende Karte, wenn wir sie als Sinnbild der emotionalen Intelligenz sehen. Bewusste Emotionen sind fruchtbare Emotionen. Der Zauber der Gefühle braucht den Zauber der Gedanken, Worte und Taten, einen Reigen der persönlichen Ausdrucksformen. Erst wenn unsere Gefühle uns ganz durchdringen, wachsen wir mit Körper, Geist und Seele zu einer Person zusammen. Dieser innere Zusammenhalt aber ist Voraussetzung und Ergebnis eines glücklichen und dauerhaften Zusammenspiels mit anderen.

Praxistipps: *Entwickeln Sie Ihr seelisches Vokabular. Lernen Sie, auch fremde Emotionen zu begreifen. Und teilen Sie Ihre eigenen Gefühle ausdrucksvoll mit. Scheuen Sie sich nicht vor „emotionalen" Reaktionen. Gehen Sie auf andere zu, oder grenzen Sie sich von ihnen ab, auch wenn es Ihnen noch ungewohnt erscheint. Ein richtiges Wort zur rechten Zeit wirkt Wunder.*

Comprendre les émotions

En évoquant les trois Grâces, les trois Nornes (fileuses de destin), les trois vœux d'un conte, cette carte nous entraîne dans une ronde cosmique : jamais deux sans trois. Les palmiers bleus et le motif esquissé de la grotte bleue sont autant d'allusions à la béatitude, à l'envoûtement et à l'allégresse. La vie devient une fête, si nous nous surpassons et sommes capables d'affirmer notre indépendance mentale même en groupe.

Tout dépend de la nature et de la qualité des sentiments. La nudité des personnages ne signifie pas seulement beauté et naturel. Elle incite symboliquement à la vérité et pour autant nous met en garde contre toute impudence (insistance déplacée et manque de pudeur). Les formes rouges dans les coins supérieurs de la carte peuvent faire figure de rideau et ne sont pas sans rappeler la méduse du SIX DE COUPE ainsi que mainte ombre fantômatique sur d'autres cartes. À gauche et à droite de l'image coulent deux sources, qui représentent les disparités, les contradictions de l'âme.

Dans l'ensemble, une carte de bonheur et annonciatrice de bonheur si nous la considérons comme le symbole de l'intelligence émotionnelle. Les émotions conscientes sont des émotions créatrices. La magie des sentiments requiert la magie des pensées, paroles et actions, une ronde de formes d'expression personnelles. Nous ne grandissons dans notre corps, esprit et âme en une seule personne que lorsque nos sentiments nous imprègnent totalement. Mais cette cohérence intérieure est la condition et le produit d'une interaction heureuse et durable.

Conseils pratiques : *Créez votre vocabulaire psychique. Apprenez à comprendre aussi les émotions des autres. Et exprimez vos sentiments avec intensité. Ne craignez pas les réactions « émotionnelles ». Allez à la rencontre des autres ou distancez-vous d'eux, même si cela vous semble encore inhabituel. Un mot juste au bon moment peut faire des miracles.*

Four of Cups
Vier der Kelche
Quatre de Coupe

Your Own Personal Motivation

The tree in the picture is a symbol of nature and also of man as a special part of nature. The young man in the picture is shown sitting at the root of the tree, meaning that he is rooted in himself. On the one hand, this card counsels you to interrupt your daily routine in order to find refuge within yourself and to contemplate your situation. On the other, it challenges you to stop your brooding, to find a new direction in life, and to reach for the stars—like the tree.

Expect new emotional experiences (note the hand!). The cup above the tree reminds us of the card the ACE OF CUPS. Here it is also a matter of ups and downs, joys and sorrows, and of finding the right balance between your own feelings and those of others. You might have to accept this new cup, no matter what its contents. Or you might refuse to accept this cup. Quite often, it is this refusal, the saying of the simple word "no," that has been missing from your life previously.

The bird in the tree warns you of your own eccentricities and flights of fancy. At the same time, it heralds the coming of new enthusiasm and new meanings. The shadowy figure on the left, uniting a bird's head with a female body, represents your emotional reserves. But beware: ancient Greek myths describe the sirens this way, soul birds or literally "bewitchers." Ulysses escaped from being lured to destruction by the power of their seductive song only by tying himself to the mast and by sealing the ears of his comrades with wax!

Practical advice: *Explore your feelings. Relax and allow your spirit to float. Define your boundaries. It is in deep meditation and in silence that you will find the right words to express your previously mute emotions and experiences.*

Eigene Gründe

Der Baum im Bild steht für die Natur und gleichzeitig für den Menschen als Teil der Natur. Wenn die Bildfigur an den Wurzeln des Baums sitzt, verweilt sie sinnbildlich an ihren eigenen. Einmal kann es darum gehen, die Alltagsroutine zu unterbrechen, um Einkehr und Besinnung zu finden. Ein anderes Mal jedoch darum, das Grübeln zu beenden, um sich persönlich neu auszurichten und weit in den Himmel zu strecken, wie es der Baum im Bild ebenfalls illustriert.

Eine neue seelische Erfahrung kündet sich im Motiv der Hand an. Der Kelch auf dem Baum erinnert an die Karte ASS DER KELCHE. Auch hier geht es um Höhen und Tiefen, um Freude und Trauer und darum, die eigenen Gefühle in das richtige Verhältnis zu den Gefühlen der Mitmenschen zu bringen. Das eine Mal müssen Sie diesen neuen Kelch annehmen, ganz gleich was er enthält. Ein anderes Mal ist es hingegen wichtig, diesen Kelch zurückzuweisen. Nicht selten ist es gerade diese Ablehnung, dieses Neinsagen, was im bisherigen Leben gefehlt hat.

Der Vogel im Baum warnt vor Spleens und haltlosen Gedanken; er verkündet jedoch gleichzeitig, dass eine neue Besinnung und Begeisterung möglich ist. Die Schattengestalt am linken Bildrand deutet im positiven Sinne seelische Reserven an. Sie vereint Vogelkopf und Frauenkörper. So ähnlich beschrieb allerdings der antike griechische Mythos auch die Unheil bringenden Sirenen: als „Seelenvögel", wörtlich die „Bestrickenden". Odysseus entkam ihrem verführerischen, ins Verderben führenden Gesang nur, indem er sich am Mast seines Schiffes anbinden und seinen Gefährten die Ohren mit Wachs verschließen ließ!

Praxistipps: *Gehen Sie Ihren Gefühlen auf den Grund. Lassen Sie die Seele baumeln. Ziehen Sie klare Grenzen. In der Meditation, in der Stille finden Sie Worte, wo Sie bislang sprachlos waren.*

Raisons individuelles

L'arbre de l'image symbolise la nature et aussi l'homme comme élément de la nature. Le personnage est certes assis sur les racines de l'arbre, mais il reste aussi sur les siennes. Tantôt il peut s'agir de rompre la routine quotidienne, pour recouvrer le calme et la sérénité. Tantôt il faut metttre fin aux ruminations pour se réorienter personnellement et se dresser très haut vers le ciel comme l'illustre l'arbre de l'image.

Une nouvelle expérience mentale s'annonce (la main sur l'image). La coupe sur l'arbre rappelle la carte de l'AS DE COUPE. Ici aussi il est question de hauts et de bas, de joie et de chagrin et il faut mettre ses propres sentiments dans le juste rapport avec les sentiments de ceux qui nous entourent. Si, une fois, vous devez accepter la coupe nouvelle quel que soit son contenu, une autre fois il est au contraire important de refuser ce calice. C'est probablement ce refus, cette force de dire non, qui vous a fait défaut jusqu'à présent.

L'oiseau dans l'arbre met en garde contre le spleen et les idées saugrenues; mais il révèle aussi qu'un nouvel état d'esprit et un nouvel enthousiasme sont possibles. L'ombre sur le bord gauche de l'image est une allusion aux réserves de l'âme dans un sens positif. Elle est à la fois tête d'oiseau et corps de femme. Du reste, le mythe grec antique dépeignait de manière analogue les sirènes porteuses de malheur : comme des « oiseaux-émoi », des « enchanteresses ». Ulysse échappa à leur chant séducteur et assassin en se faisant attacher au mât de son bateau après s'être fait boucher les oreilles avec de la cire !

Conseils pratiques : *Allez au plus profond de vos sentiments. Laissez votre âme vagabonder. Fixez des limites précises. Dans la méditation, dans le calme vous trouverez les mots là où vous étiez jusqu'à présent sans voix.*

Five of Cups
Fünf der Kelche
Cinq de Coupe

A Spiritual Opening—Open to New Feelings

Three cups have fallen over, two are still upright. What is bygone and what is sustainable?

Three cups—past, present, and future—indicate that conventional concepts of time are no longer useful! What counts now is inner reality and personal vision. Here and now, we are confronted with desires and fears that may issue from times long past or pertain to events in times still to come.

The image of two cups still upright means that we can always choose which emotions and needs to accept and which to reject. A beautiful new way opens up. The challenge is to walk through the doorway and this involves crossing the threshold. We thereby encounter a shadowy self, psychologically speaking, a double, the alter ego (second self). This theme is represented by the shadowy figure on the right. The shadow is a symbol of the unlived parts of the self and for unconscious desires and fears.

The nakedness of the figure at the center illustrates truth and, again, openness. So this card symbolizes that the moment of truth has come. New inner realities and new experiences lie ahead. The path at the center of the card goes past a castle (indicating security or imprisonment) and leads on to the ocean and the wide-open sky.

Practical advice: *Take note of what aspect of the card attracts you most. Reconciliation or separation, setting out or staying put: these are all possibilities. Water treatments, baths, and showers can help you to open up emotionally. Do not run away from your own feelings. This is the moment of truth. The long-awaited new beginning.*

Seelische Öffnung – Offenheit für neue Gefühle

Drei Kelche sind umgestürzt, zwei stehen aufrecht: Was ist verflossen, und was hat Bestand?

Drei Kelche, Vergangenheit, Gegenwart und Zukunft – die üblichen Zeitvorstellungen sind hinfällig! Es zählt die seelische Realität, die persönliche Betroffenheit. Unsere Wünsche und Ängste wirken jetzt, in diesem Augenblick, auch wenn ihre Ursachen auf frühe Erinnerungen zurückgehen oder auf Erwartungen an künftige Ereignisse basieren.

Zwei Kelche stehen aufrecht. Sie verdeutlichen, dass wir stets wählen können, welche Gefühle und Bedürfnisse wir annehmen und welche nicht. Der Durchgang zu einem neuen, schönen Weg steht offen. Die Herausforderung besteht darin, ihn zu durchqueren; und das heißt, eine Schwelle zu überschreiten.

Wir begegnen dem Schatten, im psychologischen Sinn ein Bild für eine Art Doppelgänger, ein Alter Ego (anderes Ich). Diese Schattenthematik wird durch die schemenhafte rechte Bildfigur gut ausgedrückt. Sie steht für ungelebte Seiten, für noch unbewusste Wünsche und Ängste.

Die Nacktheit der zentralen Bildfigur illustriert Wahrheit und noch einmal Offenheit. So signalisiert diese Karte eine Stunde der Wahrheit. Neue seelische Realitäten, neue Räume des persönlichen Erlebens öffnen sich. Der Weg in der Bildmitte führt vorbei an einer Burg (Geborgenheit oder aber umschließende Gefangenschaft) und weiter zu einem Meer und einem weiten Himmel.

Praxistipps: *Achten Sie darauf, was im Bild Sie besonders anspricht! Versöhnung und Abschied, Aufbruch und ruhiges Ausharren, all dies bietet sich hier als Möglichkeit an. Eine seelische Öffnung kann durch Wasserkuren, Baden, Duschen usw. erleichtert werden. Laufen Sie vor Ihren Gefühlen nicht weg. Dies ist die Stunde der Wahrheit, des lang ersehnten Neuanfangs.*

Ouverture de l'âme – Confiance en de nouveaux sentiments

Trois calices sont renversés, deux sont encore debout : Qu'est-ce qui s'est déversé et qu'est-ce qui est stable ? Trois coupes – passé, présent, futur – les trois notions de temps sont révolues ! Ce qui importe est la réalité de l'âme, l'émotion personnelle. Nos désirs et peurs agissent maintenant, à cet instant même, bien que leur origine remonte à des souvenirs précoces ou repose sur l'attente d'événements futurs.

Deux coupes sont debout. Elles signifient que nous pouvons toujour choisir quels sentiments et besoins nous acceptons ou non. La porte donnant sur une voie nouvelle et attrayante est ouverte. Le vrai défi consiste à traverser ce portail ; et cela veut dire franchir un seuil.

Nous rencontrons l'ombre, au sens psychologique un symbole pour une sorte de sosie, un alter ego. Cette thématique de l'ombre est parfaitement exprimée par la vague silhouette située à droite. Celle-ci représente le non-vécu, les désirs et craintes encore inconscients.

La nudité du personnage central illustre la vérité et, une fois de plus, la sincérité.

Cette carte signalise ainsi l'heure de vérité. De nouvelles réalités mentales, de nouveaux domaines de la vie personnelle s'ouvrent à nous. Le chemin au centre de l'image longe une forteresse (sécurité ou bien captivité) et se dirige loin vers la mer et l'immensité du ciel.

Conseils pratiques : *Examinez bien dans l'image ce qui vous parle vraiment ! Réconciliation et adieu, départ et paisible repos, toutes ces chances s'offrent ici à vous. Une ouverture de l'âme peut être facilitée par des cures d'eaux, des bains, des douches, etc. Ne fuyez pas vos sentiments. L'heure de vérité, d'un renouveau tant attendu, a sonné.*

Six of Cups
Sechs der Kelche
Six de Coupe

Back to the Future

This is the only card showing the cups filled with flowers—representing the blossoming of inner life. The card clearly indicates what is needed: even as a grown-up, you can and may be a child again. Leave the pain of childhood behind and return to the openness and joy of your early days. This is, of course, easier said than done.

The card shows the outline of a jellyfish, demonstrating how difficult it is to grasp the true influence of early conditioning. Although experiences from childhood and early adolescence fill every cell of our being, they are very often hard to grasp.

The bird has a double meaning. It warns you to be aware of your eccentricities and pipe dreams and, at the same time, encourages you to be true to your personal ideals and higher perspectives. In order to differentiate between a pipe dream and an ideal, you have to deal with your childhood days (and with the children in your life).

Carefully evaluate your emotional experience. What was good and what less so? How can you re-create the beauty of yesteryear and how can you prevent past pain from resurfacing? How can you cope with old threats or old negative feelings should these reoccur? Today, you have more alternatives and many more possibilities. Sort out your feelings. Seize the chance to let go of old fears and to fulfill your true desires. This will rejuvenate and empower you.

Practical advice: *Dig up your memories until you can bury old feuds. Talk to your "inner child." Leave your childish behavior behind and do what you as a grown-up have wanted to do for a long time.*

Zurück in die Zukunft

Nur auf dieser Karte sind die Kelche mit Blumen gefüllt: Es geht hier ganz besonders um ein blühendes Seelenleben! Die Karte zeigt deutlich, was man dazu braucht: Man muss und darf als Erwachsener wieder Kind sein. Und das heißt auch, Abschied nehmen von schlimmen Erfahrungen der Kindheit und zurückkehren zur Offenheit und Freude der Kinderzeit. Doch dies ist leichter gesagt als getan.

Das Bild zeigt die Umrisse einer Qualle als Bild dafür, wie schwer zu fassen unsere frühkindlichen Prägungen sind. Erfahrungen aus Kindheit und früher Jugend durchfluten uns bis ins Innere jeder Zelle und sind doch nur mit Mühe dingfest zu machen.

Der Vogel besitzt demnach eine Doppeldeutung: Er warnt vor der Unbeständigkeit so mancher seelischer Blütenträume; doch er fordert uns gleichzeitig auf, unseren persönlichen Idealen und Perspektiven treu zu bleiben. Um aber Spleen und Ideal zu unterscheiden, brauchen wir eine erneute Auseinandersetzung mit unseren Kindertagen (und mit den Kindern in unserem Leben).

Setzen Sie sich behutsam mit emotionalen Erfahrungen auseinander. Was war damals gut, was nicht? Wie kann das Schöne von früher auch heute wieder gelingen, wie kann man das Schlimme von einst heute verhindern? Wie gehe ich heute mit früheren Bedrohungen oder alten unguten Gefühlen um? Sie verfügen heute als erwachsener Mensch über mehr Alternativen, mehr Möglichkeiten.

Sortieren Sie Ihre Gefühle. Nutzen Sie die Gunst der Stunde, um alte Ängste abzulegen und tiefe Wünsche zu erfüllen. Das wird Sie verjüngen und Ihre Kräfte beflügeln.

Praxistipps: *Graben Sie in Ihren Erinnerungen, bis Sie alte Zwistigkeiten begraben können. Sprechen Sie mit dem „inneren Kind"! Verabschieden Sie sich von kindlichen Reaktionsweisen und tun Sie, was Sie als erwachsene Frau oder erwachsener Mann schon lange tun wollten!*

Retour vers le futur

Cette carte est la seule où le calice est rempli de fleurs : il s'agit ici d'une vie mentale très florissante ! La carte présente clairement ce dont nous avons besoin à cet effet : nous, adultes, devons et pouvons redevenir des enfants. Et cela signifie aussi de se séparer des expériences traumatisantes de l'enfance et de revenir à la sincérité et à la joie enfantines. Mais ceci est difficile à réaliser.

L'image montre les contours d'une méduse pour prouver à quel point les souvenirs de nos premières années sont difficiles à saisir. Les expériences de l'enfance et de la prime jeunesse nous marquent jusqu'au plus profond de chaque cellule et ne sont pourtant qu'à peine perceptibles.

L'oiseau possède donc un double sens : il met en garde contre l'instabilité, maint rêve fleuri ; mais il nous incite en même temps à demeurer fidèle à nos idéaux et perspectives personnelles. Pour différencier spleen et idéal, nous devons nous pencher à nouveau sur notre enfance (et sur les enfants présents dans notre vie).

Examinez avec précaution vos expériences émotionnelles. Quel était le bon autrefois ou le mauvais ? Comment les belles choses d'autrefois peuvent-elles aujourd'hui aussi se reproduire, comment éviter aujourd'hui les écueils du passé ? Comment dois-je aborder les menaces passées et les vieux sentiments de malaise ? Vous disposez aujourd'hui à l'âge adulte de plus d'alternatives, de plus d'opportunités.

Triez vos sentiments. Saisissez le moment propice pour vous débarasser de vos peurs anciennes et réaliser vos désirs profonds. Cela vous rajeunira et stimulera vos forces.

Conseils pratiques : *Fouillez dans vos souvenirs jusqu'à ce que vous puissiez enterrer les vieilles querelles. Parlez à l'enfant qui habite en vous ! Abandonnez les réactions enfantines et faites ce que vous vouliez faire depuis longtemps comme femme adulte et comme homme adulte !*

Seven of Cups
Sieben der Kelche
Sept de Coupe

Live Your Dream

The card stands for having reached a new peak of development. Worlds beyond imagination open up. We dance with
our dreams and are victims of ever-changing illusions.

The card shows the resurrection scene from the
Isenheim Altarpiece by Matthias Grünewald (1505-16). It
is also a picture puzzle showing man as master, sculptor,
and creator of his desires and needs. The central figure is
framed by the outline of a big head. Maybe it's all in your
head? Is reality only a figment of your imagination? Is
your life lived purely symbolically?

The seven cups are fashioned after the Waite Tarot.
Their contents are drawn rather sketchily, emphasizing
their symbolic character. The seven cups represent the
promising yet deterrent character of gifts and presents.
The head evokes not only beauty but also vanity. The
tower-like castle represents might and greatness, but also
arrogance and loneliness. Pearls and precious gems speak
for themselves as objects of beauty but also point to a passion for grandeur. The next cup contains a laurel wreath
symbolizing success or futility, a funeral wreath or the lau-
rels of victory. The dragon stands for the forces of the un-
derworld, which could devour you or bring you luck.

The serpent represents not only wisdom but also false-
ness and base instincts. The seventh cup is empty, hinting
at new possibilities or chances missed.

There is nothing left but to fathom the depths of your
own needs and personal goals. Sometimes, your greatest
longing and most unrealistic yearning turns out to be the
most appropriate desire. Other times, the smallest of
temptations and the most harmless of promises might
turn out to be evil.

Practical advice: *Examine your fears and follow those desires that contain the most energy. Judging by the fruit of
your desire, you will realize what is right and what is wrong.
Create and live according to your own set of rules—especially in matters of the heart and in regard to your most
intimate desires.*

Gelebte Träume

Diese Karte steht für einen neuen Höhepunkt, neue Welten eröffnen sich. Wir erfahren uns als Traumtänzer/in und als Opfer schwankender Illusionen.

Die Karte zeigt die Auferstehungsszene aus dem Isenheimer Altar von Matthias Grünewald (1505/16) und hält gleichzeitig eine Art Vexierbild bereit. Sie präsentiert den Menschen als Meister, Künstler und Schöpfer seiner Wünsche und Bedürfnisse. Die Figur im Bildzentrum ist jedoch von den größeren Umrissen eines Kopfes umgeben. Möglicherweise spielt sich alles nur im Kopf ab: eingebildete Realitäten, ein symbolisches Leben.

Auch die Inhalte der sieben Kelche (nach dem Vorbild des Waite-Tarot) sind nur wenig ausgearbeitet, sie wirken eher skizzenhaft und unterstreichen das Symbolische, Modellhafte. Die Kelche präsentieren Gaben und Geschenke, gleichsam verheißungsvoll und abschreckend. Der Kopf symbolisiert Anmut, doch auch Eitelkeit. Die turmartige Burg steht für Macht und Größe, aber auch für Abgehobenheit und Einsamkeit. Perlen und Edelsteine sind ein Sinnbild für Schönheit, aber gleichzeitig auch für Prunksucht. Der Kelch daneben trägt einen Lorbeerkranz: Toten- oder Siegerkranz, Erfolg oder Vergeblichkeit. Der Drache stellt die verschlingenden oder aber glücksbringenden Kräfte der Unterwelt dar. Die Schlange symbolisiert Weisheit, aber auch Falschheit und niedere Motive. Der siebte Kelch schließlich ist leer; er steht für neue Möglichkeiten, jedoch auch für verpasste Chancen.

Somit bleibt hier nichts anderes übrig, als die eigenen Bedürfnisse und persönlichen Ziele auf den Prüfstand zu stellen. Manchmal sind selbst die größte Sehnsucht und das „unrealistischste" Begehren gerade richtig. Im anderen Fall aber sind selbst die kleinste Verlockung und das harmloseste Versprechen von Übel.

Praxistipps: *Gehen Sie Ihren Befürchtungen auf den Grund und folgen Sie den Wünschen, von denen die stärkste Energie ausgeht. An den „Früchten" werden Sie erkennen, was für Sie stimmt und was nicht. Entwickeln und vertreten Sie einen eigenen Maßstab, gerade auch in Liebesdingen und intimen Wünschen.*

Rêves vécus

Cette carte symbolise un apogée, des mondes nouveaux s'ouvrent à nous.

Livrés à des illusions flottantes, nous vivons l'expérience d'un utopiste. La carte représente la scène « Résurrection » de l'autel d'Isenheim, peinte par Mathias Grünewald (1505/16), et propose en même temps une image déformée. Elle montre l'être humain comme maître, artiste et créateur de ses souhaits et besoins. Toutefois, le personnage central se trouve encastré entre les contours grossiers d'une tête. Peut-être tout ne se passe que dans la tête : réalités imaginées, vie symbolique.

Les contenus des sept calices (à l'instar du tarot de Waite) sont, eux aussi, peu élaborés, comme des esquisses ils soulignent le côté symbolique, l'archétype. Les coupes présentent dons et cadeaux, à la fois prometteurs et repoussants. La tête symbolise la grâce mais aussi la vanité. Le château-fort avec ses hautes tours figure la puissance et la grandeur, mais aussi l'isolement et la solitude. Les perles et pierres précieuses sont le symbole de la beauté, mais expriment aussi le goût du luxe. Le calice voisin est orné d'une couronne de laurier : couronne mortuaire ou couronne du vainqueur, réussite et inutilité. Le dragon incarne les forces infernales dévorantes ou encore bienveillantes. Le serpent symbolise la sagesse mais aussi l'hypocrisie et les basses intentions. Enfin le septième calice est vide ; il représente les chances nouvelles mais aussi les occasions manquées.

Ainsi, il ne reste ici rien d'autre que de tester ses propres besoins et ses objectifs personnels. Parfois, même la plus grande aspiration et le souhait le plus « irréaliste » représentent le désir profond. Mais à l'inverse, la plus petite tentation et la promesse la plus innocente sont néfastes.

Conseils pratiques : *Analysez à fond vos angoisses et obéissez aux désirs chargés de la plus grande énergie. Aux « résultats » vous reconnaîtrez ce qui vous convient ou non. Créez et suivez vos propres critères, surtout dans le domaine de l'amour et des désirs intimes.*

Eight of Cups
Acht der Kelche
Huit de Coupe

On the Journey to Your Personal Destiny

Dreams and visions that cannot be easily grasped are nevertheless an important part of our inner world. They help our consciousness to expand and our power of discernment to grow. Begin your search now.

Like the cups, the moon (in the upper left corner) stands for spiritual needs. The card encourages you to start your journey and to keep moving. But it warns you not to become too restless, because then you might hurry past your goal (represented by the village in the background) without noticing it.

The flies depicted on the card thus have a central meaning. They symbolize the autonomic nervous system and, therefore, the tension alternating with relaxation that regulates our biorhythms. Replace nervousness or sluggishness with purposeful action. Go where your heart wants you to go! It is your task to become aware of your inner flow. This is the best remedy against addiction as well as loneliness. It is said that "everything flows" but sometimes, the inner life has dried up, or overflowed and submerged all.

Think of your life as a journey. Be like the journeymen of old, who used to travel in order to become masters of their craft. Where do you come from? Where are you headed? Don't force your feelings and inclinations to fit into a preconceived logic. You will find your own destiny in the balance of your own feelings and thoughts. You will discover it at the place where the experience of the flow is the strongest. This is not only a wonderful spiritual experience; it is also a very practical way of dealing with everyday life. "The lazy ones are the clever ones." The person who succeeds in going with the flow exerts relatively little energy and yet achieves the most!

Practical advice: *Feel and trust your inner flow. Be aware of your own personal rhythm and make it an integral part of daily life. Feast and fast—there is a time for everything.*

Wanderschaft – persönliche Bestimmung

Ein wertvoller Teil unserer Gefühle sind nicht unmittelbar zu begreifende Träume und Visionen. Lassen Sie Ihr Bewusstsein und Ihr Urteilsvermögen daran wachsen. Begeben Sie sich auf die Suche.

Wie die Kelche, so steht auch der Mond (links oben im Bild) für seelische Bedürfnisse. Die Karte ermuntert dazu, sich auf den Weg zu machen und in Bewegung zu bleiben. Sie warnt aber auch vor einer Ruhelosigkeit, die möglicherweise am Ziel (das Dorf im Bildhintergrund) vorbeiläuft.

Die Fliegen im Bild besitzen daher eine entscheidende Bedeutung: Sie symbolisieren das vegetative Nervensystem, also die Ruhe oder die Anspannung, die unbewusst unseren Lebensrhythmus bestimmen.

Setzen Sie an die Stelle von Nervosität oder Trägheit eine bewusste Leidenschaft. Geh, wohin dein Herz dich trägt! Ihre Aufgabe ist es, sich dem inneren Strömen zu öffnen. Das ist das beste Mittel sowohl gegen eine Sucht wie gegen Einsamkeit. Man sagt zwar „alles fließt", doch manchmal ist der innere Fluss ausgetrocknet, und manchmal fließt er nicht, sondern überflutet alles.

Begeben Sie sich auf Wanderschaft, wie früher die Handwerksgesellen, und machen Sie Ihren Meister (Ihre Meisterin) in eigener Sache. Wo kommen Sie her? Wo gehen Sie hin? Zwingen Sie Ihre Gefühle und Neigungen nicht in eine vorgegebene Logik.

In der Summe erkennen Sie so die richtige Bestimmung für Ihr Leben. Sie finden sie eben dort, wo Sie dem Fluss am nächsten sind. Das ist eine große spirituelle Erfahrung und gleichzeitig eine Methode der Alltagsbewältigung: „Wer faul ist, ist auch schlau" – wer dem Fluss der Energien folgt, der oder die strengt sich vergleichsweise am wenigsten an und erreicht am meisten!

Praxistipps: *Finden Sie Zutrauen und spüren Sie den Fluss in sich. Achten Sie auf Ihren persönlichen Rhythmus und verbinden Sie ihn mit Ihrem Alltag. Feiern Sie genussvolle Feste und fasten Sie – alles ist wichtig, alles zu seiner Zeit.*

En chemin – vocation personnelle

Une part précieuse de nos sentiments est constituée de rêves et de visions qui ne nous sont pas directement accessibles. Laissez votre conscience et votre faculté de jugement mûrir. Commencez votre recherche.

Comme les coupes, la lune (en haut à gauche) symbolise les besoins de l'âme. La carte encourage à se mettre en route et à rester en mouvement. Mais elle met en garde contre la fébrilité qui pourrait passer à côté du but à atteindre (voir le village à l'arrière-plan).

Les mouches sur cette image jouent donc un rôle important : elles symbolisent le système nerveux végétatif, à savoir le calme ou la tension qui régissent insconsciemment notre rythme de vie.

Remplacez la nervosité ou l'oisiveté par une passion consciente. Va où ton cœur te porte ! Votre tâche est de vous ouvrir aux courants intérieurs. C'est le meilleur remède contre l'addiction et contre la solitude. Certes, on dit « Tout baigne », mais tantôt le fleuve intérieur est tari, et tantôt non seulement il coule, mais il inonde tout.

Mettez-vous en route, comme les compagnons artisans d'autrefois et soyez votre propre patron. D'où venez-vous ? Où allez-vous ? N'enfermez pas vos sentiments et vos inclinations dans une logique préconçue. Ainsi, au final, vous reconnaîtrez la vocation profonde de votre vie. Vous la trouverez au point le plus proche du fleuve. C'est une immense expérience spirituelle et aussi une méthode pour assumer le quotidien : « Qui est paresseux est aussi rusé », qui suit le courant des énergies se fatigue le moins et obtient le plus !

Conseils pratiques : *Gagnez confiance et sentez le fleuve en vous. Observez votre rythme personnel et intégrez-le à votre quotidien. Célébrez des fêtes grandioses et jeûnez – un temps pour chaque chose et chaque chose en son temps.*

Nine of Cups
Neun der Kelche
Neuf de Coupe

Emotional Merry-Go-Round

What moves you emotionally? Nine cups represent strong feelings and manifold passions. The cylinder-like vase (floating above the head of the central figure) symbolizes substantial spiritual capacity as well as your desire to control all emotions.

It might also indicate the attitude you adopt when something doesn't work out exactly as planned, when "everything has gone down the drain." Are you playing a game of all or nothing?

The two faces representing (grand)father and (grand)mother show the influence of two strong superegos. Foreign or your own "higher" demands keep you from living your own life, despite the fact that you have very definite ideas regarding your own happiness.

Have the courage to make a difference. Don't let embarrassments hold you back nor be unduly fascinated by things strange and exotic. Define your long-term goals. Explore your life dreams. This is the meaning of the picture, tablet, mirror, or book in the right hand of the central figure. The challenge is to reshape your own life.

Learn from your own experiences and define your own standards! Find out what kind of support you can muster and try to distinguish between needs that can be ignored and those you should take into consideration. This way, you will protect your great emotional store.

Practical advice: *Learn to go with the flow and to swim against the current if necessary. Write yourself a "letter of intent" stating your goals for the next nine weeks. Write down (nine) important desires or fears. Establish specific goals for your personal growth and well-being.*

Karussell der Emotionen

Was bewegt Sie innerlich? Neun Kelche stehen für große Gefühle und vielfältige Leidenschaften. Die zylinderartige Vase (über dem Kopf der Bildfigur schwebend) symbolisiert großes (seelisches) Fassungsvermögen, aber vielleicht auch den Drang, alle Emotionen „in den Griff", unter Kontrolle zu bekommen. Vielleicht betrifft dieses Gefäß auch Ihre Neigung, anzunehmen, alles sei „im Eimer", wenn etwas nicht funktioniert. Das könnte heißen, Sie gehen aufs Ganze.

Die beiden großen Gesichter stehen für (Groß-)Vater und (Groß-)Mutter – sie zeigen den Einfluss von zwei starken „Über-Ichs". Fremde oder eigene Ansprüche halten Sie zunächst davon ab, Ihr eigenes Leben zu führen. Zugleich verfügen Sie aber über durchaus eigene Vorstellungen vom großen Glück.

Haben Sie den Mut, einen Unterschied zu machen. Lassen Sie sich nicht von Peinlichkeiten erschrecken oder von Sonderbarem faszinieren. Definieren Sie Ihre langfristigen Ziele, erforschen Sie Ihre Lebensträume. Die Bildfigur hält in ihrer Rechten eine Tafel, einen Spiegel oder ein Buch und fordert so: Machen Sie Ihren eigenen Lebensentwurf.

Verstehen Sie Ihre eigenen Erfahrungen und definieren Sie die zu Ihnen passenden Ansprüche! Stellen Sie fest, welche Unterstützung Sie dafür gewinnen können, welche Bedürfnisse Sie künftig mehr berücksichtigen und welche Sie künftig ignorieren sollten. So bewahren Sie sich Ihren großen Reichtum an Gefühlen.

Praxistipps: *Lernen Sie, sich freizuschwimmen; sich mit dem Strom wie auch gegen ihn zu bewegen. Entwerfen Sie einen „Letter of intent", in dem Sie Ihre Ziele für die nächsten neu(e)n Wochen festlegen. Notieren oder merken Sie sich (neun) wichtige Wünsche oder Ängste. Setzen Sie sich konkrete Ziele für Wachstum und Wohlbefinden.*

Carrousel des émotions

Qu'est-ce qui nous touche intérieurement ? Neuf calices représentent les grands sentiments et passions diverses. Le vase en forme de cylindre (flottant au-dessus de la tête du personnage) symbolise une grande capacité (mentale), mais peut-être aussi le besoin de d'« avoir en mains » toutes les émotions, de les contrôler. Ce récipient fait peut-être également allusion à votre tendance à accepter que tout est « dans le seau » (synonyme de « fichu » en allemand N. d. T.), si quelque chose ne fonctionne pas. Cela pourrait signifier que vous jouez le tout pour le tout.

Les deux grands visages figurent le (grand-) père et la (grand-) mère – ils expriment l'influence de deux « surmoi » puissants. Les exigences des autres et les vôtres vous empêchent d'abord de mener votre propre vie. Mais vous avez pourtant vous-même votre idée bien personnelle du grand bonheur.

Ayez le courage de faire la différence. Ne vous laissez pas rebuter par des moments embarrassants ou fasciner par des choses étranges. Définissez vos objectifs à long terme, analysez les rêves de votre vie. En tenant dans sa main droite une planche, un miroir ou un livre, la figure centrale vous conseille d'élaborer vous-même votre projet de vie.

Déchiffrez vos expériences et définissez les besoins qui vous conviennent ! Fixez quel soutien vous pouvez y gagner, quels désirs vous devriez prendre en considération et lesquels vous devriez ignorer. Ainsi vous préservez votre grande richesse de sentiments.

Conseils pratiques : *Apprenez à vous libérer, à nager avec, mais aussi contre le courant. Rédigez une « lettre d'intention » dans laquelle vous fixez vos projets pour les prochaines semaines. Notez ou relevez neuf désirs ou angoisses essentiels. Donnez-vous des buts concrets pour votre évolution et votre bien-être.*

Ten of Cups
Zehn der Kelche
Dix de Coupe

Intense Feelings

This is the card of great emotion and high times. Fire and water unite to form a rainbow. High (heaven) and low (fish) begin to move and unite. The red, wavy lines indicate how the blood boils and how the pressure in your cups (emotions) has built up. This is the card of great desires and passions coming true, but also of false romanticism and intoxication. How can you have the one and avoid the other?

Ten cups in a rainbow signify a well-rounded sense of security and the safety that comes from trust. In a negative sense, it signifies a defensive force field, a magnetic shield, or a glass ceiling, which are all hard to penetrate. Any hermetic ideas about life, love, or faith function at best as a sort of hothouse. They provide shelter and warmth, but they keep real life out. They create a force field, but cannot fulfill the essential needs of the individual.

The two central figures have been taken from a painting by Giuseppe Bonito and the three peaches from the 1638 painting *The Five Senses* by Jacques Linard. A wise combination, since all forms of false and harmful passions dull the senses, whereas joyful and wholesome passions are uplifting. It is this deep sensitivity that determines our happiness in high times of great emotion.

Practical advice: *Don't be afraid of "oceanic feelings." This is a perfect opportunity to take a fearless look at powerful and bold passions. The more you learn to assess the degree to which you can truly trust yourself and others, the more secure you will feel. This is a test of your self-awareness and knowledge of human nature.*

Hochdosierte Gefühle

Eine Karte der großen Emotionen und der Hoch-Zeiten des Lebens. Feuer und Wasser verbinden sich im Regenbogen. Höhen (Himmel) und Tiefen (Fisch) geraten in Bewegung und finden sich vereint im Bild. Die roten Wellenlinien deuten an, wie sehr das Blut in Bewegung ist und wie sehr die Kelche unter „Dampf" stehen. Eine Karte der Erfüllung großer Wünsche und Leidenschaften, aber auch der falschen Romantik und des Rausches. Wie lässt sich das Eine erreichen und das Andere vermeiden?

Die zehn Kelche im Regenbogen bedeuten im guten Sinne Geborgenheit, Schutz und Vertrauen. Im negativen aber stehen sie für Abschirmung, wie unter einer Käseglocke, einem Glasdach oder einem Magnetschirm, die nur mühsam zu durchbrechen ist. Solche hermetischen Lebens-, Glaubens- oder Liebesverhältnisse wirken bestenfalls wie ein Treibhaus: Sie schützen, halten jedoch das wirkliche Leben fern. Sie schaffen zwar ein Kraftfeld, aber wesentliche Bedürfnisse der/des Einzelnen bleiben dabei außen vor.

Die beiden Personen im Bild entstammen einem Gemälde von Giuseppe Bonito. Darunter präsentiert Dalí einen weiteren Bildausschnitt, die drei Pfirsiche aus dem Bild „Die fünf Sinne" (1638) von Jacques Linard. Beide Motive thematisieren Leidenschaft und Sinnlichkeit und ihre schädliche wie auch ihre erhebende Wirkung. Die Qualität dieser Leidenschaft entscheidet, wie glücklich wir mit unseren Emotionen und unseren Hoch-Zeiten werden.

Praxistipps: *Haben Sie keine Angst vor „ozeanischen Gefühlen"! Jetzt ist eine gute Gelegenheit, sich Ihren Leidenschaften zu stellen. Sie werden sich dabei umso sicherer fühlen, wenn Sie unterscheiden können, wie weit Sie sich und anderen trauen können. Ihre Selbsterfahrung und Ihre Menschenkenntnis werden hier auf eine Probe gestellt.*

Sentiments à haute dose

Une carte des grandes émotions et des grands moments de la vie. Le feu et l'eau se rejoignent dans l'arc-en-ciel. Les hauts (ciel) et les bas (poisson) se mettent en mouvement et se trouvent réunis dans l'image. Les lignes rouges et ondulées expriment à quel point le sang est en mouvement et combien les coupes sont sous pression. Une carte de la réalisation des grands désirs et passions, mais aussi du faux romantisme et de la griserie. Comment atteindre l'un et éviter l'autre ?

Les dix calices de l'arc-en-ciel symbolisent au sens positif sécurité, protection et confiance. Mais, au sens négatif, ils représentent isolement, comme sous une cloche à fromage, un toit de verre ou un blindage électromagnétique difficile à transpercer. De telles conditions hermétiques de vie, de foi et d'amour ressemblent dans le meilleur des cas à une serre. Elles protègent, mais éloignent de la vie réelle. Elles créent certes un champ de force, mais les besoins essentiels de l'individu restent en dehors.

Les deux personnages sont tirés d'un tableau de Giuseppe Bonito. En dessous, Dalí a ajouté un autre extrait de tableau, les trois pêches de l'œuvre de Jacques Linard, « Les Cinq sens » (1638). Les deux détails de tableaux thématisent la passion et la sensualité, leurs effets néfastes autant qu'exaltants. La qualité de cette passion détermine la façon dont nous sommes heureux dans nos émotions et les moments forts de notre vie.

Conseils pratiques : *N'ayez pas peur des « sentiments océaniques » ! Voici une bonne occasion de faire face à vos passions. Vous vous sentirez d'autant plus sûr que vous pourrez distinguer dans quelle mesure vous pouvez avoir confiance en vous et autrui. Votre expérience personnelle et votre connaissance du genre humain sont mis ici à l'épreuve.*

Queen of Swords
Königin der Schwerter
Reine d'Épée

QUEEN OF SWORDS

Conscious Living

The QUEEN OF SWORDS has two faces. She is a stern judge and at the same time a cheerful elf queen embodied in the picture by the red being (superego, ghost, conscience) above her and the butterfly below.

One of the most splendid tasks of the suit of swords is to reveal alternative ways to realize your unfulfilled needs. Use the weapons of your mind to liberate yourself from internal and external constraints. Stand up for yourself. Do not be impressed by superficialities or delusions. Refine your power of discernment.

The queen's lofty location in a cloud constitutes a warning to beware of castles built in the air and of other pipe dreams. In a more positive sense, the image indicates that the realm of the mind is a world of its own with special opportunities. It celebrates the capacity to recognize and to define vague desires or fears. One of the major strengths of this mistress of perception lies in dispelling unfounded fears.

Prejudices and fears constitute self-imposed obstacles, and may prove to be unfounded when carefully analyzed. In other cases, they express authentic needs and experiences, which cannot be communicated in any other way. Swords as weapons of the mind have the power to develop and refine our mental capacities. Being able to discern and assess experiences that have previously gone unnoticed, about which you were ignorant, is an important aspect of that power.

Practical advice: *Ensure clarity in your decisions and your behavior. If necessary, use a magnifying glass or a pair of binoculars to look at your concerns from all possible angles. Refine love, longing, and passion. This is a card of release from your fears and of new openings in matters of the heart.*

Bewusstes Leben

Die KÖNIGIN DER SCHWERTER hat zwei Gesichter: Sie ist zugleich strenge Richterin und lustige Elfen-Königin. Beide Seiten zeigen sich im Bild durch den Schmetterling unter ihr und das rote Wesen (Über-Ich, Gespenst, Gewissen) über ihr.

Eine der schönsten Aufgaben der Schwerter ist es, Alternativen für die Verwirklichung unerfüllter Bedürfnisse aufzuzeigen. Nutzen Sie also die Waffen des Geistes, um sich von inneren und äußeren Abhängigkeiten zu befreien. Richten Sie sich auf. Lassen Sie sich nicht durch Vordergründigkeiten oder Kulissenzauber beeindrucken. Schärfen Sie Ihr Urteil.

Der Platz der Königin in den Wolken stellt sicherlich eine Warnung vor Luftschlössern und Illusionen dar. Im positiven Sinne aber zeigt das Bild das Reich des Geistes als eine Welt für sich, mit eigenen Möglichkeiten und der Gelegenheit, bisher unerkannte Wünsche und Ängste wahrzunehmen und zu benennen. Gerade der Abbau von unberechtigten Ängsten ist eine der wesentlichen Stärken dieser Meisterin der Erkenntnis.

Vorurteile und Ängste behindern unsere persönliche Entwicklung, solange sie nicht auf ihren Gehalt überprüft werden. Sie können aber auch Ausdruck berechtigter Bedürfnisse sein, die noch kein besseres Sprachrohr gefunden haben. Die Macht der Schwerter sind die Waffen des Geistes, sie helfen, unsere geistigen Kapazitäten zu entfalten und zu verfeinern. Und dazu gehört auch, die Erfahrungen zu beurteilen, bei denen bislang Unwissen oder Bewusstlosigkeit vorherrschten.

Praxistipps: *Sorgen Sie für Klarheit in Ihren Entscheidungen und in Ihrem Verhalten. Nehmen Sie bei Bedarf eine Lupe oder ein Fernglas zu Hilfe, betrachten Sie Ihre Angelegenheiten aus allen Perspektiven. Verfeinern Sie Liebe, Lust und Leidenschaft. Eine Karte des Abbaus von Ängsten und der neuen Chancen für die Liebe.*

Vie consciente

La REINE D'ÉPÉE a deux visages : elle est à la fois juge sévère et joyeuse reine des elfes. Sur l'image ces deux faces apparaissent dans le papillon sous elle et dans la silhouette rouge (sur-moi, fantôme, conscience) au-dessus d'elle.

L'un des plus beaux rôles de l'épée est de montrer les alternatives permettant la réalisation de désirs inassouvis. Utilisez les armes de l'esprit pour vous libérer de vos chaînes intérieures et extérieures. Redressez-vous. Ne vous laissez pas impressionner par des futilités ou des escamotages. Aiguisez votre jugement.

L'emplacement de la reine dans les nuages signifie certainement un avertissement contre les châteaux en Espagne et les illusions. Mais dans un sens positif l'image présente le royaume de l'esprit comme un monde à part, avec ses possibilités propres et l'opportunité de percevoir des désirs et angoisses jusqu'alors inconnus et de les appeler par leur nom. L'extinction des peurs injustifiées est une des forces principales de cette maîtresse de la connaissance.

Préjugés et craintes font obstacle à notre évolution personnelle tant qu'ils ne sont pas examinés dans leur étendue. Mais ils peuvent aussi être l'expression de besoins justifiés qui n'ont pas encore trouvé de meilleur porte-voix. Les armes de l'esprit ont le pouvoir des épées, elles aident à épanouir nos facultés mentales et à les raffiner. Y compris à jauger les expériences jusqu'alors empreintes d'ignorance ou d'inconscience.

Conseils pratiques : *Mettez de la clarté dans vos décisions et dans votre attitude. Au besoin prenez une loupe ou une paire de jumelles, observez les affaires qui vous concernent sous tous les angles. Raffinez l'amour, le plaisir et la passion. Une carte du rejet des angoisses et des nouvelles chances en amour.*

King of Swords
König der Schwerter
Roi d'Épée

Knowledge and Breadth

At first glance, it seems quite surprising that a man of the Church should represent the suit of swords, which symbolize the air element of the mind. It would be more reasonable to expect him as a HIGH PRIEST or in the suit of cups. But the KING OF SWORDS is the master of swords, the master of knowledge. His lofty realm of the mind begins high above the mountaintops. Either he has his head in the clouds, or develops an independent consciousness—free and independent in his thinking, down-to-earth, and well-grounded.

The bishop or man of the Church highlights the danger of entertaining false beliefs in a state of worldly innocence. In a positive sense, he reminds us that each piece of knowledge includes its paradoxical opposite: not-knowing. The peaks of knowing include the limits of our knowledge as well as the realm in which knowing is transformed into believing.

Heaven and earth represent mental absoluteness and practical necessity. He who knows much will also have to define his place between heaven and earth, between God and the world. Success or failure depend very much upon your ability to question yourself and to view yourself from the outside. The shadowy figure on the left indicates the positive ability to look at yourself from a neutral perspective with loving and, at the same time, critical eyes. But the shadow also warns you to beware of splitting yourself in two halves, a potentially extremely serious state.

Use your mental powers to better understand your needs and how to fulfill them. It is your conscious handling of the unconscious that will result in a better understanding of yourself and help you to overcome half-truths, superstition, and disbelief.

Practical advice: *Try to understand what it is that you do not know about yourself and others—and what you cannot know. Make sure you understand your most important needs and expectations. In order to achieve this end, it is most helpful to have all the mirrors of your mind well-polished and to know your own star!*

Wissen und Weite

Auf den ersten Blick mag es überraschen, ausgerechnet bei den Schwertern, die für das Luftelement des Geistes stehen, einen Kirchenmann anzutreffen. Beim HOHE-PRIESTER oder bei den KELCH-Karten würde man ihn möglicherweise eher erwarten. Und doch: Der KÖNIG DER SCHWERTER ist der Meister der Schwerter, der Meister des Wissens. Hoch über den Gipfeln beginnt sein luftiges Reich des Geistes. Entweder ergeht er sich im Negativen in völliger Abgehobenheit, oder er entwickelt ein souveränes Bewusstsein, frei und ungebunden im Denken, bodenständig und verankert in seiner Existenz.

Der Bischof oder Kirchenmann kann zwar die War-nung vor Weltfremdheit und einem falschen Glauben her-vorheben, gleichzeitig kann er aber auch daran erinnern, dass jedes Wissen auch das Nichtwissen einschließt. Die Gipfel des Wissens schließen die Grenzen der Erkenntnis ein – und jenen Bereich, in dem Wissen zu Glauben wird.

Himmel und Erde stehen für geistige Unbedingtheit und praktische Notwendigkeit. Wer viel weiß, wird auch seinen Platz zwischen Himmel und Erde, zwischen Gott und Welt zu bestimmen haben. Erfolg oder Misserfolg hängen entsprechend davon ab, dass wir uns selbst infrage stellen und gleichsam von außen betrachten können.

Die Schattenfigur im Bild steht für diese Fähigkeit, sich aus einer neutralen Perspektive, wie von außen, mit liebe-vollen, aber auch kritischen Augen selbst zu überprüfen. Sie warnt allerdings gleichzeitig vor der Abspaltung eines zweiten Ichs, einer Halbierung, und stellt uns damit vor eine schwere Aufgabe.

Nutzen Sie Ihre geistigen Kräfte, um Ihre Bedürfnisse besser zu verstehen und zu erfüllen. Ein bewusster Umgang mit dem Unbewussten führt Sie zu einem per-sönlichen Selbstverständnis, das Halbwissen, Aberglauben und Unglauben überwindet.

Praxistipps: *Machen Sie sich bewusst, was Sie von sich, aber auch von anderen nicht wissen und nicht wissen können. Kümmern Sie sich darum, dass die wesentlichen Bedürfnisse und Erwartungen klar sind. Dabei hilft es, wenn alle Spie-gel klar sind und Sie Ihren eigenen Stern kennen!*

Savoir et immensité

Au premier abord il peut paraître surprenant de découvrir un homme d'Église muni d'épées qui représentent l'élé-ment aérien de l'esprit. On s'attendrait plutôt à le trouver avec LE PAPE ou dans les cartes de COUPE. Et pourtant, le ROI D'ÉPEE est le maître des épées, le maître du savoir. Son royaume aérien commence bien au-dessus des som-mets. Soit il s'élève et s'isole totalement au sens négatif, soit il dispose d'une conscience souveraine, libre et indé-pendante de pensée, solide et bien ancrée dans son exis-tence.

L'évêque ou le prêtre peut certes incarner l'avertissement face à un manque de réalisme ou une fausse croyance, mais il peut aussi rappeler que chaque savoir inclut égale-ment le non-savoir. Les sommets du savoir contiennent les limites de la connaissance – et ce domaine où le savoir devient croyance.

Ciel et terre représentent l'inconditonnalité spirituelle et la nécessité pratique. Celui qui est très savant aura à choisir sa place entre ciel et terre, entre Dieu et le monde. De fait, réussite ou échec dépendent de la faculté de nous remettre nous-mêmes en question et de nous observer de l'extérieur. La silhouette d'ombre figure la faculté de s'exa-miner dans une perspective neutre, comme de l'extérieur, d'un œil bienveillant tout en étant critique. Mais elle met en garde aussi contre un partage, la désunion d'un second moi et nous place devant un grand défi.

Mettez à profit vos forces spirituelles pour mieux saisir et mieux réaliser vos désirs. Une approche consciente de l'inconscient vous conduit à une identité personnelle qui surmonte connaissances superficielles, superstition et impiété.

Conseils pratiques : *Prenez conscience de ce que vous ne savez pas et ne pouvez pas savoir de vous, mais aussi des autres. Faites en sorte que les besoins et attentes essentiels soient évidents. Veillez à ce que tous les miroirs soient clairs et à bien connaître votre étoile !*

Knight of Swords
Ritter der Schwerte
Cavalier d'Épée

KNIGHT OF SWORDS

Personal Consequences

Dalí's picture emphasizes the pompous and the playful. Besides their hard and metallic aspect, swords always have a lighter, elf-like quality, which on this card (and in many other tarot decks) is symbolized by the butterfly. What is highly unusual is the presentation of the key motif on a bowl or a dish. The knight appears to be more like a little tin soldier or a trophy to be put on a shelf.

But this is nevertheless a very wise depiction. Living a purely symbolic life is one of the greatest of dangers, but when acknowledged, a great task. If you live completely within and for the realm of the mind, you will be completely absorbed in your imagination, your ideas, and your perceptions. You might think the title of a doctor or a professor, an award, or a medal will bring you the greatest happiness. To gather such trophies might become your most important goal in life. But because these trophies are nothing but symbols, your life becomes merely symbolic. In this rather chilling version of mental radicalism, you ultimately sacrifice your humanity for the sake of amassing trophies. This will lead to a shrivelling up of your personality, which then can be shown around on a silver platter.

Positive alternatives may vary, but they always have to do with overcoming the dangers of symbolic life and using the power of your mind to deal with real problems and to experience real happiness.

In a positive sense, the pomp and the adornments of the horseman represent a colorful, rich, and liberated life—including a clear conscience (see the white color of the hat and the horse) and plenty of love (see the red color of the horse and its rider.)

Practical advice: *Take your thoughts further than usual. Risk greater commitment and be more consequential and steadfast. Leave old thought patterns behind. Take your thoughts seriously and interpret them like dreams.*

Persönliche Konsequenz

Dieses Dalí-Bild betont den Pomp und das Verspielte. Immer haben die Schwerter neben ihrer harten, metallischen Komponente auch eine leichte, feenhafte Seite, die hier (und in vielen anderen Tarot-Karten) durch den Schmetterling symbolisiert wird.

Ungewöhnlich ist die Präsentation des Hauptmotivs auf einer Schüssel oder Schale. So wirkt der Ritter eher wie ein Zinnsoldat oder wie eine Trophäe, die man sich ins Regal stellt. Dies aber ist eine überaus weise Bildidee. Eine große Gefahr stellt das rein symbolische Leben dar, in dessen Überwindung aber liegt auch eine große Aufgabe. Wer konsequent und radikal mit dem Geist und für den Geist lebt, der geht ganz in seinen Phantasien, Einfällen und Erkenntnissen auf. Ein Doktor- oder Professorentitel, Preise und Auszeichnungen erscheinen dann wie das höchste Glück. Der Erwerb dieser Trophäen wird zum wichtigsten Lebensziel. Sofern diese Trophäen aber nichts als Symbole darstellen, verwandelt sich auch das Leben in ein symbolisches Leben. In dieser eher abschreckenden Version der Radikalität des Geistes opfert man seine Menschlichkeit und stellt sie in den Dienst der Erreichung eines ersehnten Ziels. Die eigene Persönlichkeit schrumpft und wird gleichsam auf dem Silbertablett herumgereicht.

Eine positive Deutung legt nahe, das symbolische Leben zu überwinden und die Kraft des Geistes zu nutzen, um wirkliche Probleme zu lösen und reale Glückserfahrungen zu ermöglichen. Der Schmuck und die Pracht des Ritters stehen im positiven Sinne für ein farbenprächtiges, reiches und erlöstes Leben mit einem reinen Gewissen (die Farbe Weiß – Hut und Pferd) und mit viel Liebe (die Farbe Rot – Ross und Reiter).

Praxistipps: *Gehen Sie in Ihren Gedanken weiter als sonst. Wagen Sie (mehr) Verbindlichkeit und Konsequenz. Lassen Sie die Schubladen des Denkens hinter sich. Nehmen Sie Ihre Gedanken ernst und deuten Sie sie wie Träume.*

Conséquence personnelle

Cette image de Dalí met en valeur la pompe et le ludique. En plus de leurs composantes dures et métalliques, les épées ont toujours un côté léger, féérique qui est symbolisé ici (et dans d'autres jeux de tarot) par le papillon. La présentation du motif central sur un plat ou un plateau est inhabituelle. Le cavalier ressemble ainsi plutôt à un soldat de plomb ou à un trophée qu'on range sur une étagère.

Pourtant, c'est une idée de portrait tout à fait judicieuse. La vie purement symbolique présente un grand danger, mais la surmonter constitue un réel défi. Celui qui vit de manière conséquente et radicale avec et pour l'esprit s'épanouit vraiment dans ses fantasmes, ses idées et ses connaissances. Un titre de docteur ou de professeur, les prix et récompenses apparaissent alors comme le bonheur suprême. L'obtention de ces trophées devient l'objectif de vie essentiel. Mais dans la mesure où ces trophées ne représentent que des symboles, la vie même se transforme en vie symbolique. Dans cette version plutôt repoussante de la radicalité de l'esprit on sacrifie son caractère humain et l'exploite pour recevoir un trophée convoité. La personnalité s'atrophie et passe en quelque sorte de main en main sur un plateau d'argent.

Une interprétation positive s'impose, de surpasser la vie symbolique et d'utiliser la force de l'esprit pour résoudre les vrais problèmes et permettre de réelles expériences de bonheur. Les bijoux et le luxe affichés par le cavalier symbolisent dans un sens positif une vie riche en couleurs, fastueuse et libérée avec une conscience tranquille (la couleur blanche du chapeau et du cheval) et beaucoup d'amour (la couleur rouge du cavalier et de sa monture).

Conseils pratiques : *Allez plus loin dans vos pensées. Osez plus de complaisance et de conséquence. Laissez derrière vous les tiroirs de la pensée. Prenez vos pensées au sérieux et interprétez-les comme des rêves.*

Page of Swords
Page der Schwerter
Valet d'Épée

PAGE OF SWORDS

Mental Agility

By adding air to a flame in the fire, to a body immersed in water, or to an object floating in air, it will become more buoyant and rise up. This is also true of the human mind, which is symbolically equivalent to the fire element. A well-functioning mind makes many things easier. Traditionally, the PAGE (KNAVE, PRINCESS) OF SWORDS represents mental renewal and new thoughts, judgments, and decisions. In addition, Dalí depicts a possible contradiction between apparently peaceful intentions, represented by the green twig in the figure's hand, and dangerous consequences, visible as the demon in the background.

In a general sense, this card stands for everything new, for playful and experimental thinking. It warns you to beware of gullibility and ignorance, which might lead to powerless protests, general distrust, and erratic or dogmatic decision-making.

Remain mentally fit. Look for rewarding tasks and challenges. Exploit your humor and your charm. Discover a new lightness of being. Avoid made-up statements and arguments. Work in a creative and attentive manner with the images that are in your head and in the heads of others.

Practical advice: *Take things more "lightly." Take the "sword" into your own hands. Do not delegate your power of discernment to others. The value of a new idea cannot be judged by that which is, but only by that which will be. You might sense that the little bit that man can comprehend is much smaller than that which is. It makes a big difference whether or not you comprehend your individual contribution and put your abilities to good use in order to make life easier, more deliberate, and more fun for yourself and for your fellow human beings.*

Die Leichtigkeit des Geistes

Eine Flamme im Feuer, ein Körper im Wasser oder ein Objekt in der Luft bekommen Auftrieb, wenn Luft zugeführt wird. Das gilt auch im übertragenem Sinn für den menschlichen Geist, dem in der Symbolik das Luftelement gleichgesetzt wird. Ein funktionierender Geist manifestiert sich darin, dass er vieles leichter macht.

Traditionell wird der PAGE (BUBE, PRINZESSIN) DER SCHWERTER als ein Sinnbild oder ein Bote der geistigen Erneuerung betrachtet, er steht für neue Gedanken, Urteile und Entscheidungen. Das Dalí-Bild weist zusätzlich auf einen möglichen Widerspruch zwischen friedlichen Absichten, dargestellt duch den Zweig in der Hand im Vordergrund, und eher gefährlichen, hinterrücks wirkenden Folgen hin, sichtbar in der Darstellung des Dämons im Hintergrund.

So steht diese Karte insgesamt für Neuigkeiten, für spielerische, experimentelle Gedanken. Und sie warnt zugleich vor Gutgläubigkeit und Ahnungslosigkeit, die in der Folge zu hilflosem Protest, zu allgemeinem Misstrauen oder zu beliebigen oder dogmatischen Entscheidungen führen können.

Bleiben Sie geistig fit, suchen Sie sich lohnende Aufgaben und Herausforderungen. Bauen Sie auf Ihren Witz und Ihren Charme – und finden Sie zu einer neuen Leichtigkeit. Meiden Sie Behauptungen und „Argumente", die lediglich aus der Luft gegriffen sind. Gehen Sie kreativ und aufmerksam mit den Vorstellungen um, die Sie und Ihre Mitmenschen im Kopf haben.

Praxistipps: *Bringen Sie mehr „Luft" ins Spiel. Halten Sie das „Schwert" selbst in der Hand. Geben Sie Ihr Urteilsvermögen nicht an andere ab. Der Wert einer neuen Idee misst sich nicht an dem, was ist, sondern an dem, was sein wird. Vielleicht spüren Sie, dass der Teil, den ein Mensch begreifen kann, kleiner ist als das, was ist. Nutzen und begreifen Sie Ihren Teil, und Ihr Leben und das Ihrer Mitmenschen wird leichter, bewusster und unterhaltsamer werden.*

La légèreté de l'esprit

Une flamme dans le feu, un corps dans l'eau ou un objet dans l'air se met en mouvement si on lui insuffle de l'air. Cela vaut aussi au sens figuré pour l'esprit humain, qui est comparé à l'élément de l'air dans le symbolisme. Un esprit qui fonctionne se manifeste en faisant beaucoup de choses avec légèreté. Traditionnellement, le VALET (PAGE, PRINCESSE) D'ÉPÉE est considéré comme un symbole ou un messager du renouveau spirituel, il incarne les pensées, décisions et jugements nouveaux. En outre, l'image de Dalí souligne une contradiction possible entre les intentions pacifiques, symbolisées par la branche dans la main au premier plan, et des suites dangereuses et sournoises, visibles dans la représentation du dragon à l'arrière-plan.

Dans son ensemble cette carte représente les nouveautés, les pensées ludiques et expérimentales. Et elle met aussi en garde contre la naïveté et l'inconscience qui peuvent mener de fait à une protestation impuissante, à une méfiance générale ou à des décisions arbitraires ou dogmatiques.

Restez vif d'esprit, recherchez des tâches ou des défis qui en valent la peine. Comptez sur votre humour et votre charme – et essayer d'atteindre une nouvelle légèreté. Fuyez les affirmations et « arguments » en l'air. Ayez une approche créative et attentive des idées que vous et vos contemporains ont en tête.

Conseils pratiques : *Aérez votre jeu. Tenez vous-même l'épée en main. Ne cédez pas votre capacité de jugement à d'autres. La valeur d'une idée ne se mesure pas à ce qui est, mais à ce qui sera. Peut-être sentez-vous que la partie qu'un être humain peut comprendre est plus petite que ce qui existe. Utilisez et saisissez votre part, et votre vie comme celle de votre entourage en deviendra plus légère, plus consciente et plus divertissante.*

Ace of Swords
Ass der Schwerter
As d'Épée

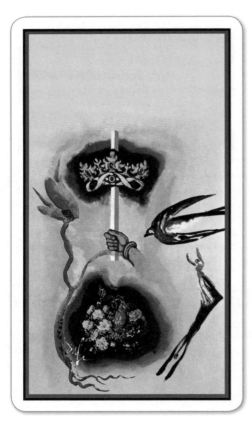

The Crowning Achievement of the Mind

In Tarot, swords stand for the mind's weapons. This symbolism dates back to the figure of Justitia from antiquity. The attributes of the goddess of justice—one of the four cardinal virtues—were tools in the form of a pair of scales and a sword. Not only an executioner's instrument of power, the sword was a means to form a judgment, like the scales. While the scales measure, the sword examines and discerns, being used to make deep cuts and to draw the line, separating that which belongs from that which does not belong.

On this picture, a bare hand holds the sword at the blade, indicating the pain that might be inflicted by this weapon. However, the image also emphasizes that this card is not just about fighting or other martial uses of arms. Accept this hint as a gift, enabling you to view the sword in a different manner.

The realm of the mind is the air. The swallow and the angel remind us of the heights and depths of the world of the mind and of spirits.

A single sword already expresses the ambiguity of the human mind. On the one hand, it is the crowning achievement of creation, on the other, it represents the greatest possible alienation and distance from nature in all its glory. To develop the former and avoid the latter, it is up to us to learn to fly.

The fruitfulness of the mind is measured by the refinement and fulfillment of practical needs. The ACE OF SWORDS stands for the opportunity to gain a better understanding of your unexpressed desires and fears, (note the red being at the left-hand margin).

Practical advice: *Rise and stand up straight! Gain strength from your knowledge and delve into everything you don't yet know. You possess and you will need clear reasoning and staying power. Brain jogging and physical exercise will support your mental facilities. Enjoy your newfound clarity!*

Die Krönung des Geistes

Schwerter stehen im Tarot für die Waffen des Geistes. Diese Symbolik geht unter anderem auf das antike Bild der Justitia zurück. Die Göttin der Gerechtigkeit – eine der vier antiken Kardinaltugenden – besaß als Werkzeuge Waage und Schwert. Das Schwert war dabei nicht nur ein Machtmittel zur Urteilsvollstreckung, sondern wie die Waage auch ein Werkzeug zur Urteilsbildung: Mit der Waage wird abgewogen und mit dem Schwert wird untersucht und unterschieden. Mit dem Schwert werden Einschnitte gemacht und Trennungslinien gezogen; es zeigt sich, was zusammengehört und was nicht.

Im vorliegenden Bild greift die bloße Hand an die Schneide des Schwertes. Entweder weist dies auf die durch Schwerter verursachten Schmerzen hin, oder aber es wird betont, dass es hier eben nicht nur um den gewaltsamen Gebrauch des Schwertes geht. Nehmen Sie es als Geschenk, das Schwert in diesem Sinne neu zu begreifen.

Das Reich des Geistes aber ist die Luft. Die Schwalbe und der Engel erinnern an die Höhen und Tiefen in der Welt des Geistes und der Geister.

Schon das eine Schwert verweist auf die Bedeutungsebene der Zweischneidigkeit des Geistes. Der menschliche Geist stellt auf der einen Seite die Krone der Schöpfung dar, auf der anderen Seite die maximale Entfernung und Entfremdung von der blühenden Natur. Um das eine zu entwickeln und das andere zu meiden, müssen wir selbst fliegen lernen.

Die Fruchtbarkeit des Geistes misst sich an der Verfeinerung und Erfüllung praktischer Bedürfnisse. Das ASS DER SCHWERTER steht auch für die Chance, undefinierte Wünsche und Ängste (wie das rote Wesen am linken Bildrand) besser zu verstehen.

Praxistipps: *Erheben Sie sich, richten Sie sich auf und stärken Sie sich an dem, was Sie wissen; untersuchen Sie, was Sie nicht wissen. Nutzen Sie ihr gutes Denkvermögen und Ihren kraftvollen, langen Atem. Gehirnjogging und Körpertraining unterstützen Ihre geistigen Kräfte. Genießen Sie eine neue Klarheit!*

Le couronnement de l'esprit

Dans le tarot les épées représentent les armes de l'esprit. Ce symbole remonte, entre autres, à l'effigie antique de la Justitia. La déesse de la Justice – l'une des quatre vertus cardinales – avait comme attributs la balance et l'épée. L'épée ne représentait pourtant pas seulement un instrument de puissance pour l'exécution d'un jugement, mais était aussi comme la balance un moyen de discernement : la balance soupesait, et l'épée examinait et différenciait. L'épée sert à trancher et à tracer des limites ; elle montre ce qui va ensemble ou non.

Dans cette image une main nue saisit le tranchant de l'épée. Soit ceci évoque les douleurs que provoquent les épées, soit il est question de souligner que l'épée n'est pas que d'un usage violent. Considérez comme un cadeau de voir l'épée sous un jour nouveau.

Mais l'air est le royaume de l'esprit. L'hirondelle et l'ange rappellent les hauts et les bas dans le monde de l'esprit et des esprits.

En soi, cette épée contient le niveau de sens du double tranchant de l'esprit. D'une part, l'esprit humain représente le couronnement de la création, d'autre part l'éloignement maximal et le détachement de la nature florissante. Afin de cultiver l'un et d'éviter l'autre, il nous faut apprendre à voler de nos propres ailes.

La fécondité de l'esprit se mesure au raffinement et à la réalisation de désirs pratiques. L'AS D'ÉPÉE symbolise aussi la chance de mieux comprendre les souhaits et craintes indéfinies (comme le personnage rouge au bord de l'image).

Conseils pratiques : *Levez-vous, redressez-vous et fortifiez-vous de ce que vous savez ; analysez ce que vous ne savez pas. Utilisez votre bonne capacité de réflexion et votre long et puissant souffle. Gymnastique mentale et exercice physique stimulent vos forces mentales. Profitez de cette nouvelle transparence !*

Two of Swords
Zwei der Schwerter
Deux d'Épée

New Insights

This card shows that your thoughts and your discerning powers are in the process of transcending your previous limits. The moon at the top of the card represents the cycles of life. The bull (cow or calf?) in the lower part of the picture stands for your physicality, for your moods and irritability as well as your sense of security and tranquillity.

Subtle sentiments and unexpressed needs demand your attention, unvoiced desires and fears await a response. And yet those louder and more insistent opinions and intentions are in no less need of closer scrutiny. You need to use the weapons of your mind—thinking, knowing, and discerning—to probe your emotions and wants.

The blindfold warns against a lack of attention or inadequate mental vigilance. And yet the blindfolded eyes also represent impartiality and the transition to a more spiritual vision. The frontiers of the realm of the mind, within which your current questions are focused, are to be found beyond the concrete and the obvious.

The body of the bull contains drawings of several little boats, depicting a voyage or a maritime battle, perhaps. If you consider the bull, the picture of a saint at the center of the picture, and the moon above as representing the sum total of a human being, you will note: down below in the realm of the unconscious or in the lower abdomen, there is growing unrest. Little boats move to and fro in the waves. In the middle region, the realm of your normal waking consciousness, everything is clearly de- fined but also rather rigid. Noble aims and ideals, represented by the moon, float overhead.

The challenge is to penetrate new spaces with the weapons of your mind and to shed the light of consciousness on all aspects of your personality.

Practical advice: *Do not become entrenched in uncertainty. Do not pretend to be blind or not to understand. Expand your horizons. Search within to grow beyond yourself.*

Neue Erkenntnisse

Hier wachsen Ihre Gedanken und Ihr Urteilsvermögen weit über den bisherigen Rahmen hinaus. Der Mond im oberen Bildteil steht für die Zyklen des Lebens, und der Stier (Kuh, Kalb?) im unteren Bildteil verweist auf die eigene Körperlichkeit mit ihren Launen und Reizbarkeiten, aber auch mit einer eigenen Ruhe und Sicherheit.

Unerkannte Gefühle und Bedürfnisse rufen nach Beachtung, unausgesprochene Wünsche und Ängste warten auf ein Echo. Andererseits sind da lautstarke, gleichsam überdeutliche Meinungen und Absichten, die jedoch nicht weniger einer genaueren Unterscheidung bedürfen. Die Waffen des Geistes – Denken, Wissen, Urteilen – sind nötig, um Ihre Gefühle und Bedürfnisse zu prüfen.

Die Augenbinde stellt eine Warnung vor mangelnder Aufmerksamkeit oder fehlender geistiger Wachheit dar. Auf der anderen Seite bedeuten die verbundenen Augen im positiven Sinne auch Unparteilichkeit und den Übergang in ein geistiges Schauen. Jenseits des Augenscheins und jenseits des Konkreten beginnt das Reich des Geistes, in dem Sie sich mit Ihren aktuellen Fragen bewegen.

In den Umriss des Stierkörpers sind kleine Schiffe eingezeichnet, eine Seereise oder eventuell auch ein Seegefecht könnten sich darin darstellen. Sieht man den Stier, das Heiligenbild in der Mitte und den Mond darüber als Bild für die Gesamtheit eines Menschen, so zeigt sich: Unten, im Unbewussten oder im Unterleib, rumort es, Schiffchen ziehen hin und her. Im mittleren Bereich, dem Alltagsbewusstsein, hat alles einen klaren, aber auch starren Rahmen. Darüber schweben hehre Ziele und Ideale, die sich im Mond darstellen.

Die Aufgabe besteht nun darin, mit den Waffen des Geistes in neue Räume vorzudringen und das Bewusstsein auf alle Bereiche der eigenen Persönlichkeit auszudehnen.

Praxistipps: *Verschanzen Sie sich nicht hinter Ihrem Unwissen. Flüchten Sie nicht in Blindheit oder Unverständnis. Erweitern Sie Ihren Horizont, gehen Sie in sich, um über sich hinauszuwachsen.*

Connaissances nouvelles

Vos pensées et votre capacité de jugement dépassent ici de loin le cadre usuel. La lune en haut de l'image représente les cycles de la vie, et le taureau (vache, veau?) en bas de l'image renvoie à la corporalité individuelle avec ses caprices et susceptibilités, mais aussi son équilibre et son assurance. Les sentiments et besoins méconnus réclament de l'attention, les désirs et peurs inexprimés attendent un écho. D'autre part, il existe des avis et intentions impétueux, en quelque sorte limpides, qui cependant exigent une différenciation tout aussi exacte. Les armes de l'esprit – penser, savoir, juger – sont indispensables pour tester vos sentiments et vos besoins.

Le bandeau exprime un avertissement contre une attention médiocre ou un manque de vigilance spirituelle. D'autre part, les yeux bandés signifient aussi dans un sens positif la neutralité et le passage à un regard mental. Au-delà de l'apparence et au-delà du concret commence le domaine de l'esprit dans lequel vous vous mouvez avec vos sujets actuels.

Sur le contour du taureau sont gravés des petits bateaux, représentant une croisière ou éventuellement aussi une bataille navale. Si l'on considère le taureau, le saint au centre de l'image et la lune au-dessus de lui comme image figurant l'intégralité d'un être humain, force est de constater: en bas, dans l'inconscient ou le bas-ventre il y a beaucoup d'agitation, les petits bateaux vont et viennent. Au centre, siège de la conscience du quotidien, tout a un cadre clair mais aussi rigide. Au-dessus flottent les buts et idéaux nobles symbolisés par la lune.

Le défi consiste à pénétrer dans d'autres sphères à l'aide des armes de l'esprit et d'étendre la conscience à tous les domaines de la personnalité.

Conseils pratiques: *Ne vous retranchez pas derrière votre ignorance. Ne vous réfugiez pas dans l'aveuglement ou l'incompréhension. Élargissez votre horizon, rentrez en vous-même pour vous surpasser.*

Three of Swords
Drei der Schwerter
Trois d'Épée

Conscious Love

This is a very powerful card, an homage to love and to the liberating power of the mind. The card depicts a scene from the painting *Roger Rescuing Angelica* (1819), by Jean-Auguste-Dominique Ingres, framed by a big red heart. As ever, the message is ambiguous: perhaps a great abyss is opening up at the center of your heart— or maybe swords are about to free you from affliction and distress.

The picture is based on the classical motif of a battle with a dragon: a black serpent-like monster visible at the bottom of the big heart. The image warns against hurt feelings—old wounds reopened by the sword. The positive message is that whatever problems we may encounter, the weapons of the mind and the eyes of love will enable us to find a solution, in a happy alliance of heart and sword.

Most problems arise out of a separation of abstract thoughts and your real feelings. Obsessive views and rigid ideas refuse to be checked against actual experience, paralyzing your mental and emotional faculties. Like a thorn in the side, they are a source of constant pain and irritation.

Give love a chance, including a love of truth and honesty. Shed light on your memories and expectations. Do not be afraid of painful truths. All wounds will heal if you tend to them.

Practical advice: *Do not give up! Risk being more honest and authentic. Let go of your prejudice, pretence, and reserve. Feel the great relief that will be yours when your heart is set free again.*

Bewusste Liebe

Eine starke Karte, eine Hommage an die Liebe – und an die befreiende Kraft des Geistes: Die Karte zeigt, eingerahmt von einem angedeuteten roten Herz, einen Ausschnitt aus dem Bild „Roger befreit Angelika" von Jean-Auguste-Dominique Ingres (1819). Wie immer ist die Botschaft doppeldeutig: Möglicherweise tut sich hier ein tosender Abgrund inmitten des Herzens auf. Oder die Schwerter führen zur glücklichen Befreiung aus Bedrängnis und Trübsal.

Das Bild von Ingres greift das klassische Motiv des Drachenkampfs auf. Der schwarze Drache ist auf dem Boden des großen Herzens zu erkennen. Das Bild warnt auf der einen Seite vor verletzenden Gefühlen – vor Wunden, die mit den Schwertern weiter aufgerissen werden. Die positive Botschaft aber lautet: Welche Probleme uns auch begegnen mögen, mit den Waffen des Geistes und den Augen der Liebe, in der glücklichen Verbindung von Schwert und Herz, können sie überwunden werden.

Die meisten Probleme entstehen aus der Trennung abstrakter Ideen und echter Gefühle. Fixe Ideen und Vorstellungen widersetzen sich einer Überprüfung durch Erfahrung und lähmen unsere geistigen und emotionalen Fähigkeiten. Wie ein Dorn im Fleisch bereiten sie ständig Schmerzen.

Geben Sie der Liebe eine Chance, auch der Liebe zu Wahrheit und Ehrlichkeit. Durchleuchten Sie Ihre Erinnerungen und Erwartungen. Haben Sie keine Angst vor unbequemen Wahrheiten. Die Wunden heilen, wenn man sich um sie kümmert.

Praxistipps: *Geben Sie nicht auf! Riskieren Sie mehr Aufrichtigkeit. Bauen Sie Vorbehalte, Vorwände und Vorurteile ab. Spüren Sie die große Erleichterung, wenn Ihr Herz wieder frei wird!*

Amour conscient

Une carte puissante, un hommage à l'amour – et à la force libératrice de l'esprit : encadrée d'un cœur rouge juste esquissé, la carte représente un fragment du tableau de Jean-Auguste-Dominique Ingres « Roger délivrant Angélique » (1819). Comme toujours, le message est ambigu : en plein cœur pourrait s'ouvrir ici un abîme fracassant. Ou bien les épées délivrent avec bonheur de la détresse et de la dépression.

Le tableau d'Ingres reprend le thème classique du combat contre le dragon. Le dragon noir apparaît au fond du grand cœur. D'une part, l'image met en garde contre les sentiment blessants – contre les plaies que les épées déchirent encore davantage. D'autre part le message positif nous dit : Quels que soient les problèmes que nous pouvons affronter, ils peuvent être surmontés avec les armes de l'esprit et les yeux de l'amour, dans une heureuse union de l'épée et du cœur.

La plupart des problèmes résultent de la séparation entre idées abstraites et sentiments réels. Les idées fixes et les chimères empêchent un contrôle de l'expérience et bloquent nos capacités spirituelles et émotionnelles. Comme une épine implantée dans la chair elles nous font sans cesse souffrir.

Donnez une chance à l'amour, à l'amour de la vérité et de la sincérité aussi. Passez au crible vos souvenirs et vos espérances. N'ayez pas peur des vérités gênantes. Les plaies guérissent si on les soigne.

Conseils pratiques : *Ne baissez pas les bras ! Osez plus de sincérité. Abolissez les réserves, les prétextes et les préjugés. Ressentez le grand soulagement de votre cœur à nouveau libre !*

Four of Swords
Vier der Schwerter
Quatre d'Épée

Holistic Thinking

The picture on this card picks up on a motif from the tarot deck by A. E. Waite and P. C. Smith. It shows a detail of the painting *The Death of Marat* (1793), one of the great radicals of the French Revolution, by Jacques-Louis David. Jean-Paul Marat's life came to a violent end.

This particular scene warns of the dangers of the hypnotic effect of ideas and of fanaticism in general, which turns people into martyrs and into politically or religiously motivated criminals. The serpent to the right is an ambiguous symbol. On the one hand, it tells you to beware of your base drives and animal instincts, on the other, it is a symbol of wisdom.

Drawing on the four points of the compass, four swords represent the completeness of the weapons of the mind. Thoughts and ideas form a composite whole. Ideally, your thoughts should be "well-rounded." They should complement and inspire each other, as a sign of wisdom and expanded consciousness.

In less ideal circumstances, unmitigated thought manifests itself in disastrous convictions that can only lead to dire consequences. Then you will become a victim or a perpetrator, a fundamentalist or a martyr. There is not just a very real danger to life and limb—as in the case of Jean-Paul Marat. In a metaphorical sense, you are warned against human and spiritual bleakness, when convictions become more important than love or life.

Practical advice: *You've got some tough nuts to crack! But you will be able to resolve major contradictions and master complicated issues. Relax both inwardly and outwardly by letting go of negative thoughts. In order for your mind to concentrate on the task at hand, you must relax. A new dimension and a life beyond your expectations await you.*

Ganzheitliches Denken

Dieses Bild knüpft an ähnliche Bilder aus dem Tarot von A. E. Waite und P. C. Smith an und zeigt einen Bildausschnitt aus „Der Tod des Marat" von Jacques-Louis David (1793). Jean-Paul Marat war eine der großen radikalen Gestalten der französischen Revolution, sein Leben nahm ein gewaltsames Ende.

Die Bedeutung dieses Bildzitats liegt in dem Hinweis auf die hypnotische Wirkung und den Fanatismus des Geistes, der Menschen zu Märtyrern oder zu Überzeugungstätern werden lässt. Die Schlange am rechten Bildrand ist ein ambivalentes Symbol, sie warnt vor niederen Trieben und Instinkten, gilt aber auch als Zeichen der Weisheit.

In Anlehnung an die vier Himmelsrichtungen deuten vier Schwerter auf eine Vollständigkeit der Waffen des Geistes hin. Gedanken und Vorstellungen setzen sich zu einem Ganzen zusammen. Im Idealfall werden Ihre Gedanken dadurch richtig „rund", sie ergänzen und beflügeln sich in einem Moment der Weisheit und des sich entwickelnden Bewusstseins.

Im weniger erfreulichen Fall äußert sich jedoch die Vollständigkeit des Denkens darin, dass fatale Grundüberzeugungen ebenso fatale Folgen haben. Man wird zum Opfer oder zum Täter, zum Fundamentalisten oder zum Märtyrer. Die Gefahr liegt nicht nur im unmittelbaren Verlust von Leib und Leben, so wie es Jean-Paul Marat traf. Im übertragenen Sinn warnt uns diese Karte vor menschlicher und geistiger Kälte, die unsere Überzeugungen über die Liebe und das Leben stellt.

Praxistipps: *Sie haben einige Widersprüche zu lösen! Sie sind in der Lage, auch schwierige Gegensätze zu vereinen. Sorgen Sie für Entspannung, nach innen wie nach außen, indem Sie negative Vorstellungen loslassen. Entspannen Sie sich, damit Ihr Geist sich konzentrieren und schärfen kann. Eine neue Dimension, ein größeres Leben, erwartet Sie.*

Pensée globale

Cette image est inspirée d'images analogues du tarot de A. E. Waite et P. C. Smith et représente un fragment du tableau « La Mort de Marat » de Jacques-Louis David (1793). Jean-Paul Marat fut une des personnalités marquantes de la Révolution française, il connut une mort violente.

L'importance de cette référence picturale réside dans l'indication d'un effet hypnotique et du fanatisme de l'esprit qui transforme les hommes en martyrs ou en criminels idéologiques. Le serpent sur le bord droit de la carte est un symbole ambivalent, il met en garde contre les basses pulsions et les instincts, mais figure aussi la sagesse.

Suivant le principe des quatre points cardinaux, quatre épées soulignent l'intégralité des armes de l'esprit. Pensées et fantasmes se réunissent pour faire un tout. Dans le cas idéal, vos pensées sont bien « rondes », elles se complètent et se stimulent en un moment de sagesse et d'une conscience en pleine évolution.

Toutefois, dans un cas moins favorable l'intégralité de la pensée s'exprime dans le fait que des convictions fondamentales fatales ont aussi des conséquences fatales. On devient victime ou bourreau, fondamentaliste ou martyr. Le danger ne réside pas seulement dans un brutal trépas, comme ce fut le destin de Jean-Paul Marat. Au sens figuré, cette carte nous met en garde contre la froideur humaine et spirituelle qui place nos convictions au-dessus de l'amour et de la vie.

Conseils pratiques : *Il vous faut démêler plusieurs contradictions ! Vous êtes à même de concilier des différences même complexes. Cherchez à vous relaxer, intérieurement et extérieurement, en vous débarassant des pensées négatives. Détendez-vous afin que votre esprit puisse se concentrer et s'aiguiser. Une nouvelle dimension, une vie plus exaltante vous attend.*

Five of Swords
Fünf der Schwerter
Cinq d'Épée

The Essence of Mind

A man with esprit and charm looking towards the woman on the left, with his feet firmly planted on the ground, is an image of the liberated mind and the freedom of a butterfly.

Skeptically interpreted as a warning, the card shows a self-conceited man, who is content with only those swords he has managed to grab. An abyss opens beneath his feet as he looks at the woman, who has no way of getting hold of the swords. He sees her only as a blur. This is for both parties involved—man as well as woman—a picture of uncertainty, flightiness, and ultimately of misunderstanding.

How do we use the air element of the mind? You may be totally ruled by your moods or have suppressed them by the use of the sword. A fertile mind is able to distinguish between good and bad emotional states, enabling you to live according to your own rhythm. The essence of the mind is a developed consciousness and personal clarity, which will make your life easier and more fulfilled.

Learn from experience. Probe deeper into the meaning of your victories and your defeats. Use the weapons of your mind as tools for healing. It is never too late, and only very rarely too early, to draw conclusions from your experiences and to learn the necessary lessons. Do not allow difficulties to bring you down. Be clear and honest. You have nothing to lose, but much to gain.

Practical advice: *Use your knowledge fruitfully. Consider the two swords lying on the ground and ask yourself whether you understand the power of your untapped thoughts and can appreciate the joy of overcoming and discarding old doubts. Beware of empty promises and unfounded speculation. Live fully in the present moment. Reassess what you consider to be good and beautiful. You know you are on the right track when you are happy and have learned to marvel again.*

Quintessenz des Geistes

Ein Mann mit Esprit – der Frau gegenüber, mit beiden Beinen fest auf der Erde, als Bild von befreitem Geist und schmetterlingshafter Freiheit.

Dasselbe Bild in einer warnenden, skeptischen Beschreibung: Ein selbstgefälliger Mann, der sich mit dem Teil der Schwerter zufrieden gibt, den er gerade zu erfassen vermag; er steht in einem Abgrund, nimmt die Frau nur schemenhaft wahr; die Frau hat keinerlei Zugriff auf die Schwerter. Für beide Seiten, Mann wie Frau, ein Bild der Unbeständigkeit, der Flatterhaftigkeit und letztlich der Verständnislosigkeit.

Wie nutzen wir das Luftelement des Geistes? Es ist möglich, dass nur die Laune regiert, ebenso, dass die Laune mit Schwertern unterdrückt wird. Ein fruchtbarer Geist jedoch kann positive und negative Launen unterscheiden und helfen, den eigenen Rhythmus zu leben. Die Quint-essenz des Geistes ist ein geeignetes Bewusstsein, eine persönliche Klarheit, die Sie bereichert und erleichtert.

Lernen Sie aus Ihren Erfahrungen. Suchen Sie nach der tieferen Bedeutung Ihrer Siege und Niederlagen. Nutzen Sie die Waffen des Geistes als Mittel zur Heilung. Es ist nie zu spät und selten zu früh, Erfahrungen zu verarbeiten und die erforderliche Lektion zu lernen. Lassen Sie sich von Schwierigkeiten nicht entmutigen. Stehen Sie zu Klarheit und Aufrichtigkeit. Sie haben nichts zu verlieren, aber viel zu gewinnen.

Praxistipps: *Machen Sie Ihr Wissen fruchtbar. Beachten Sie die beiden auf dem Boden liegenden Schwerter: Wissen Sie um die Macht Ihrer ungenutzten Gedanken, aber auch um die Freude des überwundenen und abgelegten Zweifels. Schützen Sie sich vor leeren Versprechungen und grundlosen Vermutungen. Leben Sie im Mittelpunkt des Augenblicks. Finden Sie neu heraus, was aktuell gut und schön ist. Wenn Sie sich freuen und wenn Sie wieder staunen können, liegen Sie richtig.*

Quintessence de l'esprit

Un homme d'esprit – face à la femme, les deux pieds bien sur terre, symbole du libre-penseur léger comme un papillon.

La même image décrite avec scepticisme et méfiance : un homme imbu de sa personne, s'estimant heureux d'avoir une seule partie des épées qu'il est tout juste capable de tenir, est dans un abîme, ne perçoit la femme que schématiquement, la femme, elle, n'a aucun accès aux épées. Pour l'homme comme pour la femme, une image d'instabilité, d'inconstance et au final d'incompréhension.

Comment utilisons-nous l'air, élément de l'esprit ? Il se peut que seule l'humeur régisse. Il se peut aussi bien que l'humeur soit réprimée par les épées. En revanche, un esprit fécond peut distinguer les humeurs positives des humeurs négatives et vivre selon son propre rythme. La quintessence de l'esprit est une conscience acquise, une perspicacité individuelle qui enrichit et apaise.

Tirez des enseignements de vos expériences. Cherchez le sens profond de vos victoires et de vos défaites. Employez les armes de l'esprit comme remède de guérison. Il n'est jamais trop tard et rarement trop tôt pour élaborer ses expériences et en apprendre la leçon. Ne vous laissez pas décourager par les difficultés. Tenez-vous en à la clarté et à la franchise. Vous n'avez rien à perdre mais beaucoup à gagner.

Conseils pratiques : *Faites prospérer votre savoir. Regardez bien les deux épées jonchant le sol : prenez conscience de la puissance de vos pensées encore en friche, mais aussi du bonheur d'avoir surmonté et rejeté le doute. Gardez-vous des promesses vaines et des suppositions sans fondement. Vivez au centre de l'instant. Redécouvrez ce qui maintenant est bon et beau. Si vous pouvez vous réjouir et à nouveau être étonné, alors vous êtes sur la bonne voie.*

Six of Swords
Sechs der Schwerter
Six d'Épée

At a superficial level, the scene from Eugène Delacroix's 1822 painting *Dante and Virgil in Hell* represents movement, translocation, or any other external change. However, it also points to the faculties of the mind that enable different worlds to become interlinked. It challenges you to be mentally alert and always up-to-date.

Ferrying someone from one shore to the other can be likened to translating words from one language into another. Different people and their respective truths are like two shores or two different worlds, which need to be connected.

The archetype of the ferryman represents the controlling power and transformational abilities of the human mind. In many traditional stories, such as "The Devil with the Three Golden Hairs," the ferryman is condemned for all eternity to ferry back and forth. In his novel *Siddhartha,* Hermann Hesse created such an inspiring version of the ferryman that this archetype has become a symbol of the dignity of human consciousness as a bridge between two realms.

Whether or not we can cope with our current situation depends to a great extent on our mental clarity and openness. Useless thoughts are like old baggage, carried along to each new destination. Useful thoughts, on the other hand, plumb the depths of any issue, just as the ferryman can only advance if his pole makes contact with the bottom of the river.

Practical advice: *Be thorough in all your dealings. Use your mental agility and the intensity of the moment to find out which needs really motivate you and others. Communicate to them your needs.*

Übersetzen

Vordergründig stellt die Szene im Boot (ein Ausschnitt aus „Dante und Virgil in der Hölle" von Eugène Delacroix, 1822) eine Fortbewegung, einen Umzug oder eine andere äußere Veränderung dar. Es verweist jedoch auch auf die Fähigkeiten des Geistes, verschiedene Welten, insbesondere die der Lebenden und der Toten, miteinander zu verbinden, geistig rege und auf dem Laufenden zu bleiben bleiben, trotz der Allgegenwärtigkeit des Todes.

Das Übersetzen von einem zum anderen Ufer kann vom Übersetzen von der einen in die andere Sprache handeln; auch verschiedene Menschen mit ihren verschiedenen Wahrheiten sind wie zwei Ufer oder unterschiedliche Welten, die es miteinander zu verbinden gilt.

Der Archetyp des Fährmanns steht für die besonderen Steuerungs- und Transformationsleistungen des menschlichen Geistes. In zahlreichen Überlieferungen, so etwa im Märchen vom Teufel mit den drei goldenen Haaren, ist der Fährmann ohne Hoffnung auf Erlösung auf ewig dazu verdammt, die Fähre zu steuern. Ganz anders hat Hermann Hesse in seiner Erzählung *Siddharta* eine so leuchtende Version des Fährmanns geschaffen, dass der Fährmann seitdem auch zu einem Symbol der Erleuchtung, zu einem Sinnbild für die Würde des menschlichen Bewusstseins als Mittler zwischen den Welten geworden ist.

Von der Klarheit und der Durchlässigkeit unserer Gedanken hängt es ab, ob wir in unserer aktuellen Situation gut vorankommen. Untaugliche Gedanken sind wie alter Ballast, den man in jede neue Situation hineinträgt. Taugliche Gedanken aber stützen sich auf die wirklichen Gründe einer Angelegenheit, so wie der Fährmann im Bild nur vorankommt, wenn sein Staken Kontakt zum Grund hat.

Praxistipps: *Seien Sie also gründlich in Ihren Auseinandersetzungen. Nutzen Sie Ihre geistige Beweglichkeit und die Intensität des Augenblicks, um herauszufinden, welche Bedürfnisse Sie und andere tatsächlich bewegen. Teilen Sie anderen Ihre Bedürfnisse verständlich mit.*

Passage

À première vue la scène du bateau (un fragment de « Dante et Virgile aux enfers » d'Eugène Delacroix, 1822) représente un transfert, un déplacement ou un autre changement extérieur. Pourtant, il souligne aussi les aptitudes de l'esprit à relier différents univers entre eux, à rester vif d'esprit et informé.

Le passage d'une rive à l'autre peut évoquer la traduction d'une langue dans une autre ; des individus différents porteurs de vérités différentes sont aussi comme deux rivages ou mondes distincts qu'il s'agit de relier.

L'archétype du passeur symbolise les efforts remarquables de guidage et de transformation de l'esprit humain. Dans de nombreux écrits, dans le conte des « Trois Cheveux d'or du diable » entre autres, le passeur est condamné pour l'éternité à conduire son transbordeur sans espoir de rédemption. En revanche, dans son œuvre « Siddartha » Hermann Hesse a créé une version si lumineuse du passeur que celui-ci est devenu depuis un symbole de la révélation, de la dignité de la conscience humaine comme médiateur entre les mondes.

La clarté et la transparence de nos pensées est capitale pour l'évolution de notre situation actuelle. Les pensées incongrues sont un vieux fardeau que l'on porte dans chaque nouvelle situation. Mais les pensées adéquates s'appuient sur les fonds réels d'une situation, comme le passeur de l'image qui ne peut avancer qu'en touchant de sa perche le fond du fleuve.

Conseils pratiques : *Allez donc au fond des choses dans vos réflexions. Exploitez votre mobilité mentale et l'intensité du moment pour trouver quels désirs vous animent, vous et autrui. Transmettez clairement vos souhaits aux autres.*

Seven of Swords
Sieben der Schwerter
Sept d'Épée

Riddles and Solutions

Diana, the virgin huntress, appears with dog, bow, and arrow. The blood red, sketchily drawn creature (on the left) represents the second ego, the inner being, and a special kind of energy, which is—already or still—separate from you.

Each human being brings a new truth into this world. As long as we are separated from our inner qualities, we will be forever searching! You are faced with contradictions and riddles that have one purpose only: to enable you to find the answer that is in true harmony with your personality.

This card stands in a negative sense for failing to know yourself or others, a permanent division of your outer personality and inner being. You are searching without being aware of what you are looking for.

However, there is an alternative. The best way to broaden our minds is to look at familiar things from a different perspective! This occurs quite naturally when, on returning from a vacation, we see our familiar surroundings in a different light. Similarly, when we are in love, hurt, angry, or relieved, we suddenly see the world through new eyes. The card challenges you to do what often happens spontaneously on purpose. If you draw this card, it means you should bury old feuds and ban the ghosts of yesteryear from your life for good.

Practical advice: *Reevaluate all that you take for granted. Take a break—for an hour or a whole day. Allow yourself to do something "foolish." See to your needs so that they may benefit yourself and others in the long term. Say good-bye to aims and ambitions, which no longer serve you. Pay attention to your dreams and your life's wishes.*

Rätsel und Lösungen

Diana, die jungfräuliche Jägerin, tritt mit Hund, Pfeil und Bogen auf. Das blutrote schemenhafte Wesen (am linken Bildrand) steht für ein zweites Ich, für eine innere Gestalt und eine eigene Energie, die (schon oder noch) getrennt existiert.

Jeder Mensch bringt eigene Qualitäten mit in die Welt, und solange wir von diesen inneren Qualitäten getrennt sind, befinden wir uns auf der Suche! Wir stoßen auf Widersprüche und treffen auf Rätsel, die gleichsam nur dazu da sind, dass wir die Lösungen finden, die der eigenen Persönlichkeit gerecht werden.

Eine negative Bedeutung hat diese Karte immer dann, wenn man sich und andere nicht versteht, wenn es zu einer dauerhaften Abspaltung der äußeren Person von ihrem inneren Wesen kommt. Dann suchen wir, haben aber kein Ziel; wir sind in Bewegung, wissen aber nicht, was wir zu erreichen suchen.

Doch es gibt bessere Alternativen. Zu einem erweiterten Selbstverständnis verhilft nichts so sehr wie der Blick auf Selbstverständliches aus einer veränderten Perspektive! Diesen Vorgang erleben wir manchmal, wenn wir nach einem Urlaub nach Hause kommen und, voll von fremdartigen Eindrücken, das vertraute Zuhause in anderem Licht sehen. Das Gleiche erfahren wir, wenn wir verliebt oder verletzt, wütend oder erleichtert sind und die Welt mit einem Mal mit anderen Augen sehen.

Was Sie dabei spontan erleben, macht die Karte nun zur bewussten Aufgabenstellung. Wenn Sie diese Karte ziehen, heißt es, alte Gräben zu überwinden und alte Gespenster endgültig aus Ihrem Leben zu verbannen.

Praxistipps: *Diese Karte fordert Sie zu einer Überprüfung Ihrer Selbstverständlichkeiten auf. Legen Sie eine Pause ein, eine Stunde oder einen Tag. Erlauben Sie sich, etwas „Unvernünftiges" zu tun. Widmen Sie sich Bedürfnissen, die Ihnen und anderen nachhaltig guttun, und verabschieden Sie sich von vordergründigen Zielen und Ambitionen. Arbeiten Sie mit Ihren Träumen und Lebenswünschen.*

Énigmes et solutions

Diane, la vierge chasseresse, apparaît avec chien, flèche et arc. La silhouette rouge sang (à gauche de l'image) figure le deuxième moi, le personnage intérieur et une énergie individuelle qui existe à part (déjà ou encore).

Chaque être humain apporte au monde ses qualités propres et, tant que nous sommes séparés de ces qualités, nous sommes toujours en quête ! Nous nous heurtons à des contradictions et butons sur des énigmes qui ne servent en fait qu'à nous aider à trouver des solutions conformes à notre personnalité. Cette carte a toujours un sens négatif si l'on n'est pas en accord avec soi et les autres, si une scission durable survient entre la personne extérieure et le caractère intérieur. Alors nous cherchons, mais n'avons aucun but ; nous sommes en marche, mais ne savons pas pourquoi.

Pourtant, il existe de meilleures alternatives. Rien n'est plus profitable au développement de l'assurance personnelle que le regard sur les choses simples à partir d'une perspective nouvelle ! Parfois, nous faisons cette expérience en rentrant de vacances et, la tête pleine d'impressions exotiques, nous regardons notre demeure sous un jour nouveau. Le processus est le même quand nous sommes amoureux ou blessés, furieux ou soulagés et que nous voyons d'un seul soup le monde d'un regard neuf. Cette carte transforme ce type d'expérience en un défi conscient. Tirer cette carte signifie surmonter les vieux fossés et chasser pour toujours les vieux spectres de votre existence.

Conseils pratiques : *Cette carte vous invite à analyser les choses qui vous semblent tomber sous le sens. Faites une pause. D'une heure ou d'un jour. Osez faire quelque chose de « fou ». Consacrez-vous aux désirs qui vous font durablement du bien, à vous et aux autres, et abandonnez les ambitions et objectifs superficiels. Élaborez vos rêves et vos projets de vie.*

Eight of Swords
Acht der Schwerter
Huit d'Épée

Expanded Consciousness

Spiritual life connects heaven and earth. All conscious thought and knowledge has a spiritual dimension that helps us to recognize our own limitations and sense a reality that is much greater than ourselves. The central figure in the picture is hidden by a butterfly, but her pose suggests that she is holding a child in her arms. Children symbolize everything that goes beyond our earthly existence—our offspring and our metaphorical spiritual children—representing new truths and realities.

Beyond the boundaries of the ego lies eternal life, which is represented by the "heavenly" city above the figure. In this instance, eternity is but another term for purposefully lived uniqueness. This card is about saying farewell to castles in the sky and childish inhibitions.

Free yourself from all dependencies! The city or castle in the background symbolizes parental powers. Parents can influence you even from afar, in a kind of remote control operating through the air element of the mind. Come into contact with your own emotional basis, with your own "inner child" and with all that you want to contribute to the world.

In many situations, this card should encourage you to withdraw for a while. Retreat or hide in a self-made cocoon like a caterpillar, in order to get in touch with yourself, and to generate new and original thoughts.

Become the master of your life and the center of your world. Always remain in harmony with yourself. You will become comfortable and relaxed in everyday life when you reestablish your own way of thinking, acting, and desiring.

Practical advice: *Werner Sprenger said, "There are thoughts that you cannot comprehend, unless you change your life." But the opposite is also true: "There are changes in your life that cannot be realized, unless you comprehend your thoughts."*

Bewusstseinserweiterung

Das geistige Leben verbindet Himmel und Erde. Zum bewussten Denken und Wissen gehört die spirituelle Dimension, das Erkennen der eigenen Grenzen und der Realität dessen, was größer ist als wir. Ein Schmetterling verdeckt den Blick auf die zentrale Bildfigur, deren Haltung vermuten lässt, dass sie ein Kind in Ihren Armen hält. Kinder stehen für das, was über unsere irdische Existenz hinausgeht – leibliche Kinder und im übertragenen Sinn geistige „Kinder" – also neue Wahrheiten und Realitäten.

Jenseits der Grenzen des Ichs liegt das ewige Leben, die „himmlische" Stadt, die im oberen Bildteil zu sehen ist. Ewigkeit steht in diesem Fall für bewusst gelebte Einzigartigkeit. Hier zeichnet sich ein Abschied von Wolkenschlössern sowie von kindischen Befangenheiten ab.

Befreien Sie sich aus Abhängigkeiten! Die Stadt oder die Burg im Hintergrund symbolisiert mütterliche und väterliche Kräfte. Deren Einflüsse können auch von Weitem wirken, wie eine „Fernsteuerung" durch das Luftelement des Geistes übertragen werden. Finden Sie Kontakt zu Ihrer emotionalen Basis, zu Ihrem „inneren Kind" und zu dem, was Sie in die Welt bringen möchten.

Oft bedeutet die Karte eine Empfehlung, sich für eine gewisse Zeit bewusst zurückzuziehen, Einkehrtage einzulegen oder sich wie eine Raupe in einen Kokon einzuspinnen, um zu sich selbst und zu neuen Gedanken zu finden.

Werden Sie zum Meister, zum Zentrum Ihres eigenen Reichs. Bleiben Sie mit sich im Einklang, und erleben Sie die (ent-)spannende Geborgenheit im Alltag, wenn Sie Ihren eigenen Standpunkt im Denken, Handeln und Wollen wiederfinden.

Praxistipps: *„Es gibt Gedanken, welche Du nicht begreifen kannst, wenn Du nicht Dein Leben änderst" (Werner Sprenger). Und auch die Umkehrung gilt: Es gibt Änderungen in Deinem Leben, welche Du nicht verwirklichen kannst, wenn Du nicht Deine Gedanken begreifst.*

Élargissement de la conscience

La vie spirituelle réunit ciel et terre. La dimension spirituelle fait partie de la pensée et du savoir conscients, la reconnaissance de ses propres limites et la réalité de ce qui est plus grand que nous. Un papillon empêche de bien voir la figure centrale dont l'attitude laisse supposer qu'elle tient un enfant dans ses bras. Les enfants représentent ce qui dépasse notre existence terrestre – les enfants biologiques et au sens figuré les « enfants » spirituels –, donc les vérités et réalités nouvelles.

Au-delà des limites du moi se situe la vie éternelle, la ville « céleste » qui apparaît en haut de l'image. Dans ce cas l'éternité symbolise l'unicité consciemment vécue. Ici se profile l'abandon des projets chimériques ainsi que des inhibitions puériles.

Délivrez-vous des addictions ! La ville ou le château-fort à l'arrière-plan symbolise les forces maternelles et paternelles. Leurs influences peuvent s'exercer même de loin, être transportées par l'élément aérien de l'esprit telle une « commande à distance ». Prenez contact avec votre base émotionnelle, avec l'enfant qui est en vous et avec tout ce que vous aimeriez apporter au monde.

Souvent la carte porte le message de se mettre consciemment en retrait pour un certain temps, de planifier des journées de méditation ou comme la chenille de s'envelopper dans son cocon, pour se retrouver avec soi-même et de nouvelles pensées.

Devenez le maître, au centre de votre propre domaine. Restez en phase avec vous-même et découvrez la tranquillisante sécurité au quotidien en retrouvant votre point de vue personnel qu'il s'agisse de pensée, d'action ou de volonté.

Conseils pratiques : *« Il y a des pensées que tu ne peux pas saisir si tu ne changes pas ta vie » (Werner Sprenger). Et l'inverse est tout aussi juste : il existe des changements dans ta vie que tu ne peux pas réaliser si tu ne saisis pas tes pensées.*

Nine of Swords
Neun der Schwerter
Neuf d'Épée

A Wealth of Knowledge

Nine swords symbolize a very broad mental horizon. If it becomes dark on the horizon, you will experience a deep personal crisis. The swallow and angel that can be seen on the ACE OF SWORDS stand for the hope of spiritual guidance in difficult and eventful times.

As soon as a person starts going their own way, they enter dimensions of being that are uncharted, because no one has been there before. Once we redefine our own individuality and comprehend the uniqueness of each and every life, our horizon will shift. Nightmares and nagging thoughts are an integral part of this process.

Do not be afraid. Take your time to digest the new state of affairs. Accept doubts and disappointments, but do not succumb to despair. Accept responsibility for your situation.

There are new possibilities and new horizons ahead. Go forth and explore them. The time has come to think about your thinking. Reevaluate your ideas from a different perspective. Try to comprehend what your thoughts really mean. Beware of irrational actions and automatic reactions. Do not let yourself be provoked. It is no mere coincidence that the structure and color of this card remind us of the "Stars and Stripes," the flag of the United States of America. The "land of unlimited opportunity" is associated with many conspiracy theories, which time and again force the country to confront its own ghosts. This is a unique aspect of the Dalí Tarot.

Practical advice: *Accept responsibility. You will find spiritual guides (see the angel and the swallow) to help you during the transition to a new horizon. Do not be too deterred by temporary obstacles or difficulties. Keep your feet firmly on the ground—and reach for the stars!*

Fülle der Erkenntnis

Neun Schwerter symbolisieren einen nahezu kompletten geistigen Horizont. Wenn sich dieser verfinstert, fallen wir in eine persönlichen Krise.

Schwalbe und Engel im Bild verweisen auf Motive der Karte ASS DER SCHWERTER und stehen für die Hoffnung auf geistiges Geleit auch in schwierigen und bewegten Zeiten.

Sobald ein Mensch seinen eigenen Weg geht, stößt er in Bereiche des Seins vor, die noch unbeleuchtet sind, da sie bisher unentdeckt waren. In den Momenten, in denen wir die eigene Individualität neu definieren und die Einmaligkeit eines jeden Lebens besser verstehen, verändert sich unser geistiger Horizont. Zu den Geburtswehen solcher Wandlungsprozesse gehören Albträume und quälende Gedanken.

Fürchten Sie sich nicht, sondern nehmen Sie sich Zeit, um den neuen Sachverhalt zu verarbeiten. Lassen Sie Zweifel und Enttäuschungen zu, aber widersetzen Sie sich der Verzweiflung. Übernehmen Sie Verantwortung.

Es gibt neue Möglichkeiten und neue Horizonte. Entdecken Sie sie. Jetzt ist es an der Zeit, „das Denken zu denken". Betrachten Sie Ihre Vorstellungen aus einem anderen Blickwinkel. Verstehen Sie, was Ihre Gedanken bedeuten! Hüten und schützen Sie sich vor Kurzschlusshandlungen und automatischen Reaktionen. Lassen Sie sich nicht provozieren. Nicht zufällig erinnern Gestaltung und Farbgebung an die „stars and stripes", an die Sterne und Streifen der US-amerikanischen Flagge. Das „Land der unbegrenzten Möglichkeiten" ist bekannt für seine zahlreichen Verschwörungstheorien und muss sich in diesem Zusammenhang immer wieder auch mit Geistern und Gespenstern auseinandersetzen. Eine interessante Besonderheit des Dalí-Tarot.

Praxistipps: *Stärken Sie Ihre Verantwortung. Dann finden Sie geistige Helfer (Engel, Schwalbe), die Ihnen den Übergang zu einem neuen Horizont erleichtern. Lassen Sie sich von vorübergehenden Blockaden oder Schwierigkeiten nicht allzusehr beeindrucken. Bleiben Sie auf dem Teppich – er fliegt ja schon!*

Plénitude de la connaissance

Neuf épées symbolisent un horizon spirituel pratiquement complet. Si celui-ci s'assombrit nous chutons vers une crise personnelle.

L'hirondelle et l'ange de l'image rappellent les motifs de la carte AS D'ÉPÉE et représentent l'espoir d'un encadrement spirituel dans des périodes difficiles et agitées.

Dès qu'un individu suit sa propre voie, il pénètre dans les domaines de l'être qui sont encore obscurs parce qu'ils étaient inconnus jusqu'à présent. Dans les moments où nous redéfinissons notre propre individualité et comprenons mieux l'unicité de chaque vie, notre horizon spirituel change. Cauchemars et pensées dérangeantes sont les douloureux symptômes de tels processus de métamorphoses.

N'ayez pas peur, prenez plutôt le temps d'élaborer le nouvel état de fait. Ne tolérez pas les doutes et les déceptions et refusez le désespoir. Assumez des responsabilités.

Il existe de nouvelles chances et de nouveaux horizons. Trouvez-les. Il est temps à présent de « penser la pensée ». Considérez vos idées sous un autre angle. Comprenez ce que vos pensées veulent dire ! Gardez-vous et protégez-vous des actions impulsives et des réactions automatiques. Ne vous laissez pas provoquer. Ce n'est guère un hasard si la conception et la coloration rappellent les « stars and stripes », les étoiles et rayures du drapeau américain. Le « pays des possibilités illimitées » est connu pour devoir particulièrement lutter contre les esprits et les fantômes. Un aspect original du Tarot de Dalí.

Conseils pratiques : *Renforcez votre responsabilité. Alors vous trouverez des complices (ange, hirondelle) qui vous faciliteront le passage vers un nouvel horizon. Ne vous laissez pas trop impressionner par des difficultés ou blocages passagers. Restez sur votre tapis – il s'envole déjà !*

Ten of Swords
Zehn der Schwerter
Dix d'Épée

The Fruit of the Mind

The card shows a scene from the painting *The Death of Julius Caesar* (1805-06) by Vincenzo Camuccini. In a negative sense, swords as weapons of the mind represent it's destructive power and, in turn, man's alienation from nature. The vicious and hurtful aspect of the sword culminates here in such a perfidious assassination. Aside from portraying an actual event that took place during the Ides of March, when Caesar fell by the dagger, the card has a more symbolic meaning. It tells us to beware of highly sophisticated and cultivated people who nevertheless succumb to their baser instincts and malice.

In a positive sense, the card has a quite different meaning: reaping the fruits of the mind. Ten swords represent the epitome of consciousness and knowledge. Breaking with traditional symbolism, this card does not depict a wise man, a philosopher-king, or a guru on a throne to represent the pinnacle of knowledge and insight. On the contrary: the TEN OF SWORDS heralds the end of all role models and idols.

For this reason, the old Zen saying "If you meet Buddha on the road, kill Buddha" has become associated with this card. This famous koan, one of the illogical riddles of the Zen Buddhists, does not intend to instigate murder and mayhem; it calls upon all of us to dispense with all role models and idols. The German word "Kaiser" (emperor) is derived from the Latin name Caesar: do not accept any emperors—worldly authorities—in your life.

Practical advice: *Strengthen your mental alertness. Treat thoughts, definitions, and decisions with care. Clear the air and take a deep breath. Beware of suspicions and harmful actions. Open up to the flow of life.*

Früchte des Geistes

In der Bildmitte sehen wir eine Szene aus Vincenzo Camuccinis „Die Ermordung Julius Caesars" (um 1805/06).

Die Schwerter als Sinnbild für die Waffen des Geistes stehen im negativen Sinn für den zerstörerischen Geist, für die Entfremdung von der Natur. Die verletzende und zerstörerische Seite der Schwerter kulminiert hier in einem heimtückischen Attentat. Über die Darstellung der konkreten historischen Begebenheit in den Iden des März hinaus, als Cäsar dem Dolch zum Opfer fiel, ist die Szenerie auch als allgemeines Gleichnis zu verstehen: Sie warnt vor kultivierten, gebildeten Menschen, die gleichwohl niederen Instinkten folgen.

Im positiven Sinne thematisiert die Karte die Möglichkeiten des Geistes. In diesem Fall verkörpern zehn Schwerter die Fülle des Bewusstseins und der Erkenntnis. Symbolisch für den Gipfel der Erkenntnis zeigt die Karte nicht wie sonst üblich einen weisen Menschen, einen Philosophenkönig oder Guru auf seinem Thron. Die ZEHN DER SCHWERTER stellen im Gegenteil das Ende aller Vorbilder dar.

Aus diesem Grund wird bei der Interpretation der ZEHN DER SCHWERTER oft ein alter Zen-Spruch herangezogen: „Triffst du Buddha unterwegs, töte Buddha." Mit diesem berühmten Koan, diesem Rätselspruch der Zen-Buddhisten, wird nicht zu Mord und Totschlag aufgerufen, sondern zur geistigen Überwindung von Vorbildern und Idolen. Auch die Ermordung Cäsars, von dessen Name sich das Wort Kaiser ableitet, steht hier sinnbildlich für die Überwindung von weltlichen Autoritäten.

Praxistipps: *Stärken Sie Ihre Geistesgegenwart. Gehen Sie sorgsam mit Ihren geistigen Fähigkeiten um. Sorgen Sie für gute Luft und einen wachen Atem. Hüten und schützen Sie sich vor Verdächtigungen und niederträchtigen Aktionen. Öffnen Sie sich dem Strom des Lebens.*

Fruits de l'esprit

Au centre de l'image apparaît une scène du tableau de Vincenzo Camuccini « La Mort de César » (vers 1800).

Les épées, symboles des armes de l'esprit, représentent au sens négatif l'esprit destructeur, le détachement de la nature. L'aspect ravageur et blessant de l'épée culmine ici en un perfide attentat. Au-delà de la représentation d'un événement historique concret aux ides de Mars, au cours duquel César mourut poignardé, la scène présente aussi un parabole universelle. Elle met en garde contre les personnes cultivées qui obéissent néanmoins aux bas instincts.

L'interprétation positive de la carte est tout autre, elle thématise ici aussi les possibilités de l'esprit. Dans ce cas, dix épées figurent la plénitude de la conscience et de la connaissance. Symbolique pour l'apothéose de la connaissance, la carte ne montre pas comme d'habitude un homme sage, un roi philosophe ou un gourou sur son trône. Au contraire, le DIX D'ÉPÉE évoque la fin de tous les modèles.

Pour cette raison un vieux dicton zen s'est imposé pour l'interprétation du DIX D'ÉPÉE : « Si tu rencontres Bouddha sur la route, tue-le. » Ce célèbre koan, phrase énigmatique des bouddhistes zen, n'appelle pas au meurtre ou à l'homicide mais à la victoire spirituelle sur les modèles et idoles. Aussi l'assassinat de César, dont le titre d'empereur en allemand « Kaiser » est dérivé, surmonte-t-il ici symboliquement les autorités terrestres.

Conseils pratiques : *Accentuez votre présence d'esprit. Traitez vos possibilités spirituelles avec beaucoup de précaution. Veillez à une respiration active au grand air. Gardez-vous et protégez-vous des accusations et des actions infâmes. Ouvrez-vous au courant de la vie.*

Queen of Coins
Königin der Münzen
Reine de Denier

QUEEN OF COINS

Talent as a Calling

It is certainly not your destiny to go through life as a nameless being, but neither are you called upon to sacrifice something absolutely essential in the name of duty: your uniqueness and the value of your existence.

The "demon" in the upper right corner symbolizes a lack of scruples, and a tenuous conscience, and a pernicious consciousness, which constantly grab us by the hair. Feelings of superiority and inferiority are equally dangerous. Do not foolishly play around with your opportunities or your problems. You possess special talents, as well as certain handicaps. They are part of what makes you unique, so learn more about them. Understand the value of your life's experiences. Every human being is a unique product of nature—just like the flowers on the card.

The arches in the background appear light and delicate, as if made of flowers—cascades of gentleness and tenderness, but also of fragility. Their shape is reminiscent of the arches shown on THE MAGICIAN card.

Respect for the experience of each individual is addressed here. It is the great art of this queen to absorb from many people their experiences and to fashion them into something extraordinary and of lasting value (for more on the significance of the pentagram, see p. 164).

Practical advice: *You have at your disposal the strength to pursue happiness and to make your fortune. Your love for yourself and your fellow human beings, as well as your ability to accept your present circumstances, whatever they may be, will allow you to get out of life what is most important. Go into the hills and climb a peak. Organize your everyday routine in such a way that you will move mountains in your daily life. As the saying goes, "First do what is necessary, then what is possible, and suddenly you will find that you can do the impossible." (Francis of Assisi)*

Talent als Auftrag

Sie sind nicht dazu berufen, als namenloses Wesen das Leben zu fristen; und auch nicht dazu, für vermeintliche Pflichten und Dienste etwas Wesentliches zu opfern: nämlich Ihre Besonderheit, den Wert Ihrer Existenz.

Der „Dämon" in der oberen rechten Kartenecke symbolisiert Skrupellosigkeit, ein fehlendes Gewissen, ein ungutes Bewusstsein, das uns an den Haaren zerrt. Das Gefühl von Überheblichkeit ebenso wie das von Minderwertigkeit sind gefährlich, kokettieren Sie nicht mit Ihren Chancen oder Schwierigkeiten. Sie besitzen besondere Begabungen, ebenso wie besondere Handicaps. Diese Prägungen sind Ihr Talent – erforschen Sie es. Nutzen Sie den Wert Ihrer Erfahrungen. Jeder Mensch ist ein besonderes Geschöpf der Natur, so wie die Blumen im Bild.

Die Bögen im Bildhintergrund wirken leicht, wie aus Blüten gemacht, Kaskaden der Zartheit und der Zärtlichkeit – auch der Zerbrechlichkeit. In ihrer Form erinnern sie an die Arkaden der Karte des MAGIERS und unterstreichen die Botschaft der persönlichen Einzigartigkeit.

Der Respekt für die Erfahrungen des Einzelnen ist hier angesprochen. Aus den Erfahrungen vieler einzelner Menschen etwas Bedeutendes von bleibendem Wert zu machen, das ist die Kunst, auf die sich diese Königin versteht (zur Bedeutung des Pentagramms siehe Seite 165).

Praxistipps: *Sie verfügen über die Kraft, Ihr Glück zu finden und zu verwirklichen. Die Liebe zu dem, was Ihnen und Ihren Mitmenschen wichtig ist, und die Ihnen gegebenen Möglichkeiten in ihrer ganzen Vielfalt werden Ihnen erlauben, das Wesentliche zu erreichen. Begeben Sie sich in die Berge, erklimmen Sie einen Gipfel. Teilen Sie sich Ihre Aufgaben ein, um auch im Alltag Berge zu meistern: „Tue zuerst das Notwendige, dann das Mögliche, und plötzlich schaffst du das Unmögliche". (Franz von Assisi)*

Le talent, un défi

Vous n'êtes pas appelé à mener votre vie comme un individu anonyme; ni à sacrifier à de soi-disant obligations et services l'essentiel : votre originalité, la valeur de votre existence.

Le « démon », en haut dans le coin droit de la carte, symbolise le manque de scrupules, l'absence de remords, une conscience malsaine qui nous tire par les cheveux. Le sentiment de supériorité, tout comme celui d'infériorité, est dangereux.

Ne jouez pas avec vos chances ou vos difficultés. Vous possédez des dons particuliers ainsi que des handicaps particuliers. Ces qualités sont votre talent – explorez-les. Mettez à profit la valeur de vos expériences. Chaque individu est une créature à part de la nature, comme les fleurs de l'image.

Les arcs à l'arrière-plan semblent légers, comme s'ils étaient composés de fleurs, des cascades de délicatesse et de tendresse – de fragilité aussi. Dans leur forme elles rappellent les arcades du MAGICIEN et soulignent le message de l'unicité personnelle.

C'est le respect des expériences de chacun qui est exprimé ici. Faire des expériences de nombreuses personnes un tout important, de valeur durable, tel est l'art que maîtrise cette reine (Plus d'informations sur la signification du pentagramme, voir page 165).

Conseils pratiques : *Vous disposez du pouvoir de trouver votre bonheur et de le réaliser. L'amour de ce qui est important pour vous et ceux qui vous entourent, associé aux chances qui vous sont offertes dans toute leur variété, vous permettent d'atteindre l'essentiel. Allez en montagne, escaladez un ou des sommets. Répartissez vos tâches pour dominer aussi les montagnes du quotidien. « Fais d'abord le nécessaire, puis le possible, et soudain tu réussis l'impossible ». (François d'Assise)*

King of Coins
König der Münzen
Roi de Denier

KING OF COINS

Sense and Pleasure

In Tarot the suit of coins represents matter and the physical body, money and talents. The KING OF COINS is its master.

Dalí immortalized himself on this card. This choice can be interpreted in two different ways. Perhaps Dalí intended to offer himself as a financial investment of sorts, as an authority, and as a special case. Then the viewer looking at the picture will feel how small and insignificant they really are in comparison with this artistic genius. But maybe Dalí intended to portray himself as an example for every one of us. Then the viewer would understand that each person is called upon to be his or her own master in terms of wealth and well-being!

The many fingerprints on this card are intended to show you that you need to become active yourself in a hands-on approach to creating your own fortune. The ocelot on a leash with a blurred face, in the lower left corner warns against predatory instincts, becoming obsessed with material values and sensual pleasures. But at the same time, it challenges you to face fearlessly the animal and the predator in yourself and your fellow human beings. Dalí's relaxed, half-sleeping pose together with the resting bull above his head warn against carelessness and complacency. In a positive sense, it encourages you to be at ease and to feel comfortable with yourself.

You are your own greatest resource—your fields and harvest, vineyard and wine. Create a life and work style that fits your personality, your own personal culture. Become the architect, artist, and builder of your life!

Practical advice: *Reassess your financial situation as well as your talents and your desire for productivity and fulfillment. Take stock and make a survey of what you have accomplished so far and what is still lacking.*

Care for everything you have planted—in your garden as well as in your life in general. All that is meant to last needs to be reevaluated. Sense and pleasure are the measure of appropriate, personal wealth.

Sinn und Genuss

Münzen stehen im Tarot für Materie und Körper, für Geld und Talente. Der KÖNIG DER MÜNZEN ist deren Meister.

Auf dieser Karte hat sich Dalí selbst verewigt. Dies lässt zwei unterschiedliche Deutungen zu: Entweder bietet sich Dalí hier quasi als Geldanlage an, als Autorität und als Sonderfall. In diesem Fall fühlt sich der Betrachter im Vergleich mit dem künstlerischen Genie klein und unbedeutend. Oder die Karte bringt Dalí als Beispiel für jeden von uns ins Spiel. Dann würde man auf die Karte schauen und verstehen, dass jeder berufen ist, Meister seines Glücks und Wohlstands zu werden! Die zahlreichen Fingerabdrücke besagen in diesem Sinne: Es gilt, selbst Hand anzulegen und eigene Ergebnisse zu schaffen. Der Ozelot, unten links im Bild, mit schemenhaftem Gesicht, angeleint an die Hand der Bildfigur, warnt vor räuberischen Instinkten, einer Sucht nach materiellen Werten und körperlichen Reizen. Er ermuntert aber auch dazu, sich dem „Tier" und „Raubtier" in uns und in unseren Mitmenschen zu stellen. Die entspannte, halbschläfrige Pose Dalís, über seinem Kopf der liegende Stier, mahnt einerseits vor Nachlässigkeit und einer falschen Selbstzufriedenheit, fordert Sie andererseits jedoch zu Gelassenheit und Behaglichkeit auf.

Sie selbst sind Ihr Kapital – Acker und Ernte, Weinberg und Wein. Entwickeln Sie individuelle Lebens- und Arbeitsformen, eine persönliche Kultur. Betätigen Sie sich als Architekt, Künstler und Baumeister Ihres Lebens!

Praxistipps: *Klären Sie Ihre Finanzen. Das gilt aber auch für Ihre Talente und für Ihre Wünsche nach einem produktiven und erfüllten Leben. Stellen Sie eine Bilanz auf, welche wichtigen Ziele Sie erreicht haben und welche noch fehlen.*

Kümmern Sie sich um das, was Sie gepflanzt haben – insbesondere im Hinblick auf Ihr Leben insgesamt. Alles, was auf Dauer angelegt ist, will neu bedacht werden. Sinn und Genuss sind der Maßstab eines angemessenen, persönlichen Reichtums.

Sens et jouissance

Dans le tarot les deniers symbolisent la matière et le corps, l'argent et les talents. Le ROI DE DENIER en est le maître.

S. Dalí s'est immortalisé ici. Cela permet deux interprétations différentes : soit Dalí s'offre pratiquement comme un investissement financier, une autorité et un cas à part. L'observateur se sent alors petit et négligeable en comparaison du génie artistique. Soit la carte propose Dalí comme exemple pour chacun de nous. On contemplerait alors cette carte et comprendrait que chacun est appelé à devenir le maître de sa chance et de son bien-être ! Les nombreuses empreintes digitales indiquent qu'il faut mettre la main à la pâte et obtenir ses propres résultats. L'ocelot, dont la tête est esquissée en bas à gauche et que le personnage tient en laisse, met en garde contre les instincts prédateurs, une soif de valeurs matérielles et de charmes physiques. Mais il nous encourage aussi à affronter « l'animal » et le « carnassier » en nous et ceux qui nous entourent. La pose détendue, en demi-sommeil, de Dalí avec au-dessus de sa tête le taureau allongé nous prévient d'une part contre la négligence et une pseudo-autosatisfaction, mais nous invite d'autre part au flegme et à la décontraction.

Vous êtes vous-même votre capital – le champ et la récolte, la vigne et le vin. Inventez vos formes de vie et de travail individuelles, une culture personnelle. Agissez en architecte, artiste et bâtisseur de votre vie !

Conseils pratiques : *Mettez de l'ordre dans vos finances. Mais ceci vaut également pour vos talents et vos désirs d'une vie productive et épanouie. Dressez le bilan des objectifs importants déjà atteints et de ceux qui ne le sont pas encore.*

Occupez-vous de ce que vous avez planté – au jardin et surtout dans votre vie en général. Tout ce qui est fait pour durer doit être à nouveau repensé. Le sens et la jouissance sont la mesure d'une vie personnelle appropriée.

Knight of Coins
Ritter der Münzen
Cavalier de Denier

KNIGHT OF COINS

Sowing and Reaping

The card shows a person who has found his proverbial place in the sun. This is all about your ability to organize your life, to turn insights into practical solutions, instead of sweeping problems under the carpet.

There is much to be harvested in your life. The huge, billowing red flag symbolizes the tremendous strength and almost unlimited power of a person, who has found their way back to the sun, to the fire and the source of life.

By understanding your purpose and your needs, you will ensure a bountiful harvest. But you should pay attention to the fact that this card is the only one of the coins suit that does not show a coin. We see only five quite large red spots on a shining white area in the sky. This could be interpreted negatively: your talent falls to pieces for lack of a connecting circle or framework. The whole dissolves into its parts because you focus too much on details.

In a positive sense, the same symbol could be interpreted as a kind of explosion. If you truly have become yourself and found your place in the world and with God, no borders will be able to contain or limit you. It is actually the small things, the seemingly insignificant, that take on a special significance.

By exploring your current contradictions, you will gain experience and develop a deep sense of tranquillity. Do not be afraid of conflicts; on the contrary, seek them out at the right time. Strengthen your faith in your ability to solve problems, to conquer fears, and to fulfill your desires.

Practical advice: *Forgive yourself and others for not being perfect. Even the "garbage" that we all produce can still be used as manure and humus. You cannot change your fellow human beings, but you can accept them as they are and help them to use their talents to the greatest effect.*

Aussaat und Ernte

Diese Karte zeigt einen Menschen, der seinen sprichwörtlichen Platz an der Sonne gefunden hat. Hier geht es um die Fähigkeit, unser Leben in Ordnung zu bringen, Probleme nicht unter den Tisch zu kehren und Lösungsansätze in die Tat umzusetzen.

Es gibt viel zu ernten in Ihrem Leben. Die riesige rote Fahne steht für die starke, fast unbändige Kraft eines Menschen, der wieder zur Sonne, zum Feuer, der Quelle des Lebens, zurückgefunden hat.

Indem Sie Ihre Aufgaben und damit verbundene Notwendigkeiten erkennen, erzielen Sie eine optimale Ernte. Doch Vorsicht: Diese Karte ist die einzige in der Reihe der Münzen, auf der keine Münze zu sehen ist. Wir erkennen lediglich fünf größere und zahlreiche kleinere Farbflecken; die größeren streben auf das Zentrum eines explodieren gleißenden Himmelskörpers zu. Negativ gedeutet zerfällt das eigene Talent: Der verbindende Kreis oder Rahmen fehlt, das Ganze löst sich in seine Einzelteile auf, man verliert sich in Kleinigkeiten.

In der positiven Deutung erscheint dieselbe Symbolik als eine Art Explosion: Wenn ein Mensch wirklich individuell ist und seinen Platz bei „Gott" und in der Welt gefunden hat, sprengt er jeden Rahmen. Gerade die Teile und das eher Unscheinbare gewinnen besondere Bedeutung.

Durch die Beschäftigung mit unseren Widersprüchen entwickeln sich Erfahrung, Souveränität und Gelassenheit. Scheuen Sie sich nicht vor Auseinandersetzungen, sondern suchen Sie sie zur richtigen Zeit! Stärken Sie Ihr Vertrauen in die eigene Fähigkeit, Probleme zu lösen, Ängste zu besiegen und sich Ihre Wünsche zu erfüllen.

Praxistipps: *Verzeihen Sie sich und anderen, nicht perfekt zu sein. Auch der „Mist", den wir alle produzieren, ist noch nutzbar – als Dünger und Humus. Sie können Ihre Mitmenschen nicht ändern. Nehmen Sie sie so, wie sie sind, und helfen Sie ihnen, ihre Talente bestmöglich einzusetzen.*

Semence et récolte

Cette carte montre un homme qui a trouvé la proverbiale place au soleil. Il est question ici de l'aptitude à mettre de l'ordre dans notre vie, à ne pas tirer le rideau sur les problèmes et à mettre en pratique les ébauches de solution.

Il y a beaucoup à récolter dans votre vie. L'immense drapeau rouge symbolise la force presque invincible d'un homme qui a retrouvé le soleil, le feu, la source de la vie.

En reconnaissant les défis et les obligations inhérentes vous obtiendrez une récolte optimale. Mais attention, cette carte est la seule dans la série des deniers où ne figure aucun denier. Nous distinguons seulement cinq grandes taches de couleur sur une surface d'un blanc éclatant dans le ciel.

Dans une interprétation négative le talent individuel s'effrite en morceaux. Le cercle ou cadre unificateur est absent, le tout se désagrège en pièces diverses, on se perd dans les broutilles.

Dans une interprétation positive le même symbolisme apparaît comme une sorte d'explosion : si un homme est vraiment individuel et s'il a trouvé sa place auprès de « Dieu » et dans le monde, il dépasse tout cadre. Ce sont les éléments et les détails insignifiants qui gagnent une importance particulière.

Par l'analyse de nos contradictions se développent notre expérience et notre sérénité. Ne craignez pas les discussions, mais cherchez-les au moment propice ! Renforcez votre confiance en votre aptitude à régler les problèmes, vaincre les peurs et exaucer vos vœux.

Conseils pratiques : *Pardonnez à vous-même et à autrui de n'être pas parfait. Même le « fumier » que nous produisons tous est encore utilisable – comme engrais et humus. Vous ne pouvez pas changer ceux qui vous entourent. Prenez-les comme ils sont et aidez-les à employer au mieux leurs talents.*

Page of Coins
Page der Münzen
Valet de Denier

PAGE OF COINS

Proof of One's Talent, Revealing the Invisible

The coin is a gift of life. It reflects the way you are a treasure to yourself and your surroundings—if you realize your talent.

This card challenges you to rediscover and reevaluate your practical abilities. You should reassess the obvious—just like picking up a coin that has been lying on the street unnoticed. Our own talents often seem to us to be insignificant, like the big transparent dragonfly at the bottom of the picture. The in-trinsic and prototypical is often hidden in the in-visible. You do not take yourself seriously or you have the wrong idea about what talent really entails. You might think that only experts or famous entertainers possess a special gift. In reality, every person has special talents. You "only" have to learn to understand the value of your unique experiences and abilities. The process of becoming a child again often drags the ghosts of yesterday from their graves, as symbolized by the figure to the right in the picture. Do not allow yourself to be confused, but keep on searching and evaluating your experiences and results.

You will find the right answer to your questions by examining your value system. What has dwindled in importance? What has recently grown in significance? Everything can be of value if you consciously make it your own.

Practical advice: *Become an explorer. A simple walk through the town or the countryside can be an adventure full of surprising discoveries! Regard your relationships and encounters, your duties and tasks in the same spirit.*

Talentprobe, Aufhebung des Unscheinbaren

Die Münze ist ein Geschenk des Lebens. Sie spiegelt wider, dass Sie, wenn Sie Ihr Talent begreifen, selbst ein „Schatz" sind, für sich und Ihre Umgebung.

Diese Karte ist ein guter Anlass, Ihre praktischen Fähigkeiten neu zu entdecken und neu zu bewerten. Man muss das Vertraute neu betrachten: Es ist wie mit Geld, das unbemerkt auf der Straße liegt. Das eigene Talent erscheint uns oft unscheinbar wie die große transparente Libelle am Fuß des Bildes. Im Unscheinbaren steckt auch das Un-Scheinbare als das Wesentliche und Typische, das, worauf es ankommt. Man hält sich selbst für nicht wichtig genug oder hat einen falschen Begriff von Talent: Allein bei Spezialisten oder Artisten wird ein besonderes Talent vermutet. Tatsächlich aber besitzt jeder Mensch besondere Fähigkeiten. Man muss „nur" deren Prägung und deren Wert erkennen. Hierbei als Erwachsener wieder zum Kind zu werden, kann Gespenster der Vergangenheit auf den Plan rufen. Gespenster, wie die Bildfigur im rechten Hintergrund. Lassen Sie sich davon nicht irritieren, sondern suchen Sie weiter, prüfen Sie Ihre Erlebnisse und Ergebnisse.

Wenn Sie gewohnte Werte und Wertschätzungen auf den Prüfstand stellen, finden Sie Antworten auf Ihre Fragen. Was hat an Bedeutung verloren, und was ist für Sie in neuer Weise wichtig geworden? Alles hat seinen Wert, wenn Sie es sich nur bewusst zu eigen machen.

Praxistipps: *Werden Sie zum Abenteurer. Ein Spaziergang in der Natur oder durch die Stadt wird so zu einem Ausflug voller Entdeckungen! Halten Sie es so auch mit Ihren Beziehungen und Begegnungen, mit Ihren Pflichten und Aufgaben.*

Bilan des compétences, suppression de l'insignifiant

Le denier est un cadeau de la vie. Il révèle que vous êtes vous-même un « trésor » pour vous et votre entourage si vous percevez votre talent.

Cette carte est une bonne occasion de redécouvrir vos dispositions pratiques et de les réévaluer. Il faut jeter un regard neuf sur ce qui est familier : il en est comme de l'argent qui est sur la route sans qu'on le remarque. Notre propre talent nous paraît souvent anodin comme le grand insecte ailé au bas de l'image. L'insignifiant renferme aussi l'in-signifiant comme l'essentiel et le typique, ce qui compte vraiment. On ne se considère pas comme assez important ou on a une fausse idée du talent : on accorde un talent particulier aux seuls spécialistes et artistes. Mais en fait, chacun de nous a des dons particuliers. Il suffit « seulement » de distinguer leur essence et leur valeur. Le fait que dans cette démarche un adulte redevienne un enfant peut éveiller les fantômes du passé. Des fantômes analogues à la silhouette en arrière-plan à droite. Ne vous laissez pas agacer par eux, mais continuez à chercher, analysez vos expériences et vos résultats.

Si vous examinez les valeurs et les évaluations familières, vous trouverez la réponse à vos questions. Qu'est-ce qui a perdu de l'importance et qu'est-ce qui est devenu nouvellement essentiel pour vous ? Tout a sa valeur si seulement vous vous en emparez consciemment.

Conseils pratiques : *Devenez un aventurier. Une promenade dans la nature ou en ville se transforme en une excursion pleine de découvertes ! Faites-en autant en ce qui concerne vos relations et rencontres, vos tâches et devoirs.*

Ace of Coins
Ass der Münzen
As de Denier

New Values

The arm with the coin and pentagram appears to rise out of a gigantic vulva. The trees in the picture symbolize Mother Nature, who constantly gives birth to human beings as new creations.

Matter contains life and energy. The process of birth is not the only visible expression of this fact. The pentagram (the five-pointed star on the coin, also known as a pentangle) is an energy sign and a symbol for man, as its five points represent head, hands, and feet. The card emphasizes the double nature of human beings. You are like the two faces of a coin representing the influences on your character: on one side, experience and expectation, on the other, future events and results. "How have I been shaped?" on one face and, on the other, "What do I give shape to?" Each person possesses special talents as well as handicaps. By accepting all that we are made of, we will discover and develop our strengths. Each person has certain talents, which are uniquely his or hers.

Practical advice: *How do you see your role in the world? Do you want to take it easy? Or do you want to carry the weight of the world on your shoulders like the titan Atlas? Your talents become clear in the face of huge challenges, but also in the sum total of small achievements. Recognize the power within yourself. The world is waiting for your special contribution. Conquer the world with creativity and passion!*

Neue Werte

Wie aus einer riesigen Vulva ragt ein Arm und zeigt eine Münze mit Pentagramm. Die Bäume im Bild stehen für Mutter Natur, aus der wir Menschen als fortwährende Neuschöpfung geboren werden.

In der Materie stecken Leben und Energie. Das drückt sich nicht allein durch den Geburtsvorgang aus. Das Pentagramm (der fünfzackige Stern auf den Münzen, auch Drudenfuß genannt), ein bedeutungsschweres, schillerndes Symbol, das zahlreiche Interpretationen zulässt, ist nicht zuletzt ein Energiezeichen – außerdem ein Symbol für den Menschen; die fünf Spitzen markieren Kopf, Hände und Füße. Damit verweist die Karte auch auf die Doppelnatur des Menschen: Wie eine Münze mit ihren zwei Seiten ist auch der Mensch Ergebnis unterschiedlicher Prägungen – Erfahrung und Erwartung auf der einen, kommende Erlebnisse und künftige Ergebnisse auf der anderen Seite. „Wie bin ich geprägt worden?" und „Was präge ich meinerseits?" Jeder Mensch besitzt Begabungen und Handicaps. Indem wir unsere Prägungen annehmen und nutzen, entdecken und entwickeln wir unsere Stärken. Jeden von uns zeichnen herausragende Talente aus.

Praxistipps: *Wie sehen Sie Ihre Rolle in der Welt? Eine ruhige Kugel schieben? Wie der Riese Atlas den Globus, die ganze Last der Welt, auf Ihren Schultern tragen? Ihre besonderen Talente zeigen sich in Ihren großen Leistungen ebenso wie in der Summe vieler kleiner Errungenschaften. Begreifen Sie die Kraft, die in Ihnen steckt, und Ihren Beitrag, auf den die Erde wartet. Nehmen Sie die Welt mit Kreativität und Leidenschaft in Besitz!*

Valeurs nouvelles

Comme s'échappant d'une vulve géante apparaît un bras brandissant un denier orné d'un pentagramme. Les arbres symbolisent Mère Nature d'où nous, humains, sommes issus dans un renouvellement permanent de création.

Vie et énergie résident dans la matière. Cela ne s'exprime pas seulement dans le processus de naissance. Le pentagramme (étoile à cinq branches sur les deniers, appelée aussi pied du druide) est un signe d'énergie – et, de plus, un symbole pour l'homme; les cinq branches figurent la tête, les mains et les pieds. Ainsi la carte renvoie-t-elle aussi à la double nature de l'homme: comme un écu à deux faces, l'homme est, lui aussi, le produit de diverses empreintes – l'expérience et l'espoir d'un côté, les moments à venir et les résultats futurs de l'autre. D'un côté se pose la question: « Par quoi ai-je été marqué? », de l'autre « En quoi est-ce que je laisse ma marque? » Chaque individu est doté d'aptitudes comme de handicaps. En acceptant et en exploitant nos caractères nous découvrons et développons notre potentiel. Chacun de nous se distingue par des talents remarquables.

Conseils pratiques : *Que signifie le monde pour vous? Se la couler douce? Porter le globe, tout le poids du monde, sur vos épaules, tel le géant Atlas? Vos talents spécifiques se révèlent à travers vos grandes performances tout comme dans la somme des petites victoires. Saisissez la force qui est en vous et la contribution que la terre attend de vous. Emparez-vous du monde avec créativité et passion!*

Two of Coins
Zwei der Münzen
Deux de Denier

New Realities, a Greater Reality

New facts, values, and results are appearing in your current situation. As a result, you will find your perspective shifting. Something that has always been present and possible is becoming clearly visible and gaining special significance. A true change always requires a reevaluation of the old. Your focus in life will alter. Old principles will become ambiguous, formerly important habits suddenly seem questionable, and new tasks are added to old ones! You are in the midst of it all and experience yourself like never before.

This is your opportunity to liberate yourself and to let go of what formerly appeared as constraints. You are called upon to see beyond your narrow view of life and to break free from your limited reality, like the red figures in the picture outside the central frame. You are encouraged to undergo a transformation and to expand your "frame of life."

Yet the card also warns you not to take yourself too seriously and not to puff yourself up or to become the victim of empty promises. You are neither the servant nor the master of circumstance.

You have chosen in the past and you are free to choose again and to put your life into a new context. When your focus in life changes, you will experience unexpected confirmation, but also much insecurity. This is a blessing for the development of your personality, in spite all the difficulties involved.

Practical advice: *Pay attention to your knees (do not let them become too soft or too rigid). Your eyes and ears—all of your senses—may be playing up for some time to come. This is because all your perceptions are shifting, changing, and expanding as you attain a new focus in life. What is needed now are new results. They constitute your new task and will prove to be your mainstay.*

Neue Realitäten, größere Wirklichkeit

In Ihrer aktuellen Situation treten neue Fakten, Werte und Ergebnisse auf, die Ihren Standpunkt verschieben. Etwas, das immer schon vorhanden und möglich war, tritt jetzt hervor und gewinnt eine besondere Bedeutung. Jeder wirkliche Wandel ist mit einer Neubewertung verbunden. Lebensschwerpunkte ändern sich. Bisherige Grundsätze werden zweideutig, prägende Gewohnheiten erscheinen zwiespältig, und neue Aufgaben treten zu alten hinzu! Sie stehen dabei mittendrin und erfahren sich selbst neu.

Ihre Chance und Aufgabe besteht jetzt darin, sich aus vermeintlichen Sachzwängen zu befreien. Dazu ist es nötig, wie die roten Gestalten außerhalb des Bildes in der Kartenmitte über den bisherigen Rahmen, den aktuellen Ausschnitt der Wirklichkeit hinauszugehen. Somit werden Sie hier ermuntert, sich zu wandeln, Ihren Lebensrahmen zu erweitern.

Zugleich warnt die Karte davor, „dicke Backen zu machen", sich aufzublasen und zum Opfer schwankender Verheißungen zu werden. Sie sind weder Diener noch Beherrscher der äußeren Umstände.

Sie haben in der Vergangenheit gewählt und sind frei, auch jetzt wieder zu wählen und Ihr Leben in einen neuen Zusammenhang zu stellen. Rechnen Sie mit unerwarteten Bestätigungen, doch auch mit Verunsicherungen, wenn sich Ihr Lebensschwerpunkt verschiebt. Trotz aller Mühe ist dies für die Entfaltung Ihrer Persönlichkeit schon jetzt segensreich.

Praxistipps: *Achten Sie auf Ihre Knie (lassen Sie sie nicht zu weich oder zu hart werden). Augen und Ohren – alle Sinne spielen möglicherweise etwas verrückt. Doch das ist ganz wörtlich zu nehmen: Ihre Wahrnehmungen werden ver-rückt, das heißt verschoben und erweitert, weil Ihr Standpunkt sich ändert. Was jetzt hilft, sind neue Ergebnisse. Sie sind Ihre Aufgabe und gleichzeitig Ihr Halt.*

Nouvelles réalités, grande vérité

Dans votre situation actuelle de nouveaux faits, valeurs et résultats apparaissent, qui décalent votre point de vue. Quelque chose qui était toujours présent et possible se fait jour à présent et obtient une importance particulière. Chaque changement réel est lié à une réévaluation. Les axes essentiels de la vie changent. Les principes valables jusqu'alors deviennent ambigus, les habitudes marquantes semblent ambivalentes et de nouvelles tâches s'ajoutent aux anciennes ! Vous vous trouvez au centre du jeu et vous vous redécouvrez.

La chance et le défi consistent désormais à vous libérer des contraintes matérielles. Pour ce faire, il faut dépasser le cadre précédent, le carcan actuel de la réalité, comme les silhouettes rouges à l'extérieur de l'image centrale. Ainsi êtes-vous ici invité à vous transformer, à élargir votre cadre de vie.

Parallèlement, la carte vous dissuade de « gonfler vos joues », de vous enfler et de devenir la proie de promesses incertaines. Vous n'êtes ni serviteur ni maître des circonstances extérieures.

Par le passé vous avez fait vos choix et êtes libre maintenant aussi de choisir et de placer votre vie sous d'autres augures. Attendez-vous à des confirmations imprévues mais aussi à des inquiétudes, si le centre de votre vie se déplace. Malgré tous les tourments ceci est, dès à présent, bénéfique pour l'épanouissement de votre personnalité.

Conseils pratiques : *Surveillez vos genoux (ne les laissez devenir ni trop mous ni trop durs). Les yeux et les oreilles – tous vos sens sont peut-être un peu dérangés. Pourtant, le phénomène est à prendre au pied de la lettre : vos perceptions sont dé-rangées, c'est-à dire décalées et amplifiées parce que votre point de vue change. De nouveaux résultats sont maintenant d'un grand secours. Ils sont à la fois votre défi et votre soutien.*

Three of Coins
Drei der Münzen
Trois de Denier

The Calling

Dalí, who has often been accused of godlessness and of being an enemy of the Church, uses the figure of Christ here to represent money and (new) values. For the devout Christian, the picture of Christ represents an invitation to follow in his footsteps (imitatio Dei), to heed the call of God, and to realize your own personal calling. It is precisely this question of a calling that constitutes the traditional reading of this card. Although Dalí's picture is unique in its composition, it conveys the same message as many other versions of this card.

The city or castle in the tree represents your personal goals, which are above and behind all your efforts. Do these objectives resemble a dream house or are they more like the proverbial castle in the sky? All your ideals and aims are being questioned now. You will not be able to achieve any peak performances if you do not call upon and use all your hidden energies, your "latent talents." The circles on the robe of Christ or saintly figure may be interpreted as a labyrinth, probably hinting at the great effort and all the searching involved before you reach your personal summit. If you look at the labyrinth from a different angle, it resembles the shell of a great tortoise. This symbol encourages you to be consistent and patient, but to beware of reclusive and standoffish behavior. Only top-class achievements that enhance your personal well-being and expand your consciousness are of any lasting value.

Each person has his or her own peak to climb. Naturally, there are mountains of varying heights, but each has a summit. Your personal task is to reach your own zenith.

Practical advice: *Find the task that requires and focuses all your energies. Do not only ask what you want. Ask what God and the world want from you. Then your life will be much easier and more rewarding.*

Berufung

Der oftmals als gottlos oder kirchenfeindlich eingestufte Dalí verwendet in diesem Bild die Christus-Gestalt, um sich mit dem Thema des Geldes und der (neuen) Werte auseinanderzusetzen. Für einen überzeugten Christen bedeutet das Bild Jesu eine Aufforderung zur Nachfolge, zur Imitatio Dei – ein Aufruf, dem „Ruf Gottes" zu lauschen und die persönliche Berufung zu erkennen. Gerade die Frage der Berufung gehört auch zum überlieferten Inhalt dieser Karte. So ist Dalís Bild in seiner Gestaltung einzigartig und vermittelt dennoch das, was auch viele andere Varianten dieser Karte zeigen.

Die Stadt oder Burg auf dem Baum symbolisiert dabei die persönlichen Zielvorstellungen, die über und hinter allem stehen. Sind sie ein Traumhaus oder ein Wolkenschloss? Ziele und Ideale werden hier auf den Prüfstand gestellt. Wir erreichen keine persönliche Spitzenleistung ohne verborgene Energien und „latente Talente", zu wecken und zu nutzen. Die Kreislinien auf dem Gewand der Christus- oder Heiligenfigur lassen sich als Zeichen eines Labyrinths deuten und verweisen damit möglicherweise auf die bevorstehenden Mühen und Irrwege, die es zu überwinden gilt, bis man schließlich seinen persönlichen Gipfel erreicht. Im Querformat betrachtet ähneln dieselben Kreislinien dem Panzer einer großen Schildkröte. Darin mag eine Ermutigung zu Beharrlichkeit und Geduld liegen, aber auch eine Warnung vor allzu großer Abkapselung und menschlicher Unzugänglichkeit. Nur diejenigen Spitzenleistungen sind wertvoll, die das persönliche Bewusstsein und Wohlsein auf Dauer erhöhen.

Auf jeden von uns warten neue Gipfel. Selbstverständlich gibt es Berge von unterschiedlicher Höhe, und jeder von ihnen hat seinen Gipfel. Ihren persönlichen Zenit zu erreichen, ist Ihr Auftrag.

Praxistipps: *Finden Sie die Aufgabe, die Ihnen am meisten Energien abverlangt. Fragen Sie nicht nur danach, was Sie selbst wollen; schauen Sie danach, was „Gott" und die Welt von Ihnen wollen. Umso leichter und lohnender wird es für Sie!*

Vocation

Dalí, souvent considéré comme athée ou hostile à l'Église, crée dans cette image une représentation du Christ où il est question d'argent et de valeurs (nouvelles). Pour un chrétien convaincu l'image de Jésus signifie une invitation à le suivre, une imitation de Dieu – à entendre un appel, « l'appel de Dieu » et à discerner la vocation personnelle. La question de la vocation est précisément aussi un élément de cette carte. Aussi la gravure de Dalí est-elle unique dans sa conception et transmet cependant ce que de nombreuses autres variantes de cette carte révèlent.

La ville ou le château-fort sur l'arbre y symbolise les projections personnelles qui se trouvent au-dessus de tout et derrière tout. Ces projections sont-elles une maison de rêve ou un château en Espagne ? Ce sont les objectifs et idéaux qui sont étudiés de près ici. Nous ne réalisons aucun exploit personnel sans activer et employer les énergies secrètes, les « dons latents ». Les cercles sur l'habit du Christ ou du saint peuvent être interprétés comme les signes d'un labyrinthe et renvoyer aux efforts et fausses pistes futures qu'il s'agira de surmonter avant d'accéder finalement à des sommets personnels. Vus à l'horizontale, les mêmes cercles ressemblent à la carapace d'une grande tortue. Ils peuvent être interprétés comme un encouragement à la persévérance et à la patience, mais aussi comme une mise en garde contre la misanthropie et une trop grande isolation. Seuls sont précieux les exploits qui rehaussent durablement la conscience personnelle et le bien-être.

De nouvelles cimes attendent chacun de nous. Naturellement, il y des montagnes d'altitude différente, chacune d'elles a ses points culminants. Atteindre vos sommets personnels, tel est votre défi.

Conseils pratiques : *Recherchez la tâche qui booste la plupart de vos énergies et les dilate. Ne vous demandez pas seulement ce que vous voulez ; interrogez-vous sur ce que « Dieu » et le monde attendent de vous. Tout n'en sera que plus facile et profitable pour vous !*

Four of Coins
Vier der Münzen
Quatre de denier

Personal Values

Each person creates his or her own world. On the one hand, this card tells you to beware of "fact-bound superstition," of putting your faith in hard data and material things only.

In a more positive sense, it is a card of completeness. You restructure and discard all that is no longer appropriate for you, creating new forms and new habits. You complete the framework in which you choose to live your life, an environment in which your talents, your personal strengths and weaknesses will all find their proper place.

The statue of Buddha represents the values and customs that you hold dear. They are the glue that holds the different aspects of your actions together. The black outlines together with the black areas around the figures and the rose and lotus flowers coalesce to form a lion's or bear's head. Our personal objectives and our own god can sometimes turn out to be a dangerous animal! Even our most exalted values will have to be put to the test.

Do not play the hero or the loser! Do not waste your time with show-offs or yes-men. Every human being possesses something unique that is his and his alone. Neither good nor bad behavior will help you to succeed. You will advance only by developing your greatest talents.

Practical advice: *Your most precious talents are those that are the most useful. They will benefit you most by helping you to fulfill your desires and let go of your fears. Sometimes, it is better to clearly draw the line and to emphasize your uniqueness. But sometimes, it is better to improve your communicative abilities and to include as many people as possible in your endeavors.*

Persönliche Werte

Jeder Mensch baut sich seine eigene Welt. Auf der einen Seite warnt die Karte vor einem „sachlichen Aberglauben", vor einem falschen Glauben an Fakten und materielle Werte.

Im positiven Sinn ist dies jedoch eine Karte der Vollständigkeit. Sie bauen um und verwerfen, was nicht zu Ihnen passt. Sie schaffen neue Formen und neue Gewohnheiten. So vervollständigen Sie den Rahmen, in dem Sie leben möchten und schaffen Bedingungen, in denen sich der Wert Ihrer Talente, Ihrer persönlichen Stärken und Schwächen segensreich auszahlen.

Die Buddhafigur steht für die Werte, die Ihnen heilig sind. Sie sind die übergeordnete Klammer, welche die verschiedenen Aspekte Ihres Handelns zusammenfasst. Die schwarzen Umrisslinien zusammen mit den schwarzen Flächen um den Buddha und die Rosen/Lotus-Blumen erinnern an einen Tiger- oder Bärenkopf. Die persönlichen Werte, der eigene Gott können sich als ein gefährliches Tier entpuppen. Eine genaue Überprüfung unserer höchsten Werte bleibt uns nicht erspart.

Spielen Sie nicht den Helden oder den Versager! Halten Sie sich nicht mit Angebern und Duckmäusern auf. Jeder Mensch besitzt etwas Einzigartiges, das „einzig und nicht artig" ist. Nicht Bravheit oder Bosheit bringen Sie voran, sondern der Ausbau, die Verewigung Ihrer besten Talente.

Praxistipps: *Die wertvollsten Talente sind die, die am meisten Nutzen stiften. Und sie nutzen am meisten, wenn möglichst viele Wünsche damit erfüllt und möglichst viele Ängste damit abgebaut werden können. Manchmal ist es wichtig, sich bewusster abzugrenzen und den persönlichen Eigenwert herauszustellen. Manchmal kommt es aber auch darauf an, sich besser mitzuteilen und an den eigenen Fähigkeiten möglichst viele Menschen teilhaben zu lassen.*

Valeurs personnelles

Chaque être humain se construit son propre univers. D'un côté la carte avertit contre une « superstition concrète », contre une fausse croyance à des faits et valeurs matérielles.

Au sens positif, toutefois, cette carte est celle de l'intégrité. Vous remodelez et rejetez ce qui ne vous ressemble pas. Vous instaurez de nouvelles formes et de nouvelles routines. Ainsi complétez-vous le cadre dans lequel vous aimeriez vivre et créez des conditions dans lesquelles la valeur de vos talents, de vos forces et faiblesses personnelles est largement productive.

La figure de Bouddha représente les valeurs qui vous sont sacrées. Elles sont la parenthèse qui inclut les divers aspects de votre action. Les lignes de contour noires s'ajoutant aux surfaces noires qui enveloppent Bouddha et les roses / fleurs de lotus rappellent une tête de tigre ou de lion. Les valeurs personnelles, le dieu auquel on croit peuvent se révéler être un animal dangereux. Un examen précis de nos valeurs les plus nobles ne nous est pas épargné.

Ne jouez pas au héros ou au raté ! Évitez les frimeurs et les poules mouillées. Chaque individu possède quelque chose d'exceptionnel, « unique mais non mièvre ». Ni la gentillesse ni la méchanceté ne vous font avancer, mais bien le perfectionnement et l'immortalisation de vos meilleurs talents.

Conseils pratiques : *Les talents les plus précieux sont ceux qui procurent le plus grand profit. Et ils profitent le plus si le plus grand nombre de désirs sont exaucés et si le plus grand nombre de peurs peuvent être ainsi supprimées. Parfois, il est important de se délimiter et de faire ressortir sa propre valeur personnelle. Mais parfois aussi, il convient de mieux s'exprimer et de faire participer le plus grand nombre de personnes possible à ses propres capacités.*

Five of Coins
Fünf der Münzen
Cinq de Denier

Compassion

The red, gnarled roots running across the card and over the great arch in the background raise questions: what have heaven and earth, wish and reality in common and what is the difference? The answer: human community and individual uniqueness. The communal aspect is given special prominence in the left half of the card. In the right half, however, the figures are hidden by big flowers, which symbolize the flourishing of each individual's magic and the sheltering of private life.

Five coins represent the essence of the earth element: the full blossoming of your talents. This transformation is emphasized by the caterpillar in its cocoon (directly above the lower four coins) and the butterflies that have already emerged. It takes both community and individuality to succeed. Personal assets (property as well as ability) create enough of value to rule out avoidable human hardships and make unavoidable distress bearable. There are hardships caused by hunger or sickness, but also others, which arise from unfulfilled needs: the hunger for meaning, the thirst for love, or the longing for roots. Each and every type of human plight is a tragedy. Where the need is greatest, our talents can achieve the most.

Make a virtue of necessity. Where the darkness is deepest, your light is needed most. Where your talents shine, walls become transparent and you will stand on firm ground in all situations. Take care of your strengths as well as your weaknesses and of big and small things alike. Build a bridge between heaven and earth. Become involved without becoming constrained.

Practical advice: *Refuse to fulfill unfounded demands. But discharge meaningful obligations with a glad heart! Put an end to unnecessary suffering. Make the world a more human, a more livable, comfortable—and valuable place!*

Mitmenschlichkeit

Die roten Wurzeln quer im Bild und der große Torbogen im Hintergrund werfen Fragen auf: Was verbindet und was unterscheidet Himmel und Erde, Wunsch und Wirklichkeit? Die menschliche Gemeinschaft und die persönliche Einzigartigkeit sind die Antwort. Das Miteinander zeigt sich besonders in der linken Hälfte des Bildes. In der rechten Bildhälfte dagegen sind die Figuren von großen Blumen verdeckt: Der Zauber des Eigenen blüht, die Privatsphäre ist geschützt.

Fünf Münzen beschreiben die Quintessenz des Elements Erde: das volle Erblühen der Talente. Diese Entfaltung wird durch die Raupe im Kokon (direkt über den unteren vier Münzen) und durch die geschlüpften Schmetterlinge deutlich. Gemeinschaft und Eigenwert machen es möglich. Jedes menschliche Vermögen (Besitz und Fähigkeiten) schafft soviel Wert, wie es braucht, vermeidbare Notlagen auszuschließen und unvermeidliche Notlagen erträglich zu machen. Es gibt jene Nöte, die durch Katastrophen und Krankheit entstehen, und jene anderen Nöte, die aus unerfüllten Bedürfnissen erwachsen: etwa der Hunger nach Sinn, der Durst nach Liebe, die Sehnsucht nach Heimat. Jede Art von Not ist belastend. Wo sich die Fülle unserer Möglichkeiten mit den dringendsten Notwendigkeiten verbindet, bewirken unsere Talente am meisten.

Machen Sie aus der Not eine Tugend. Wo Finsternis ist, wird Ihr Licht am meisten gebraucht. Wo Ihre Talente aufleuchten, da werden Mauern durchlässig, und Sie gewinnen in jeder Beziehung festen Boden unter den Füßen. Wenn Sie sich um Stärken wie um Schwächen, um Großes wie um Kleines kümmern, bauen Sie die Brücke zwischen Himmel und Erde: Anteil nehmen und persönlich frei bleiben.

Praxistipps: *Kündigen Sie unbegründete Ansprüche. Erfüllen Sie sinnvolle Verpflichtungen mit leichtem Herzen! Beenden Sie unnötiges Leid. Machen Sie die Welt menschlicher, wohnlicher, komfortabler – und wertvoller!*

Sollicitude

Les racines rouges en travers de l'image et le grand arc de portail à l'arrière-plan soulèvent des questions : qu'est-ce qui unit et qu'est-ce qui différencie le ciel et la terre, le désir et la réalité ? La communauté humaine et l'unicité personnelle sont la réponse. Le phénomène de groupe apparaît particulièrement sur la moitié gauche de l'image. Sur la moitié droite en revanche les personnages sont cachés par de grandes fleurs : la magie de l'individualité fleurit, la sphère privée est protégée.

Cinq pièces décrivent la quintessence de l'élément terre : la complète éclosion des talents. Cet épanouissement est visible à travers la chenille dans son cocon (en bas de l'image, juste au-dessus des quatre deniers) et à travers les papillons éclos. Communauté et individualité le rendent possible. Chaque capital humain (biens matériels et aptitudes) produit autant de valeur qu'il est nécessaire pour exclure les mauvaises passes évitables et rendre supportables les mauvaises passes inévitables. Certaines détresses sont causées par des maladies ou des catastrophes et d'autres détresses sont provoquées par des besoins inassouvis : par exemple la faim d'orientation, la soif d'amour, le mal du pays. Toute forme de détresse est pesante. Nos talents atteignent la plus grande efficacité là où la multitude de nos chances s'unit aux nécessités les plus urgentes.

Faites de nécessité vertu. Votre lumière est la plus utile là où l'obscurité règne. Les murs deviennent étanches là où vos talents rayonnent, et vous avez à tous égards un sol ferme sous vos pieds. Si vous vous penchez sur les forces comme sur les faiblesses, sur les grandes choses comme sur les petites, vous bâtirez un pont entre ciel et terre : participez tout en restant libre.

Conseils pratiques : *Abandonnez les exigences infondées. Acquittez-vous d'obligations intelligentes d'un cœur léger ! Mettez fin à la souffrance inutile. Rendez le monde plus humain, plus agréable, plus confortable – et plus attrayant !*

Six of Coins
Sechs der Münzen
Six de Denier

Productive Needs

The three figures represent different aspects of giving and taking. Whenever coins are spent to satisfy real needs, both parties involved win—the one spending the coins as well as the one receiving them. Do not waste your time giving alms or appealing to someone's charity. Much more is needed here.

The figure on the right has a halo around his head. Again, Dalí can be credited with emphasizing the divine dimension (cf. THREE OF COINS, FOUR OF COINS, TEN OF WANDS). Whenever giving and taking become one, whenever strengths and weaknesses are reconciled, a divine blessing can be felt. This benediction is represented by the sketchily drawn figure with the raised arms in the background. Inside this hazy apparition, a red chalice or a glass with red wine and a tablet with eight rolls of dough can be seen. These items symbolize the Christian concept of transmutation: bread and wine provide physical as well as spiritual nourishment.

Whenever you use your talents to satisfy your needs and use your needs to stimulate your talents, there is always something to be gained. Both aspects will benefit by the result—a true win-win situation. In this manner, you can transform plain wants and banal necessities through blessed creative acts.

Practical advice: *New ways of realizing your own needs and of understanding the needs of others are called for. Learn to distinguish productive from unproductive needs. The value of that which you own is greatest when as many people as possible benefit from it. In this sense, you own only that which you give away. Focus upon realizing a gain for all parties involved. This is much better than managing deprivation.*

Produktive Bedürfnisse

Die drei Bildfiguren zeigen verschiedene Seiten des Gebens und Nehmens . Wenn „Münzen" wirkliche Bedürfnisse zur Geltung bringen, dann gewinnt derjenige, der sie weggibt, genauso wie derjenige, der sie entgegennimmt. Verschwenden Sie Ihre Zeit nicht mit karitativen Spenden oder mit Appellen an die Wohltätigkeit. Es geht um mehr.

Die rechte Bildfigur trägt einen Heiligenschein. Erneut betont das Dalí-Tarot die göttliche Dimension (vgl. die Karten DREI DER MÜNZEN, VIER DER MÜNZEN oder ZEHN DER STÄBE). Wo Geben und Nehmen miteinander aufgehen, wo Stärken und Schwächen miteinander versöhnt werden, da wird ein göttlicher Segen spürbar. Dieser Segen zeigt sich durch die Figur mit den erhobenen Armen im Bildhintergrund. Inmitten dieser schemenhaften Gestalt sehen wir einen roten Kelch oder ein Glas mit rotem Wein sowie ein Tablett mit sechs Gebäckröllchen, ein Bild für die christlichen Zeichen der Wandlung: Brot und Wein, zugleich materielle wie geistigseelische Nahrung.

Wenn Sie mit Ihren Talenten Bedürfnisse erfüllen und mit Ihren Bedürfnissen Talente wecken, entsteht jedesmal ein Zugewinn. Beide Seiten profitieren vom Ergebnis. Und so verwandeln Sie selbst banale Notwendigkeiten und Bedürfnisse in ein segensreiches, schöpferisches Tun.

Praxistipps: *Finden Sie neue Wege zur Verwirklichung Ihrer eigenen und zum Verständnis fremder Bedürfnisse. Unterscheiden Sie produktive von unproduktiven Wünschen. Der Wert des Eigenen ist am größten, wenn möglichst viele davon profitieren. In diesem Sinne besitzen Sie nur, was Sie weggeben. Konzentrieren Sie sich darauf, einen Zugewinn für alle Beteiligten zu realisieren, das ist besser, als einen Mangel zu verwalten.*

Résultats productifs

Les trois personnages présentent différentes facettes du donner et du prendre. Si les « deniers » mettent les véritables besoins en valeur, alors celui qui donne est tout aussi gagnant que celui qui prend. Ne gaspillez pas votre temps en dons caritatifs ou en appels à la générosité. L'enjeu est plus important.

La figure de droite porte une auréole.Une fois de plus, Dalí souligne la dimension divine (voir les cartes TROIS DE DENIER, QUATRE DE DENIER ou DIX DE BÂTON). Là où donner et prendre vont de pair, où les forces et les faiblesses sont réunies, une bénédiction divine est tangible. Celle-ci se manifeste à travers le personnage aux bras levés au fond de l'image. Au centre de cette figure schématique nous distinguons un ciboire rouge ou un verre contenant du vin rouge ainsi qu'un plateau où sont posés six biscuits roulés, motifs chrétiens de la transsubstantiation : le pain et le vin, nourriture à la fois matérielle et spirituelle.

Si vous satifaisez vos besoins grâce à vos talents et si vous éveillez vos talents par vos besoins, cela représente chaque fois un avantage. Les deux parties profitent du résultat. Et vous transformez même de banales nécessités et besoins en une action bénéfique et créative.

Conseils pratiques : *Cherchez de nouvelles voies pour la réalisation de vos propres besoins et la compréhension des besoins d'autrui. Faites la différence entre les désirs productifs et les désirs caduques. La valeur de votre bien est la plus élevée si le grand nombre en profite. En ce sens, vous ne possédez que ce que vous offrez. Veillez surtout à réaliser un profit pour tous les participants, cela vaut mieux que de gérer un déficit.*

Seven of Coins
Sieben der Münzen
Sept de Denier

Balance Sheet

Whether a mountain of hardships and sorrows is already behind us or still to be climbed, this card is all about reviewing results and determining new goals. Are we satisfied with the results of past efforts? Are we happy about the way we have achieved our goals? Our results are the mirror of our lives. Emotional and mental clarity are only of value if put to good use. The fruits of our efforts will only make us happy and satisfied if we relate to them as true expressions of our authentic selves.

Facing contradictions offers a special chance to contemplate the self and to be contemplative. We will gain our own measure and recognize our true talents only by evaluating our own experiences. Every one of us possesses special talents.

Talent is not something exotic but shows itself in always mastering the next step and accomplishing the tasks of your daily life in your own way and according to your own standards. Through your personal talent, you make a difference to the world. If you examine social norms, you will find out whether or not they function for you. Objective facts and subjective questions are linked, and yet different.

There are objective matters that you will only be able to solve by realizing your own destiny, your own purpose in life, your own individuality. Each success will confirm that you are indeed on the right track. But even failures are important if they reveal to you what is not your purpose in life and not your destiny.

Pratical advice: *In your current situation, you are called upon to look for signs and interpret them. Sometimes, even stumbling blocks can give you important clues. Search and find until you see clearly. If you can find your own measure, you will grow with your tasks and your tasks will grow with you!*

Bilanz

Wir mögen einen Berg von Mühen und Sorgen vor oder hinter uns haben – hier geht es um die Bilanz unserer bisherigen Leistungen und die Festlegung neuer Ziele. Sind wir mit unseren Leistungen zufrieden? Damit, wie wir gearbeitet haben? Unsere Leistungen sind der Spiegel unseres Lebens. Es zeigt sich, dass emotionale oder gedankliche Klarheit letztlich nur insofern von Wert sind, als wir sie in fruchtbare Resultate umsetzen; und ebenso, dass die Früchte unserer Bemühungen nur dann Glück und Befriedigung bringen, wenn sie mit uns in Verbindung stehen und Ausdruck unserer selbst sind.

Gerade in der Konfrontation mit diesen Ambivalenzen liegt aber eine besondere Chance der Selbstbesinnung und der Betrachtung. Nur aus der Erfahrung gewinnen wir einen eigenen, einen geeigneten Maßstab und erkennen unsere wirklichen Talente. Wir alle verfügen über besondere Talente.

Talent ist nicht eine exotische Sonderbegabung, sondern der nächste Schritt, die konkrete Tagesaufgabe, die in eigenem Stil und eigenem Ermessen gelöst wird. Das persönliche Talent ist der Unterschied, den das eigene Dasein in der Welt macht. Untersuchen Sie geltende Normen, und finden Sie heraus, ob sie für Sie funktionieren. Sachliche Entscheidungen und persönliche Fragen hängen zusammen und sind doch zwei verschiedene Dinge.

Es gibt sachliche Aufgaben, deren Lösung Sie in dem Moment finden, in dem Sie auch Ihre Bedeutung, den persönlichen Sinn, Ihre Lebensaufgaben entziffern. Jede gelöste Aufgabe zeigt Ihnen, dass Sie auf dem richtigen Weg sind. Selbst ein Fehlschlag ist wertvoll, denn er macht deutlich, worin Ihre Aufgabe und Ihre Bestimmungen nicht bestehen.

Praxistipps: *Suchen Sie nach Spuren und versuchen Sie, die Zeichen zu deuten. Manchmal geben auch Stolpersteine wichtige Hinweise. Suchen und finden Sie so lange, bis sich Ihnen das Geheimnis offenbart. Bilden Sie Ihren eigenen Maßstab heraus, dann werden Sie mit Ihren Aufgaben wachsen und Ihre Aufgaben mit Ihnen!*

Bilan

Même si nous pouvons bien avoir devant ou derrière nous une montagne d'efforts et de soucis, ici il s'agit du bilan de nos résultats antérieurs et de la détermination de nouveaux objectifs. Sommes-nous satisfaits des résultats ? De notre méthode de travail ? Nos résultats sont le miroir de notre vie. Il se trouve que la transparence émotionnelle ou mentale n'a finalement de valeur que dans la mesure où nous la transformons en résultats fructueux ; et de même, les fruits de nos efforts ne nous procurent bonheur et satisfaction que s'ils sont en rapport avec nous et l'expression de nous-mêmes.

Mais justement dans la confrontation avec ces contradictions réside une chance extraordinaire d'autoréflexion et d'observation. Seule l'expérience nous permet de fixer nos critères individuels et adéquats et de reconnaître nos réels talents spécifiques. Nous disposons tous de talents spécifiques.

Un talent n'est pas un don spécial et exotique mais le prochain pas, la tâche concrète du jour qui est effectuée dans un style personnel selon une échelle individuelle. Le talent personnel est la différence que notre existence fait dans le monde. Analysez les normes en vigueur et cherchez à savoir si elles fonctionnent pour vous. Décisions concrètes et questions personnelles sont liées et cependant deux éléments bien distincts.

Il existe des tâches concrètes dont vous trouvez la solution au moment où vous déchiffrez votre importance, le sens personnel, vos défis pour la vie. Chaque tâche exécutée vous prouve que vous êtes sur le bon chemin. Même un échec est important, car il souligne en quoi votre tâche et vos prédispositions ne consistent pas.

Conseils pratiques : *Partez à la recherche de pistes et essayez d'interpréter les signes. Parfois, des obstacles donnent aussi des indices importants. Cherchez et trouvez jusqu'à ce que le mystère s'ouvre à vous. Développez votre échelle individuelle, vous grandirez avec vos défis et vos défis avec vous!*

Eight of Coins
Acht der Münzen
Huit de Denier

Mastery

It is a paradox that you have to rise above yourself to find yourself. This is represented by the great variety of figures on the card as well as the fruit and the tree at the bottom and by the ancestral portrait above.

In a certain sense, this card, which is full of frames, is all about going out of the ordinary and breaking free. The small hiker at the bottom left hints at something extraordinary that lies beyond the current framework.

Your contribution to a great task is called for now. Review your personal responsibilities and necessities. Your current questions will help you to find your calling and to create a framework, in which you will get the best results with the means you presently have at your disposal. Do not wear yourself out with tasks set by others. Find the purpose that only you can fulfill!

Like every human being, you too possess special talents that will make your own life happy and the world more humane and a better place to live in. There are typical talents and tasks that await you—and you only. If you focus on them, you will be able to banish all gurus and masters— for it is you who will gain mastery of your life! Create many results that are uniquely yours, with your signature and style, and through which you can express yourself. In this manner, you will create a sort of healthy luxury: an abundance of well-being, accomplished ideas, and fulfilled desires.

Practical advice: *Reflect on your experiencecs. The clearer your assets and handicaps become, the easier it will be for you to discover your true purpose in life. Focusing on this will prove to be the basis and the secret of your mastery.*

Meisterschaft

Wir müssen über uns hinauswachsen, um zu uns selbst zu finden. Dieser Zusammenhang ist deutlich erkennbar in der Vielfalt der Bildfiguren, auch in den Früchten und dem Baum am Fuß der Karte sowie in dem Gemälde und dem Ahnenbild am Kopf der Karte.

In gewisser Weise heißt es hier, aus dem Rahmen zu fallen, denn das Bild enthält gleich mehrere Rahmen. Einen Hinweis auf das Außerordentliche außerhalb der Rahmen gibt der kleine Wanderer unten links.

Ihr Beitrag in einer großen Angelegenheit ist jetzt gefragt. Finden Sie zu einer Neubewertung Ihrer persönlichen Aufgaben und Pflichten. Ihre aktuellen Fragen helfen Ihnen, Ihre Bestimmung zu finden und sich den Rahmen zu schaffen, in dem Sie mit den vorhandenen Mitteln das beste Ergebnis erzielen. Verausgaben Sie sich nicht für fremde Ziele; finden Sie stattdessen die Aufgaben, für die Sie wirklich gebraucht werden!

Wie jeder Mensch bringen Sie Begabungen mit, um das eigene Leben als glücklich zu erleben und die Welt insgesamt menschlicher und angenehmer zu gestalten. Es gibt Begabungen und Aufgaben, die auf Sie allein warten – sie funktionieren bei niemand anderem als bei Ihnen. Wenn Sie sich darauf konzentrieren, brauchen Sie keine Gurus und Meister – Sie erwerben die Meisterschaft für Ihr Leben! Sorgen Sie für zahlreiche Ergebnisse, die Ihre Handschrift, Ihren Zuschnitt tragen und in denen Sie sich selbst wiedererkennen. So schaffen Sie Stück für Stück einen Zustand von gesundem Luxus: einen Überfluss an Wohlbehagen, verwirklichten Ideen und befriedigten Wünschen.

Praxistips: *Denken Sie über Ihre Erfahrungen nach. Je klarer Ihnen Ihre Vorzüge und Ihre Handicaps werden, um so leichter finden Sie die Aufgaben, für die Sie besonders begabt sind. Solange Sie sich darauf konzentrieren, liegt gerade in dieser Beschränkung die Grundlage und das Geheimnis Ihrer Meisterschaft.*

Maîtrise

Nous devons nous dépasser pour nous retrouver en nous-mêmes. Ce postulat se manifeste dans la diversité des personnages peints, dans les fruits et l'arbre au bas de la carte ainsi que dans le tableau et le portrait d'ancêtre en haut de la carte.

Il s'agit ici en quelque sorte de sortir du cadre car l'image comporte plusieurs cadres à la fois. À l'extérieur des cadres, le petit randonneur en bas de l'image à gauche personnifie ce qui sort de l'ordinaire.

Votre participation à une affaire importante est maintenant indispensable. Établissez une réévaluation de vos tâches et besoins personnels. Vos questions actuelles vous aideront à trouver votre orientation et à créer le cadre dans lequel vous obtiendrez le meilleur résultat avec les moyens à votre disposition. Ne vous dépensez dans des projets insolites ; trouvez au contraire les missions pour lesquelles vous êtes d'une réelle utilité.

Comme tout un chacun vous portez en vous des talents pour vivre une vie heureuse et construire un monde en somme plus humain et plus agréable. Il existe des dons et missions qui n'attendent que vous – ils ne fonctionnent pour personne d'autre. Si vous les focalisez, vous n'aurez besoin ni de maître ni de gourou – vous obtiendrez la maîtrise de votre vie ! Provoquez de nombreux résultats qui portent votre signature, votre empreinte, et dans lesquels vous vous reconnaissez. Vous créerez ainsi pas à pas un état de luxe salutaire : un excès de bien-être, des idées réalisées et des besoins contentés.

Conseils pratiques : *Assimilez vos expériences. Plus vos qualités et vos handicaps vous apparaissent évidents, plus vous trouverez facilement des missions pour lesquelles vous êtes particulièrement doué. Tant que vous les focalisez, le fondement et le secret de votre maîtrise résident justement dans cette restriction.*

Nine of Coins
Neun der Münzen
Neuf de Denier

Mature Talents

It makes a big difference whether or not you are in this world, because you brought something unique with you that will make it a better place. Do not hide your talents! Be generous and show your fellow human beings the treasures you have to offer. You yourself are a treasure.

The key to unfolding inner wealth is love. Love is not just an emotion; it is the basis and the result of the blossoming of all your needs and talents! This card is all about the love you feel for your fellow human beings, for animals and plants, for things, events, and anything else. Love is not just the right measure in a partnership; love is a way of encountering the world. The more talents and needs of as many people as possible are being realized, the greater the love and the greater the benefit for all involved. Any material gain that does not fulfill needs or support talents is really of no value.

If you encounter the world with respect and love, you add to it. A greater whole is created, in which many people with their strengths and weaknesses, their advantages and disadvantages feel included. You cannot gain more than this, and you should not be satisfied with less.

Practical advice: *Stop the internal dialogue, the nervous chattering of your inner voice. Find inner peace, your "blue hour," by giving loving attention to your tasks and by joyfully recognizing your results. Stop parroting the ideas of others or imitating their ever-changing moods. Find the fitting framework for your high-flying plans and your blossoming talents.*

Reife Talente

Ob Sie auf der Welt sind oder nicht, macht einen großen Unterschied. Sie bringen etwas mit, das die Erde reicher macht. Darum: Verstecken Sie Ihre Talente nicht! Seien Sie großzügig und zeigen Sie Ihren Mitmenschen, welche Schätze Sie zu bieten haben, weil Sie selbst ein Schatz sind.

Der Schlüssel zur Entfaltung dieses Reichtums ist die Liebe. Liebe ist nicht bloß ein Gefühl, sondern auch die Voraussetzung und das Ergebnis einer optimalen Förderung von Bedürfnissen und Talenten! Hier geht es um die Liebe zu Ihren Mitmenschen, zu Tieren und Pflanzen, zu Dingen, Ereignissen und allem anderen. Nicht nur für die partnerschaftliche Zweierbeziehung ist die Liebe der geeignete Maßstab. Liebe ist eine Art und Weise, der Welt zu begegnen. Je mehr Talente und Bedürfnisse von vielen Beteiligten gleichzeitig zur Geltung kommen, umso größer ist die Liebe und umso größer ist auch der insgesamt erzielte Gewinn! Jeder materielle Erfolg, der nicht dazu beiträgt, Bedürfnisse zu erfüllen und Talente zu fördern, ist letzten Endes unbedeutend.

Wenn Sie sich und der Welt mit Achtung und Liebe begegnen, entsteht ein Zugewinn, ein größeres Ganzes, in dem sich viele Menschen mit Stärken und Schwächen, mit Vorzügen und Nachteilen aufgehoben fühlen. Einen größeren Gewinn können Sie gar nicht erzielen, und mit einem geringeren sollten Sie sich nicht zufriedengeben.

Praxistipps: *Beenden Sie den inneren Dialog, das aufgeregte Plappern der inneren Stimme. Finden Sie Ihre Ruhe, Ihre „blaue Stunde" in der liebevollen Zuwendung zu Ihren Aufgaben und in der Freude über Ihre Ergebnisse. Hören Sie auf, wie ein Papagei die Ansichten anderer nachzusprechen und fremden Launen nachzugeben. Finden Sie den richtigen Rahmen für Ihre hochfliegenden Pläne und Ihre blühenden Talente.*

Talents à maturité

Le fait que vous soyez au monde ou non constitue une grande différence. Vous apportez quelque chose qui enrichit la terre. C'est pourquoi ne dissimulez pas vos talents ! Soyez généreux et montrez à autrui les trésors dont vous disposez, car vous-même êtes un trésor.

La clé de l'épanouissement de cette richesse est l'amour. L'amour n'est pas seulement un sentiment, mais la condition et le produit d'une promotion optimale de désirs et de talents ! Il est question ici de l'amour du prochain, des animaux ou des plantes, des objets, des événements, etc. L'amour n'est pas uniquement le critère adéquat dans une relation entre deux partenaires. L'amour est une manière de rencontrer le monde. Plus de nombreux talents et besoins de beaucoup de personnes sont mis en valeur, plus grand est l'amour, et plus grand est aussi le profit obtenu dans son ensemble ! Toute réussite matérielle qui ne contribue pas à satisfaire des besoins et à encourager des talents est finalement dérisoire.

Si vous allez vers vous-même et vers le monde avec respect et amour, alors un profit apparaît, un tout plus important, dans lequel beaucoup d'individus avec leurs forces et faiblesses, leurs avantages et inconvénients, se sentent chez eux. Vous ne pouvez guère obtenir de plus grand bénéfice et ne devriez pas vous contenter d'un moindre profit.

Conseils pratiques : *Cessez le dialogue intérieur, le papotage nerveux de votre voix intérieure. Trouvez le calme, faites « l'école buissonnière » en vous tournant avec amour vers vos tâches et en vous réjouissant de vos résultats. Arrêtez de rabâcher comme un perroquet les opinions des autres et de céder à des caprices extérieurs. Trouvez le juste cadre pour vos projets ambitieux et vos talents débordants.*

Ten of Coins
Zehn der Münzen
Dix de Denier

Magical Moments

The scene from the painting *The Turkish Bath* (1863) by Ingres in conjunction with the butterflies and the ten coins in a circle represents the joy of living, the best results, proliferating talents, and great wealth.

Significantly, individuality cannot be achieved in isolation. If you succeed in finding the bridge to others, loneliness—the shadow of missing individuality—will disappear, and with it, the danger of drowning in the crowd.

The communal bath represents the joys of sensuality and spiritual questions. The bath is a symbol of baptism, of rebirth, and of purification. In a spiritual sense, the card shows a true fountain of youth. If we bathe in its waters, daily contact with other people will not drain us and we will be refreshed.

The greatest wealth lies in acknowledging and fulfilling your contribution to the course of events. Your own experiences and those of others constitute a greater whole. You know that you will not be able to hold onto anything and that change is inevitable, heralding new opportunities. You are aware that your actions are based on those of your ancestors and that the younger generations will carry these forwards. Time is relative. Nothing ever gets lost. Nothing keeps you from living and from feeling your own rhythm. Nothing stops you from lingering or moving on.

Practical advice: *Cooperation, exchange, mutual support, and compromises are great as long as they are the result of each individual involved following his or her own path. They become unnecessarily limiting if based on sacrificing your independence and your individuality. Touch the moment with the magic wand of individuality and contribute to a communal style of living, in which each and every individual can walk his or her own path in joy. Then the bliss of mutuality will blossom, culminating in a culture of shared intentions.*

Magische Momente

Die Szene aus „Das türkische Bad" von Ingres (1863), verbunden mit den Schmetterlingen und den zehn Münzen im Kreis, steht für Lebensfreude, optimale Ergebnisse, blühende Talente und großen Reichtum.

Bezeichnenderweise ist Individualität nicht im Alleingang möglich. Indem wir die Brücke zum anderen finden, überwinden wir die Einsamkeit, diesen Schatten einer fehlenden Individualität, ebenso wie die Gefahr, in der Masse unterzugehen, also in einem übertragenen Sinne, „baden zu gehen".

Das gemeinsame Bad steht für körperliche Sinnesfreuden genauso wie für geistige Sinnfragen: Im Bad liegt unter anderem das Motiv der Taufe, der Reinigung und Wiedergeburt. In spiritueller Hinsicht ist hier ein Jungbrunnen gemeint, in dem das alltägliche Zusammensein uns nicht erschöpft, sondern erfrischt.

Der größte Reichtum besteht darin, den eigenen Anteil am Geschehen zu erkennen und auszufüllen. Ihre eigenen und die Erfahrungen anderer fügen sich zusammen zu einem größeren Ganzen. Sie wissen, dass Sie nichts festhalten können, dass Veränderungen unvermeidlich sind und neue Möglichkeiten beinhalten. Sie wissen, dass Ihr Handeln auf dem der Alten aufbaut und von den Jungen weitergeführt werden wird. Zeit ist relativ und kennt kein Ende. Nichts geht verloren. Nichts hält Sie davon ab, zu leben und Ihren Puls zu spüren, zu verweilen und weiterzugehen.

Praxistipps: *Kooperation, Austausch, gegenseitige Unterstützung und Kompromisse sind gut, wenn Sie das Ergebnis dessen sind, dass jede/r den eigenen Weg geht. Sie setzen uns aber Grenzen, wenn sie aus Verzicht auf Eigenständigkeit entstehen. Berühren Sie also den Augenblick mit dem Zauberstab der Individualität, und leisten Sie Ihren Beitrag zu einem gemeinschaftlichen Leben, in dem jede und jeder den eigenen Weg mit viel Freude verwirklichen kann. So entfalten sich die Wonnen der Gemeinsamkeit, so entstehen Kulte und eine Kultur des Gemeinsinns.*

Moments magiques

La scène du « Bain turc » (1863) d'Ingres, enrichie de papillons et de dix deniers encerclés, évoque la joie de vivre, les résultats parfaits, les talents débordants et la grande richesse.

De manière révélatrice l'individualité n'est pas possible en solitaire. En lançant une passerelle vers l'autre, nous surmontons la solitude, cette ombre d'une individualité déficiante, ainsi que le danger de disparaître dans la masse, donc au sens figuré de « prendre un bain » (« prendre un bain signifie » en allemand « échouer », N.d.T.).

Le bain pris en commun représente les joies physiques sensuelles tout comme les questions spirituelles fondamentales : le bain contient, entre autres, le thème du baptême, de la purification et de la renaissance. D'un point de vue spirituel est évoquée ici une fontaine de jouvence dans laquelle la communauté quotidienne ne nous épuise pas, mais nous rafraîchit.

La plus grande richesse consiste à distinguer notre part personnelle aux événements et à la réaliser. Vos propres expériences et celles des autres se fondent dans un plus grand ensemble. Vous savez que vous ne pouvez rien retenir, que des changements sont inévitables et renferment de nouvelles chances. Vous savez que votre action est basée sur celle des anciens et sera poursuivie par les jeunes. Le temps est relatif et ne connaît pas de fin. Rien ne se perd. Rien ne vous empêche de vivre et de tâter votre pouls, de vous attarder et de repartir.

Conseils pratiques : *Coopération, échange, soutien réciproque et compromis sont utiles s'ils découlent du fait que chacun(e) suit sa propre voie. Mais ils nous imposent des limites s'ils résultent du refus de l'autonomie. Touchez donc l'instant avec la baguette magique de l'individualité et apportez votre contribution à la vie communautaire, dans laquelle chacune et chacun peut réaliser sa propre voie avec une joie immense. Ainsi s'épanouissent les délices de la communauté, ainsi naissent les cultes et une culture du sens commun.*

EL LOCO

THE FOOL

THE PICTORIAL
SOURCES
IN DALÍ'S TAROT

BILDZITATE
IM DALÍ-TAROT

LES RÉFÉRENCES
ARTISTIQUES DANS
LE TAROT DE DALÍ

The Pictorial Sources in Dalí's Tarot

Bildzitate in Dalí-Tarot

Les références artistiques dans le Tarot de Dalí

In 1912, the Dalí family moved to their new home at 24 Carrer Monturiol in Figueres. One of the two laundry rooms became young Salvador's first studio.

His father gave a number of art books, published by Gowans & Gray out of London and Glasgow, to the aspiring artist. Each volume contained 60 reproductions of famous works by old masters. Dalí wrote about this collection in his book *The Secret Life of Salvador Dalí*:

"I had brought up to my laundry the whole collection of art, Gowans' little monographs which my father had so prematurely given me as a present produced an effect on me that was one of the most decisive in my life. I came to know by heart all those pictures of the history of art, which have been familiar to me since my earliest childhood, for I would spend entire days contemplating them. The nudes attracted me above all else, and Ingres' *Golden Age* appeared to me the most beautiful picture in the world and I fell in love with the naked girl symbolizing the fountain."

(The Secret Life of Salvador Dalí. [First edition 1942.] Dover Publications, New York 1993, p. 71)

With four of his fellow students, Dalí founded a school magazine in 1918. In 1919, he wrote an essay titled "The Great Masters of the Art of Painting," in which he commented on the works of Leonardo da Vinci, Michelangelo, Velázquez, Goya, El Greco, and Dürer. His comments made it plain that he possessed an intimate knowledge of their works.

One may rightfully assume that his selection of works for his tarot was by no means arbitrary, but part of the message that Dalí wanted to convey.

Im Jahr 1912 zog die Familie Dalí in ihr neues Heim an der Carrer Monturiol 24 in Figueres. Eine der beiden Waschküchen auf der Dachterrasse des Hauses wurde für den jungen Salvador zu seinem ersten Atelier.

Vater Dalí schenkte dem angehenden Künstler eine Reihe von Kunstbüchern, die vom Verlag Gowans & Gray, London und Glasgow, herausgegeben wurden. Jeder Band enthielt 60 Reproduktionen berühmter Werke alter Meister. In seinem Buch *Das geheime Leben des Salvador Dalí* äußert sich Dalí über diese Sammlung:

„Diese kleinen Monographien, die mir mein Vater so frühzeitig geschenkt hatte, hatten eine Wirkung auf mich, die zu den entscheidendsten meines Lebens gehörte. Ich lernte all diese Bilder der Kunstgeschichte auswendig, die mir seit meiner frühesten Kindheit vertraut waren, da ich ganze Tage damit verbrachte, sie zu betrachten. Vor allem zogen mich die Nackten an, und Ingres ‚Goldenes Zeitalter‘ schien mir das schönste Bild der Welt zu sein, und ich verliebte mich in das nackte Mädchen, das die Quelle (La Source) darstellte.“

(Das geheime Leben des Salvador Dalí, München 1990, Seite 95)

In der von ihm und vier weiteren Mitschülern 1918 gegründeten Schülerzeitung *Studium* kommentierte Salvador Dalí im Jahr 1919 unter dem Titel *Die großen Meister der Malerei* die Werke von Leonardo da Vinci, Michelangelo, Velázquez, Goya, El Greco und Dürer. Seine Ausführungen lassen erkennen, dass er sich minutiös mit den Kunstwerken befasst hatte.

Man darf also mit Sicherheit annehmen, dass die Auswahl der Bildzitate für die Tarot-Karten keinesfalls zufällig ist, sondern auf fundierter Kenntnis beruhte und einen dezidierten Teil der Botschaft Dalís an den Betrachter darstellt.

En 1912, la famille Dalí emménage dans sa nouvelle résidence au 24 Carrer Monturiol à Figueras. L'une des deux buanderies sur la terrasse au toit sert de premier atelier de peinture au jeune Salvador.

Le père de Dalí offre au jeune artiste des livres d'art de l'édition Gowans & Gray, London et Glasgow. Chaque volume contient soixante reproductions d'œuvres de vieux maîtres. Dans son livre *La Vie secrète de Salvador Dalí*, Dalí écrit au sujet de ces reproductions :

« Ces petites monographies que mon père m'offrit si prématurément me produisirent un des effets les plus décisifs de ma vie. Je connaissais par cœur toutes ces images de l'histoire de l'art qui m'étaient familières depuis ma première enfance, en passant des journées à les contempler. Ce sont surtout les nus qui m'attirèrent avant toute chose, et *L'Âge d'or* d'Ingres m'apparaissait la plus belle image du monde, et je tombai amoureux de la jeune fille nue symbolisant la fontaine. »

(La Vie secrète de Salvador Dalí)

En 1918, Dalí édite avec quatre de ses amis une revue mensuelle *Studium*, dans laquelle il commente sous le titre « Les grands maîtres de la peinture » les œuvres de Léonard de Vinci, Michel Ange, Velázquez, Goya, El Greco et Dürer. Ses écrits montrent la minutie avec laquelle il s'est consacré à ces œuvres.

On peut donc supposer, à juste titre, que les œuvres choisies pour les cartes de tarot ne doivent rien au hasard, mais qu'elles font partie du message que Dalí souhaite adresser à l'observateur.

I – The Magician
Top: The arches of the Sainte-Chapelle, Paris
Bottom: *The Last Supper* (1955), The
National Gallery of Art, Chester Dale
Collection, Washington, D.C.
Salvador Dalí takes the place of Christ.

II – The High Priestess
Original work by Salvador Dalí for his tarot

III – The Empress
Saint Helena at Port Lligat (1956), The
Salvador Dalí Museum, St. Petersburg,
Florida; Salvador Dalí.
Inspired by *Greece on the Ruins of Missolonghi*
(1826), Musée des Beaux-Arts, Bordeaux;
Ferdinand Victor Eugène Delacroix, born
April 26, 1798, in Charenton-Saint-Maurice
near Paris, died August 13, 1863, in Paris,
France. Dalí immortalized his lover and future
wife, Gala (born Helena Dimitriyevna
Diakonova) as Saint Helena.

IV – The Emperor
Original work by Salvador Dalí for his tarot

V – The High Priest
Further information requested. *

VI – The Lovers
Neptune and Amphitrite (1516), Gemälde-
galerie Berlin; Jan Gossaert, also known
as Mabuse, born ca. 1470-80 in Maubeuge
(Hainaut), died 1532 in Breda, the
Netherlands

VII – The Chariot
Original work by Salvador Dalí for his tarot
Further information requested. *

VIII – Justice
Justitia, painted in the style of Cranach.
Lucas Cranach the Elder, born 1472 in
Kronach (Upper Franconia), died October 16,
1553, in Weimar, Germany

IX – The Hermit
Portrait of Luca Pacioli, Museo Nazionale
di Capodimonte, Naples; Jacopo de' Barbari,
born ca. 1445 in Venice, died 1516 in Brussels
or Mechelen, Belgium.
Luca Pacioli, born ca. 1445, was one of the
most outstanding personalities of the Renaissance. In 1475, he became a lecturer at the
University of Perugia, Italy. In 1494, after
receiving his ordination as a Franciscan monk,
he wrote his epochal work *Summa de Arith-*

I – Der Magier
Oben: die Bögen der Sainte-Chapelle, Paris
Unten: *Das Abendmahl* (1955), The National
Gallery of Art, Chester Dale Collection,
Washington, DC
Salvador Dalí in der Position des Christus
(Ausschnitt)

II – Die Hohepriesterin
Salvador Dalí, neuer Entwurf für das Tarot

III – Die Herrscherin
Die Heilige Helena in Port Lligat (1956),
The Salvador Dalí Museum, St. Petersburg,
Florida; Salvador Dalí
Bildkomposition nach *Griechenland auf den
Ruinen von Missolonghi sterbend* (1826),
Musée des Barbari, Bordeaux
Ferdinand Victor Eugène Delacroix,
* 26.04.1798 St-Maurice-Charenton bei Paris,
† 13.06.1863 Paris
In der Heiligen Helena hat Dalí die Züge
seiner Lebensgefährtin und späteren Ehefrau
Gala verewigt, deren ursprünglicher Vorname
ebenfalls Helena lautete.

IV – Der Herrscher
Salvador Dalí, neuer Entwurf für das Tarot

V – Der Hierophant
Weitere Angaben erwünscht *

VI – Die Liebenden
Neptun und Amphitrite (1516), Gemälde-
galerie – Staatliche Museen zu Berlin
Jan Gossaert, genannt Mabuse, * um 1470/80
Maubeuge (Hennegau), † 1532 Breda

VII – Der Wagen
Salvador Dalí, weitere Angaben erwünscht *

VIII – Gerechtigkeit
Justitia, im Stil von Cranach
Lucas Cranach der Ältere, * 1472 Kronach
(Oberfranken), † 16.10.1553 Weimar

IX – Der Eremit
Porträt von Luca Pacioli, Museo Nazionale
di Capodimonte, Neapel
Jacopo de' Barbari, * um 1445 Venedig, † um
1516 Brüssel oder Mechelen
Der vermutlich 1445 geborene Luca Pacioli
war eine der herausragenden Persönlichkeiten
der Renaissance. Im Jahr 1475 zog er als Lehrer an die Universität von Perugia. Nachdem
er zum Franziskanermönch geweiht worden
war, schrieb Pacioli 1494 sein epochales Buch

I – Le Magicien
En haut : Les Arcs de la Sainte-Chapelle, Paris
En bas : *La Cène* (1955), The National Gallery
of Art, Chester Dale Collection, Washington.
Salvador Dalí prend la place du Christ.

II – La Papesse
Dalí, nouvelle création pour son tarot.

III – L'Impératrice
Sainte Hélène de port Lligat (1956)
The Salvador Dalí Museum, St. Petersburg,
Floride.
Salvador Dalí. Composition de tableau inspi-
rée de *La Grèce expirant sur les ruines de Mis-
solonghi* (1826), Musée des Beaux-Arts,
Bordeaux
Eugène Ferdinand Victor Delacroix, né à
Charenton-Saint-Maurice près de Paris le
26 avril 1798, mort à Paris le 13 août 1863.
Dans ce tableau, Dalí a éternisé sa compagne
et future épouse Gala en la représentant en
sainte Hélène.

IV – L'Empereur
Dalí, nouvelle création pour son tarot

V – Le Pape
Informations supplémentaires souhaitées *

VI – Les Amoureux
Neptune et Amphitrite (1516)
Gemäldegalerie, Berlin
Jan Gossaert, nommé Mabuse, né à Maubeuge
(Hennegau) entre 1470 et 1480, mort à Bréda
en 1532.

VII – Le Chariot
Dalí, nouvelle création pour son
tarot. Informations supplémentaires souhaitées *

VIII – Justice
Justitia peinte dans le style de Cranach.
Lucas Cranach l'Ancien, né à Kronach (Haute-
Franconie) en 1472, mort à Weimar le
16 octobre 1553

IX – L'Ermite
Portait de Luca Pacioli
Museo Nazionale di Capodimonte, Naples
Jacques de Barbary, né à Venise vers 1445,
mort à Bruxelles ou Malines vers 1516
Luca Pacioli, probablement né en 1445, fut
une personnalité essentielle de la Renaissance. En 1475, il enseigne les mathématiques
à l'Université de Pérouse. Devenu entre-

metica, Geometria, Proportioni et Proportionalità, a summary of the entire mathematical knowledge of the time. One of the chapters titled "Particularis de Computis et Scripturis" made him especially famous, because it was the first comprehensive treatise on double-entry accounting, also known as the "Venetian method." During the seven years he worked at the court of the Sforza family in Milan, he taught Leonardo da Vinci perspective and proportionality. This resulted in two of Leonardo's immortal works: the illustrations in Pacioli's book *De Divina Proportione* and the mural *The Last Supper* at the Dominican monastery Santa Maria delle Grazie in Milan.

X – The Wheel of Fortune
The Duke of Berry's book of hours (1413-16), Musée Condé, Chantilly
Top: The Month of August
Bottom: The Month of May
Paul, Herman, and Johan Limbourg, born between 1370 and 1380, died in 1416 (all three presumably died of the plague).

XI – Strength
Salvador Dalí, painting of a woman in the style of Lucas Cranach the Elder

XII – The Hanged Man
Young Man Among Roses, Victoria and Albert Museum, London, England;
Nicholas Hilliard, born ca. 1547 in Exeter, died January 7, 1619, in London, England

XIII – Death
Original work by Salvador Dalí for his tarot.
The illustration of his book *The Secret Life of Salvador Dalí* also shows a cypress, but with two skulls. In the accompanying text, Dalí describes how he discovered some of his beloved's letters in his rain-soaked jacket. Sitting in front of a cypress tree, he began crushing the letters in his hands until they turned into a kind of paste. The resulting balls looked very much like the seeds of a cypress tree. Dalí put them on the tree where the seeds had originally been. Then he walked to the furthest edge of a rock, where he was completely soaked by the waves of the sea. "The taste of sea salt on my lips awakened in me the myth of integrity and of immortality, which had been on my mind for some time."

Summa de Arithmetica, Geometria, Proportioni et Proportionalità, eine Zusammenfassung aller Erkenntnisse der Mathematik zur damaligen Zeit. Eines der Kapitel dieses Buches, *Particularis de Computis et Scripturis*, hat ihn berühmt gemacht, ist es doch die erste ausführliche Abhandlung über die doppelte Buchführung. In den sieben Jahren, die Pacioli am Hof der Sforza in Mailand mit Leonardo da Vinci arbeitete, unterrichtete er Leonardo im perspektivischen Zeichnen und in Proportionslehre. Daraus entstanden zwei Meisterwerke da Vincis: die Illustrationen zu Paciolis Buch *De Divina Proportione* und das Wandgemälde *Das Abendmahl* im Dominikanerkloster Santa Maria delle Grazie in Mailand.

X – Rad des Schicksals
Stundenbuch des Herzogs von Berry (1413-1416), Musée Condé, Chantilly
Oben: Monat August
Unten: Monat Mai
Paul, Hermann und Hans Limburg, zw. 1370 und 1380, † 1416 alle drei (vermutlich an der Pest)

XI – Kraft
Salvador Dalí, Frauenbildnis im Stil von Lucas Cranach dem Älteren

XII – Der Gehängte
Porträt eines Jünglings unter Rosen,
Victoria and Albert Museum, London
Nicholas Hilliard, * um 1547 Exeter,
† 07.01.1619 London

XIII – Tod
Salvador Dalí, neuer Entwurf für das Tarot
Die Illustration auf Seite 181 seines Buches *Das geheime Leben des Salvador Dalí* (3. Auflage, Schirmer/Mosel, München 1990) zeigt ebenfalls das Motiv der Zypresse, hier aber mit zwei Schädeln. Im Text dazu (Seite 180) beschreibt Dalí, wie er in seiner vom Regen durchnässten Jacke einige Briefe seiner Angebeteten fand. Vor seiner geliebten Zypresse sitzend begann er, die Briefe zwischen den Händen zu kneten, bis sich diese in eine Art Paste verwandelten. Die so entstandenen Formen sahen den Samenbällen der Zypresse sehr ähnlich. Er brachte sie an der Zypresse dort an, wo gewöhnlich die Samenbälle sitzen. Danach setzte er seinen Spaziergang bis zur äußersten Spitze eines Felsens fort, wo ihn die Wellenbrecher durchnässten: „Der Geschmack des Meersalzes auf den Lippen rief den Mythos der Unbestechlichkeit, der Un-

temps moine franciscain, Pacioli écrit en 1494 son ouvrage *Summa de arithmetica, geometria, proportioni et proportionalità*, un résumé de toutes les connaissances en mathématiques et un ouvrage qui marquera son époque. L'un des chapitres de cet ouvrage *Tractatus particularis de computis et scipturis* l'a rendu célèbre, car c'est le premier traité détaillé de la comptabilité en partie double, également connue comme la méthode vénitienne. Pacioli passe sept ans à la cour des Sforza et travaille avec Léonard de Vinci auquel il enseigne la perspective et la proportionnalité. Deux chefs-d'œuvre incomparables de Léonard de Vinci naîtront de cette collaboration : les illustrations de l'ouvrage *De Divina Proportione* de Pacioli ainsi que la peinture murale *La Cène* au couvent dominicain de Sainte-Marie-des-Grâces.

X – La Roue de Fortune
Les Très Riches Heures du duc de Berry (1413-1416), Musée Condé, Chantilly
En haut : Août
En bas : Mai
Paul, Hermann et Hans Limburg, nés entre 1370 et 1380, morts en 1416 (probablement tous trois de la peste)

XI – Force
Salvador Dalí, portrait de femme dans le style de Lucas Cranach l'Ancien

XII – Le Pendu
Young Man Among Roses
Victoria and Albert Museum, Londres
Nicholas Hilliard, né à Exeter vers 1547, mort à Londres le 7 janvier 1619

XIII – La Mort
Salvador Dalí, nouvelle création pour son tarot. Dans son livre *La Vie secrète de Salvador Dalí*, une illustration, page 181, montre également le motif du cyprès, mais représenté avec deux crânes. Dalí décrit dans le texte qui accompagne cette illustration comment il découvrit dans son blouson mouillé par la pluie quelques lettres de sa muse. Assis devant son cyprès préféré, il commença à froisser les lettres entre ses mains jusqu'à ce qu'elles se transforment en une sorte de pâte. Ces petites boules ressemblaient beaucoup aux graines du cyprès, et il les mit sur l'arbre à la place des graines. Il continua ensuite à se promener jusqu'au plus haut sommet d'une falaise où il fut complètement mouillé par les vagues : « Le goût du sel de mer sur mes lèvres fit

XIV – Temperance
Original work by Salvador Dalí for his tarot, putatively authored by Amanda Lear. In 1965, Dalí met Alain Tap, who performed under the name of Peki d'Oslo at the famous transvestite club Le Carrousel in Paris. Later, so some claim, Tap would become a famous singer under the name Amanda Lear. Lear herself claimed she has always been a woman and the sex change operation was nothing but a PR gag by her record company. Dalí was fascinated by what he called the "confusion of the sexes." Very soon, Amanda had become part of Dalí's entourage and often accompanied the master when he made public appearances. Although initially Gala could hardly tolerate her, Amanda became Dalí's most important female friend. Gala gradually changed her mind and, in the end, she wanted Amanda to take care of Dalí after her death. Amanda was the model for Dalí's painting *Roger Rescuing Angelica* (ca. 1970).

XV – The Devil
Original work by Salvador Dalí for his tarot

XVI – The Tower
The Martyrdom of Saint Sebastian (early 16th century), Galleria degli Uffizi, Florence, Italy; Girolamo Genga, born 1476 in Urbino, died 1551 in Urbino, Italy

XVII – The Star
The Source (1856), Musée du Louvre, Paris; Jean-Auguste-Dominique Ingres, born August 29, 1780, in Montauban, died January 14, 1867, in Paris, France

XVIII – The Moon
Original work by Salvador Dalí for his tarot; Manhattan skyline

XIX – The Sun
Two Young Men (1954), The Salvador Dalí Museum, St. Petersburg, Florida; Salvador Dalí

XX – Judgment
La Pietà (1485), Galleria Estense, Modena, Italy; Bartolomeo Bonascia, born ca. 1450, died 1527.
The painting was used laterally inverted

XXI – The World
Top: Original work by Salvador Dalí for his tarot
Bottom: *The Judgment of Paris* (1530), Staat-

sterblichkeit in mir wach, der mich zu dieser Zeit so sehr beschäftigte."

XIV – Mäßigkeit
Bei der Frauenfigur handelt es sich wahrscheinlich um Amanda Lear.
Salvador Dalí, neuer Entwurf für das Tarot
Im Le Carrousel in Paris, einem berühmten Transvestitenklub, lernte Dalí 1965 Alain Tapp kennen, der dort unter dem Künstlernamen Peki d'Oslo auftrat und später als Amanda Lear eine bekannte Sängerin wurde. Amanda Lear selbst verbreitete, sie sei immer Frau gewesen und die Geschlechtsumwandlung sei ein PR-Gag ihrer Plattenfirma. Dalí war jedenfalls grundsätzlich „fasziniert von der Verwirrung der Geschlechter". Seit den späten 1960er Jahren war Amanda in Dalís Gefolge integriert und begleitete den Meister bei vielen öffentlichen Auftritten. Amanda, die anfänglich von Gala kaum toleriert wurde, entwickelte sich zu einer wichtigen Freundin für Dalí. Allmählich änderte sich Galas Einstellung zu ihr. Dies ging so weit, dass sie sich schließlich wünschte, dass nach ihrem Tod Amanda die „Betreuung" von Dalí übernehmen sollte. Amanda stand bei Dalís Gemälde *Roger befreit Angelika* (etwa 1970) Modell. Es ist somit höchstwahrscheinlich, dass sie auf dieser Karte verewigt wurde.

XV – Der Teufel
Salvador Dalí, neuer Entwurf für das Tarot

XVI – Der Turm
Das Martyrium des Heiligen Sebastian (Anfang des 16. Jahrhunderts), Galleria degli Uffizi, Florenz
Girolamo Genga, * 1476 Urbino, † 1551 Urbino

XVII – Der Stern
Die Quelle (1856), Musée du Louvre, Paris
Jean-Auguste-Dominique Ingres,
* 29.08.1780 Montauban, † 14.01.1867 Paris

XVIII – Der Mond
Silhouette von Manhattan
Salvador Dalí, neuer Entwurf für das Tarot

XIX – Die Sonne
Zwei Jünglinge (1954), The Salvador Dalí Museum, St. Petersburg, Florida
Salvador Dalí

XX – Das Gericht
La Pietà, Galleria Estense, Modena
Bartolomeo Bonascia, * um 1450, † 1527

renaître en moi le mythe de l'incorruptibilité, de l'immortalité qui me préoccupait à ce moment. »

XIV – Tempérance
Probablement Amanda Lear, nouvelle création pour le tarot de Salvador Dalí. Dans le Carrousel de Paris, un cabaret célèbre de travestis, Dalí fait en 1965 la connaissance de Alain Tapp, qui montait sur scène sous le nom de Peki d'Oslo, et qui plus tard, selon une rumeur, devint chanteuse sous le nom de Amanda Lear. Amanda Lear a, quant à elle, toujours affirmé qu'elle n'avait jamais changé de sexe et que cette rumeur était à la base une ruse de sa maison de disque pour mieux lancer son album. Dalí était en tout cas absolument fasciné par ce qu'il appelait « la confusion des sexes ». À la fin des années 1960, Amanda fit partie de l'entourage de Dalí et elle accompagna le grand maître lors de plusieurs représentations publiques. Peu tolérée au début par Gala, Amanda devint une amie importante de Dalí, et Gala changea d'avis ; elle ira même jusqu'à confier à Amanda « la prise en charge » de Dalí au cas où elle mourrait.
Amanda servit également de modèle pour le tableau de Dalí *Roger délivre Angélique* (vers 1970). Il est ainsi fort probable qu'elle soit immortalisée sur cette carte de tarot.

XV – Le Diable
Dalí, nouvelle création pour son tarot

XVI – La Maison Dieu
Le Martyre de saint Sébastien (début du XVIᵉ siècle) Galleria degli Uffizi, Florence (Italie)
Girolamo Genga, né à Urbin en 1476, mort à Urbin (Italie) en 1551

XVII – L'Étoile
La Source (1856)
Musée National du Louvre, Paris
Jean-Auguste-Dominique Ingres, né à Montauban le 29 août 1780, mort à Paris le 14 janvier 1867

XVIII – La Lune
Silhouette urbaine de Manhattan
Dalí, nouvelle création pour son tarot

XIX – Le Soleil
Deux adolescents (1954)
The Salvador Dalí Museum, St. Petersburg, Floride ; Salvador Dalí

liche Kunsthalle, Karlsruhe; Lucas Cranach the Elder, born 1472 in Kronach (Upper Franconia), died October 16, 1553, in Weimar, Germany

0 – The Fool
Further information requested. *

Queen of Wands
Portrait of Marie Antoinette (1783), Palace of Versailles; Marie Louise Élisabeth Vigée-Lebrun, born April 16, 1755, in Paris, died March 30, 1842, in Louveciennes near Marly, France

King of Wands
Louis XV, King of France and Navarre (1715), Palace of Versailles; Hyacinthe Rigaud, also known as Hyacinthe Rigau y Ros, born July 18, 1659, in Perpignan, died December 29, 1743, in Paris, France

Knight of Wands
The Journey of the Magi (1459), fresco at the Palazzo Medici Riccardi, Florence; Benozzo Gozzoli, born Benozzo di Lese di Sandro in 1420 in Florence, died 1497 in Pistoia, Italy

Page of Wands
Further information requested. *

Ace of Wands
The Card Sharper (ca. 1633-39), Musée du Louvre, Paris; Georges de La Tour, born 1593 in Vic-sur-Seille (Moselle), died January 30, 1652, in Lunéville (Meurthe-et-Moselle), France

Two of Wands
Further information requested. *

Three of Wands
Further information requested. *

Four of Wands
Top: *The Five Senses with Landscape* (1638), Musée de Beaux-Arts, Strasbourg; Jacques Linard, born 1600, died 1645
Bottom: *Leda and the Swan*, Hermitage Museum, St. Petersburg; Anton von Maron, born 1731, died 1808

Five of Wands
The Kiss of Judas (ca. 1360), Collegiata San Gimignano, Italy; Barna da Siena, date of birth unknown, died 1380

Das Bild wurde seitenverkehrt verwendet.

XXI – Die Welt
Oben: Salvador Dalí, neuer Entwurf für das Tarot
Unten: *Das Urteil des Paris* (1530), Staatliche Kunsthalle, Karlsruhe
Lucas Cranach der Ältere, * 1472 Kronach (Oberfranken), † 16.10.1553 Weimar

0 – Der Narr
Weitere Angaben erwünscht *

Königin der Stäbe
Porträt von Marie-Antoinette (1783), Schloss Versailles
Marie Louise Élisabeth Vigée-Lebrun, * 16.04.1755 Paris, † 30.03.1842 Louveciennes bei Marly

König der Stäbe
Ludwig XV., König von Frankreich und Navarra (1715), Versailles, Musée National du Château et des Trianons
Hyacinthe Rigaud, eigentlich: Hyacinthe Rigau y Ros, * 18.07.1659 Perpignan, † 29.12.1743 Paris

Ritter der Stäbe
Zug der Heiligen Drei Könige (1459), Fresko im Palazzo Medici-Riccardi, Florenz
Benozzo Gozzoli, eigentlich: Benozzo di Lese di Sandro, * 1420 Florenz, † 1497 Pistoia

Page der Stäbe
Weitere Angaben erwünscht *

Ass der Stäbe
Der Falschspieler (um 1633/1639), Musée du Louvre, Paris
Georges de La Tour, * 1593 Vic-sur-Seille (Moselle), † 30.01.1652 Lunéville (Meurthe-et-Moselle)

Zwei/Drei/Vier der Stäbe
Weitere Angaben erwünscht *

Fünf der Stäbe
Der Judaskuss (um 1360), Collegiata, San Gimignano
Barna da Siena, * unbekannt, † um 1360

Sechs der Stäbe
Weitere Angaben erwünscht *

XX – Le Jugement
La Pietà, Galleria Estense, Modène
Bartolomeo Bonascia, né vers 1450, mort en 1527. Ce tableau a été utilisé en sens inverse.

XXI – Le Monde
En haut : Salvador Dalí
En bas : *Le Jugement de Pâris* (1530) Staatliche Kunsthalle, Karlsruhe
Lucas Cranach l'Ancien, né à Kronach (Haute-Franconie) en 1472, mort à Weimar le 16 octobre 1553.

0 – Le Fou
Informations supplémentaires souhaitées *

Reine de Bâton
Portrait de Marie-Antoinette (1783)
Château de Versailles
Marie Louise Élisabeth Vigée-Lebrun, née à Paris le 16 avril 1755, morte à Louveciennes près de Marly le 30 mars 1842

Roi de Bâton
Louis XV, Roi de France et de Navarre (1715)
Musée National des Châteaux de Versailles et de Trianon, Versailles
Hyacinthe Rigaud, né Hyacinthe Rigau y Ros à Perpignan le 18 juillet 1659, mort à Paris le 29 décembre 1743

Cavalier de Bâton
Le Cortège des Rois mages (1459)
Fresque de la chapelle du Palais Medici-Riccardi, Florence
Benozzo Gozzoli, né à Florence en 1420, mort à Pistoia (Italie) en 1497

Valet de Bâton
Informations supplémentaires souhaitées *

As de Bâton
Le Tricheur à l'as de carreau (vers 1635)
Musée National du Louvre, Paris
Georges de La Tour, né à Vic-sur-Seille (Moselle) en 1593, mort à Lunéville (Meurthe-et-Moselle) le 30 janvier 1652.

Deux de Bâton
Informations supplémentaires souhaitées *

Trois de Bâton
Informations supplémentaires souhaitées *

Quatre de Bâton
Informations supplémentaires souhaitées *

Six of Wands
Further information requested. *

Seven of Wands
The Fair at Imprueta (after 1622), Staatsgalerie Stuttgart; Jacques Callot, born 1592
in Nancy, France, died 1635
Callot's remarkable works were inspired by
the Thirty Years' War. From 1610 to 1621, he
lived in Florence, Italy. After returning to
Nancy, Callot produced this etching of the fair
that was held each year on October 18 in the
hamlet of Imprueta, Tuscany. In the painting
appear 1,138 people, 45 horses, 67 donkeys,
and 137 dogs.

Eight of Wands
The Oath of the Horatii (1784), Musée du
Louvre, Paris; Jacques-Louis David, born
August 30, 1748, in Paris, died December 29,
1825, in Brussels, Belgium

Nine of Wands
Further information requested. *

Ten of Wands
Further information requested. *

Queen of Cups
Elizabeth of Austria, Queen of France (ca.
1571), Musée du Louvre, Paris; François
Clouet, born 1510 in Tours, died 1572 in
Paris, France.
Inspired by Marcel Duchamp who had added
a moustache and beard to the *Mona Lisa* in
1919 in his work named *L.H.O.O.Q.*, Dalí
embellished *Elizabeth of Austria* with the
same attributes. The French phonetic
pronunciation of the letters in the title sounds
like the phrase "Elle a chaud au cul" (She has a
hot ass).

King of Cups
Saint Louis, King of France (1590-97), Musée
du Louvre, Paris; Doménikos Theotokópoulos
(El Greco), born October 1, 1541, in Fodele
(Crete), died April 7, 1614, in Toledo, Spain

Knight of Cups
Napoleon Crossing the Alps (1800), Musée
national du château de Malmaison, Rueil-
Malmaison; Jacques-Louis David, born August 30, 1748, in Paris, died December 29,
1825, in Brussels, Belgium

Page of Cups
The Indifferent Man (ca. 1717), Musée du

Sieben der Stäbe
Der Jahrmarkt von Imprueta (1610/21),
Radierung, Staatsgalerie, Stuttgart
Jacques Callot, * 1592 Nancy, † 1635
Bemerkenswert sind seine von den Schre-
cken des Dreißigjährigen Krieges inspirier-
ten Werke. Callot lebte von 1610 bis 1621 in
Florenz, wo auch die zeitgenössische Darstellung des Volksfestes entstand, das jeweils am 18. Oktober im toskanischen Ört-
chen Imprueta gefeiert wurde. Es sind auf
dem Bild nicht weniger als 1138 Personen,
45 Pferde, 67 Esel und 137 Hunde zu sehen.

Acht der Stäbe
Der Schwur der Horatier (1784), Musée du
Louvre, Paris
Jacques-Louis David, * 30.08.1748 Paris,
† 29.12.1825 Brüssel

Neun/Zehn der Stäbe
Weitere Angaben erwünscht *

Königin der Kelche
*Elisabeth von Österreich, Königin von
Frankreich* (um 1571), Musée du Louvre,
Paris
Jean Clouet, * 1510 Tours, † 1572 Paris
Das von Dalí um einen Schnurrbart und ein
„Ziegenbärtchen" ergänzte Porträt lehnt
sich an das Ready-made *L.H.O.O.Q.* von
Marcel Duchamp an. Dieser hat 1919 das
Porträt der Mona Lisa mit den gleichen At-
tributen versehen. Die phonetische Ausspra-
che des Bildtitels *L.H.O.O.Q.* auf Franzö-
sisch ergibt den Satz *Elle a chaud au cu* („Sie
hat einen heißen Hintern").

König der Kelche
Saint Louis, König von Frankreich (1590/97),
Musée du Louvre, Paris
Domínikos Theotokópoulos (El Greco),
* 01.10.1541 Fodele (Kreta), † 07.04.1614
Toledo

Ritter der Kelche
Napoleon überquert die Alpen (1800), Musée
National de Malmaison, Rueil-Malmaison
Jacques-Louis David, * 30.08.1748 Paris,
† 29.12.1825 Brüssel

Page der Kelche
L'Indifferent (um 1717), Musée du Louvre,
Paris
Jean-Antoine Watteau, * 10.10.1684 Valenci-
ennes, † 18.07.1721 Nogent-sur-Marne

Cinq de Bâton
Le Baiser de Judas (vers 1360)
La Collégiale de San Gimignano (Italie)
Barba de Siena, date de naissance inconnue,
mort en 1380

Six de Bâton
Informations supplémentaires souhaitées. *

Sept de Bâton
Foire de Imprueta (entre 1610 et 1621)
Staatsgalerie, Stuttgart ; Jacques Caillot, né à
Nancy en 1592, mort en 1635
Les œuvres remarquables de Caillot sont ins-
pirées des horreurs de la guerre de Trente Ans.
Caillot vécut de 1610 à 1621 à Florence, où il
créa cette représentation de fête populaire qui
avait lieu chaque année, le 18 octobre, dans le
village Imprueta en Toscane. Ce tableau
montre 1138 personnes, 45 chevaux, 67 ânes
et 137 chiens.

Huit de Bâton
Le Serment des Horaces (1784)
Musée National du Louvre, Paris
Jacques-Louis David, né à Paris le 30 août
1748, mort à Bruxelles le 29 décembre 1825

Neuf de Bâton
Informations supplémentaires souhaitées. *

Dix de Bâton
Informations supplémentaires souhaitées. *

Reine de Coupe
Élisabeth d'Autriche, reine de France (vers
1571)
Musée National du Louvre, Paris
Jean Clouet, né à Tours en 1510, mort à Paris
en 1572
Inspiré par Marcel Duchamp qui, en 1919,
avait ajouté au portait de la Joconde une
moustache et un bouc dans son œuvre intitu-
lée *L.H.O.O.Q.* (prononcée « elle a chaud au
cul »), Dalí surchargea de la même façon le
portrait d'Élisabeth d'Autriche.

Roi de Coupe
Saint Louis, Roy de France (1590-1597)
Musée National du Louvre, Paris
Domenicos Theotokopoulos (El Greco),
né à Fodele (Crète) le 1ᵉʳ octobre 1541,
mort à Tolède (Espagne) le 7 avril 1614.

Cavalier de Coupe
*Bonaparte franchissant le Grand-Saint-
Bernard* (1800)

Louvre, Paris; Jean-Antoine Watteau, born October 10, 1684, in Valenciennes, died July 18, 1721, in Nogent-sur-Marne, France

Ace of Cups
Allegory on the Grail; original work by Salvador Dalí for his tarot

Two of Cups
Cupid and Psyche, Musée du Louvre, Paris; François-Édouard Picot, born October 17, 1786, in Paris, died March 15, 1868, in Paris, France

Three of Cups
The Three Graces (1525), Victoria and Albert Museum, London; Giorgio da Gubbio, born ca. 1465-70 in Intra, Lago Maggiore, died 1553, in Gubbio

Four of Cups
Further information requested. *

Five of Cups
Further information requested. *

Six of Cups
Madame Royale and the Dauphin Louis Joseph (1785), Palace of Versailles; Marie Louise Élisabeth Vigée-Lebrun, born April 16, 1755, in Paris, died March 30, 1842, in Louveciennes near Marly, France

Seven of Cups
The Isenheim Altarpiece, Resurrection (1506-16), Musée d'Unterlinden, Colmar; Matthias Gothart Grünewald, also known as Matthias Neithardt, born ca. 1480 in Würzburg, died August 31, 1528, in Halle an der Saale, Germany

Eight of Cups
Further information requested. *

Nine of Cups
Circe or Melissa (ca. 1531), Galleria Borghese, Rome; Dosso Dossi, also known as Giovanni Dossi, born Giovanni di Niccolò de Luteri ca. 1479 in Ferrara, died 1542 in Ferrara, Italy

Ten of Cups
Top: *Genre Scene with Masks* (ca. 1738), Museo Nazionale di Capodimonte, Naples; Giuseppe Bonito, born November 1, 1707, in Castellammare, died May 19, 1789, in Naples, Italy

Ass der Kelche
Allegorie über den Gral
Salvador Dalí, neuer Entwurf für das Tarot

Zwei der Kelche
Amor und Psyche, Musée du Louvre, Paris
François-Édouard Picot, * 17.10.1786 Paris, † 15.03.1868 Paris

Drei der Kelche
Scheibe mit den drei Grazien (1525), Victoria and Albert Museum, London
Giorgio da Gubbio, * zw. 1465 und 1470 Intra, Lago Maggiore, † 1553 Gubbio

Vier/Fünf der Kelche
Weitere Angaben erwünscht *

Sechs der Kelche
Marie-Therèse Charlotte de France und der Dauphin Louis-Joseph Xavier de France (1785), Schloss Versailles
Marie Louise Élisabeth Vigée-Lebrun, * 16.04.1755 Paris, † 30.03.1842 Louveciennes bei Marly

Sieben der Kelche
Isenheimer Altar: *Auferstehung* (1505/1516), Musée d'Unterlinden, Colmar
Matthias Grünewald, * um 1480 Würzburg, † 31.08.1528 Halle a. d. Saale (genaue Lebensdaten umstritten)

Acht der Kelche
Weitere Angaben erwünscht *

Neun der Kelche
Circe oder Melissa (um 1531), Galleria Borghese, Rom
Dosso Dossi, auch Giovanni Dossi, eigentlich: Giovanni di Niccolò di Luteri, * um 1479 Ferrara, † 1542 Ferrara

Zehn der Kelche
Oben: *Genreszene mit Masken* (um 1738), Galleria Nazionale, Napoli
Giuseppe Bonito, * 01.11.1707 Castellamare, † 19.05.1789 Napoli
Unten: *Die fünf Sinne mit Landschaft* (1638), Musée des Beaux-Arts, Straßburg
Jacques Linard, * 1600, † 1645

Königin der Schwerter
Bildnis der Johanna von Aragón (1518), Musée du Louvre, Paris
Raffaello Santi (Raffael), * 06.04.1483 Urbino, † 06.04.1520 Rom

Musée National de Malmaison, Rueil-Malmaison
Jacques-Louis David, né à Paris le 30 août 1748, mort à Bruxelles le 29 décembre 1825

Valet de Coupe
L'Indifférent (vers 1717)
Musée National du Louvre, Paris
Jean-Antoine Watteau, né à Valenciennes le 10 octobre 1684, mort à Nogent-sur-Marne le 18 juillet 1721

As de Coupe
Allégorie du Graal
Dalí, nouvelle création pour son tarot

Deux de Coupe
L'Amour et Psyché
Musée National du Louvre, Paris
François-Édouard Picot, né à Paris le 17 octobre 1786, mort à Paris le 15 mars 1868

Trois de Coupe
Les Trois Grâces (1525)
Victoria and Albert Museum, Londres
Giorgio da Gubbio

Quatre de Coupe
Informations supplémentaires souhaitées *

Cinq de Coupe
Informations supplémentaires souhaitées *

Six de Coupe
Marie-Thérèse-Charlotte de France et le dauphin Louis-Joseph-Xavier de France (1785)
Château de Versailles
Marie Louise Élisabeth Vigée-Lebrun née à Paris le 16 avril 1755, morte à Louveciennes près de Marly le 30 mars 1842.

Sept de Coupe
Retable d'Issenheim : Résurrection (1505-1516)
Musée d'Unterlinden, Colmar
Mathis Gothart Grünewald, né à Wurtzbourg vers 1480, mort à Halle le 31 août 1529

Huit de Coupe
Informations supplémentaires souhaitées *

Neuf de Coupe
Circé la magicienne (vers 1531)
Galleria Borghese, Rome (Italie)
Dosso Dossi, de son vrai nom Giovanni di Nicolo di Lutero, né à Ferrare vers 1479, mort à Ferrare (Italie) en 1542

Bottom: *The Five Senses with Landscape*
(1638), Musée de Beaux-Arts, Strasbourg;
Jacques Linard, born 1600, died 1645

Queen of Swords
Portrait of Joanna of Aragón (1518), Musée
du Louvre, Paris; Raffaello Sanzio (Raphael),
born March 28 or April 6, 1483, in Urbino,
died April 6, 1520, in Rome, Italy

King of Swords
Further information requested. *

Knight of Swords
Louis XIV (ca. 1700), color engraving; Jean
Bérain the Elder, born October 28, 1637, in
Saint-Mihiel, died January 24, 1711, in Paris,
France.
Bérain was a painter, engraver, and creator
of ornamental engravings that had a major influence on the Régence and Louis XIV style. In
1674, he was named royal chamber and cabinet
painter by Louis XIV. Bérain designed decora-
tions and costumes for the numerous parties
and masquerades at the court of Versailles as
well as sets for plays. The image on this card
shows the Sun King dressed up by Bérain.

Page of Swords
The Paumgartner Altarpiece, St. Eustace
(1502), Alte Pinakothek, Munich; Albrecht
Dürer, born May 21, 1471, in Nuremberg, died
April 6, 1528, in Nuremberg, Germany

Ace of Swords
Still Life with Flowers by a Dutch master;
most likely from the workshop of Jan Davidsz.
de Heem (ca. 1650-60)

Two of Swords
From a gospel book, calligraphy on parch-
ment, Helmarshausen (1120-40),
J. Paul Getty Museum, Los Angeles,
California

Three of Swords
Roger Delivering Angelica (1819), Musée
du Louvre, Paris; Jean-Auguste-Dominique
Ingres, born August 29, 1780 in Montauban,
died January 14, 1867, in Paris, France

Four of Swords
The Death of Marat (1793), Musées Royaux
des Beaux-Arts, Brussels; Jacques-Louis
David, born August 30, 1748, in Paris, died
December 29, 1825, in Brussels, Belgium

König der Schwerter
Weitere Angaben erwünscht *

Ritter der Schwerter
Louis XIV. (um 1700), kolorierter Kupferstich
Jean Bérain der Ältere, * 28.10.1637 Saint-
Mihiel, † 24.01.1711 Paris
Bérain war Maler, Kupferstecher und Schöpfer von Ornamentstichen, die maßgebend den
Régence- und Louis-quatorze-Stil beeinfluss-
ten. Im Jahr 1674 wurde er von Ludwig XIV.
zum königlichen Kammer- und Kabinett-
zeichner ernannt. Für die zahlreichen Feste
und *masquerades* am Hof von Versailles
entwarf Bérain Dekorationen und Kostüme
sowie Kulissen für Theateraufführungen.
Das von Dalí verwendete Bild zeigt den Son-
nenkönig in einer Kreation Bérains.

Page der Schwerter
Paumgartner-Altar, der Heilige Eustachius
(1502), Alte Pinakothek, München
Albrecht Dürer, * 21.05.1471 Nürnberg,
† 06.04.1528 Nürnberg

Ass der Schwerter
Blumenstillleben eines holländischen
Meisters, höchstwahrscheinlich Werkstatt des
Jan Davidsz. de Heem (um 1650/1660)

Zwei der Schwerter
Evangeliar, Pergamenthandschrift, Helmarts-
hausen (1120/40), John Paul Getty Museum,
Malibu, Kalifornien

Drei der Schwerter
Roger befreit Angelika (1819), Musée du
Louvre, Paris
Jean-Auguste-Dominique Ingres,
* 29.08.1780 Montauban, † 14.01.1867 Paris

Vier der Schwerter
Der Tod des Marat (1793), Musées Royaux
des Beaux-Arts, Brüssel
Jacques-Louis David, * 30.08.1748 Paris,
† 29.12.1825 Brüssel

Fünf der Schwerter
Karl I. von England (1635), Musée du
Louvre, Paris
Anthonis van Dyck, * 22.03.1599 Antwerpen,
† 09.12.1641 London

Sechs der Schwerter
Dante und Virgil in der Hölle (1822), Musée
du Louvre, Paris
Ferdinand Victor Eugène Delacroix,

Dix de Coupe
En haut : *Scène de genre avec des masques*
(vers 1738)
Galleria Nazionale, Naples
Guiseppe Bonito, né à Castellamare le 11 janvier
1707, mort à Naples le 19 mai 1789
En bas: *Allégorie des cinq sens au paysage* (1638)
Musée des Beaux-Arts, Strasbourg
Jacques Linard, né en 1600, mort en 1645

Reine d'Épée
Portrait de Jeanne d'Aragon (1518)
Musée National du Louvre, Paris
Raffaello Santi (Raphaël), né à Urbin le
6 avril 1483, mort à Rome le 6 avril 1520

Roi d'Épée
Informations supplémentaires souhaitées *

Cavalier d'Épée
Louis XIV (vers 1700)
Gravure colorée
Jean Bérain, père, né à Saint-Mihiel le
28 octobre 1637, mort à Paris le 24 janvier
1711
Jean Bérain était peintre et graveur. Il créa
des ornements qui ont exercé une grande influence sur la Régence et le style Louis XIV.
En 1674, Bérain est nommé à la cour de Louis
XIV comme décorateur de la Chambre et du
Cabinet du Roi. Il a créé les décorations et les
maquettes de costumes pour les nombreuses
fêtes et bals masqués à la Cour de Versailles
ainsi que pour les décors des pièces de théâtre.
L'œuvre sur cette carte montre le Roi Soleil
habillé dans le style Bérain.

Valet d'Épée
*Panneau du retable Paumgartner, Saint
Eustache* (1502)
Alte Pinakothek, Munich
Albrecht Dürer, né à Nuremberg le 21 mai
1471, mort à Nuremberg le 6 avril 1528

As d'Épée
Nature morte avec des fleurs
Peintre néerlandais.
Œuvre probablement issue de l'atelier de Jan
Davidsz de Heem (entre 1650 et 1660)

Deux d'Épées
Évangéliaire, calligraphie sur feuille de par-
chemin Helmarshausen (entre 1120 et 1140)
John Paul Getty Museum, Malibu, Californie

Trois d'Épée
Roger délivrant Angélique (1819)

Five of Swords
Charles I of England (1635), Musée du Louvre, Paris; Anthony van Dyck, born March 22, 1599, in Antwerp, died December 9, 1641, in London, England

Six of Swords
Dante and Virgil in Hell (1822), Musée du Louvre, Paris; Ferdinand Victor Eugène Delacroix, born April 26, 1798, in Charenton-Saint-Maurice near Paris, died August 13, 1863, in Paris, France

Seven of Swords
Diana the Huntress (ca. 1550), School of Fontainebleau, Musée du Louvre, Paris, France

Eight of Swords
The Duke of Berry's book of hours (1413-16), The Month of March, Musée Condé, Chantilly; Paul, Herman, and Johan Limbourg, born between 1370 and 1380, died 1416 (all three presumably died of the plague)

Nine of Swords
Statue of Beata Ludovica Albertoni or possibly of St. Anne (1675), Church of San Francesco a Ripa, Rome; Gian Lorenzo Bernini, born December 7, 1598, in Naples, died November 28, 1680, in Rome, Italy

Ten of Swords
The Death of Julius Caesar (1805-06), Museo Nazionale di Capodimonte, Naples; Vincenzo Camuccini, born February 22, 1771, in Rome, died September 2, 1844 in Rome, Italy

Queen of Coins
Empress Eugénie (1857), Hillwood Museum, Washington, D. C.; Franz Xaver Winterhalter, born April 20, 1805, in Menzenschwand, died July 8, 1873, in Frankfurt am Main, Germany

King of Coins
Original work by Salvador Dalí for his tarot. The master himself is sitting on the throne. His right hand holds an ocelot on a leash. It was this companion that created quite a stir at the Hotel Meurice in Paris.

Knight of Coins
The Journey of the Magi (1459), fresco in the Palazzo Medici Riccardi, Florence; Benozzo Gozzoli, born Benozzo di Lese di Sandro in 1420 in Florence, died 1497 in Pistoia, Italy

* 26.04.1798 St-Maurice-Charenton bei Paris, † 13.08.1863 Paris

Sieben der Schwerter
Diana als Jägerin (um 1550)
Schule von Fontainebleau, Musée du Louvre, Paris

Acht der Schwerter
Oben: *Stundenbuch des Herzogs von Berry* (1413-1416), Monat März, Musée Condé, Chantilly
Paul, Hermann und Hans Limburg, * 1370-1380, † 1416 alle drei (vermutlich an der Pest)

Neun der Schwerter
Skulptur der *Beata Ludovica Albertoni*, evtl. der Heiligen Anna (1675), Kirche S. Francesco a Ripa, Rom
Giovanni Lorenzo Bernini, * 07.12.1598 Neapel, † 28.11.1680 Rom

Zehn der Schwerter
Die Ermordung Julius Caesars (1805-1806), Museo Nazionale di Capodimonte, Neapel
Vincenzo Camuccini, * 1773 Rom, † 1844 Rom

Königin der Münzen
Kaiserin Eugénie mit Florentinerhut (1857), Hillwood Museum, Washington, DC
Franz Xaver Winterhalter, * 20.04.1805 Menzenschwand, † 08.07.1873 Frankfurt am Main

König der Münzen
Salvador Dalí, neuer Entwurf für das Tarot
Auf dem Thron sitzt Dalí persönlich; auf seiner rechten Seite hält er einen Ozelot an der Leine. Bei seinen Spaziergängen versetzte Dalí mit diesem Begleiter regelmäßig das Personal des Hotels Meurice in Paris in helle Aufregung.

Ritter der Münzen
Zug der Heiligen Drei Könige (1459), Fresko im Palazzo Medici-Riccardi, Florenz
Benozzo Gozzoli, eigentlich: Benozzo di Lese di Sandro, * 1420 Florenz, † 1497 Pistoia

Page der Münzen
Master Hare (1788/89), Musée du Louvre, Paris
Sir Joshua Reynolds, * 16.07.1723 Plympton Devon, † 23.02.1792 London

Musée National du Louvre, Paris
Jean Auguste Dominique Ingres, né à Montauban le 29 août 1780, mort à Paris le 14 janvier 1867

Quatre d'Épée
La Mort de Marat (1793)
Musées Royaux des Beaux-Arts, Bruxelles
Jacques-Louis David, né à Paris le 30 août 1748, mort à Bruxelles le 29 décembre 1825

Cinq d'Épée
Charles d'Angleterre (1635)
Musée National du Louvre, Paris
Antoine van Dyck, né à Anvers le 22 mars 1599, mort à Londres le 9 décembre 1641

Six d'Épée
Dante et Virgile aux enfers (1822)
Musée National du Louvre, Paris
Eugène Ferdinand Victor Delacroix, né à Charenton, Saint-Maurice, près de Paris le 26 avril 1798, mort à Paris le 13 août 1863.

Sept d'Épée
Diane chasseresse (vers 1550)
École de Fontainebleau
Musée National du Louvre, Paris

Huit d'Épée
En haut : *Les Très Riches Heures du duc de Berry* (1413-1416), Mars
Musée Condé, Chantilly
Paul, Hermann et Hans Limburg, nés entre 1370 et 1380, morts en 1416 (probablement tous trois de la peste)

Neuf d'Épée
Sculpture de la Bienheureuse Ludovica Albertoni
ou éventuellement de sainte Anne (1675)
Église de San Francesco a Ripa, Rome
Giovanni Lorenzo Bernini, né à Naples le 7 décembre 1598, mort à Rome le 28 novembre 1680

Dix d'Épée
La Mort de César (1805-1806)
Museo Nazionale di Capodimonte, Naples
Vincenzo Camuccini, né à Rome en 1773, mort en 1844

Reine de Denier
Impératrice Eugénie au chapeau florentin (1857)
Hillwood Museum, Washington, D. C.

Page of Coins

Master Hare (1788-89), Musée du Louvre, Paris; Sir Joshua Reynolds, born July 16, 1723, in Plympton, Devon, died February 23, 1792, in London, England

Ace of Coins

The hand was taken from *The Portrait of Joanna of Aragón* (1518), Musée du Louvre, Paris; Raffaello Sanzio (Raphael), born March 28 or April 6, 1483, in Urbino, died April 6, 1520, in Rome, Italy

Two of Coins

The North Wind, miniature from a Septuagesima gradual, a liturgical text (1470), Siena Cathedral; Liberale da Verona, born Liberale de Jacopo della Biava in 1445, died 1526 or 1529

Three of Coins

Further information requested. *

Four of Coins

Bottom left: *St. Lawrence Distributing Alms* (1447-49), fresco
Bottom middle and right: *St. Lawrence Receiving the Treasures of the Church from Sixtus II* (1447-49), fresco, Cappella Niccolina, Vatican Museum; Fra Angelico—also known as Fra Giovanni da Fiesole—was born Guido di Pietro ca. 1395 in Vicchio di Mugello, and died February 18, 1455 in Rome, Italy

Five of Coins

St. Dominic Restoring Napoleone Orsini (ca. 1434), predella of the Coronation of the Virgin Altarpiece from the Convent of San Domenico, Florence, Musée du Louvre, Paris; Fra Angelico–also known as Fra Giovanni da Fiesole—was born Guido di Pietro ca. 1395 in Vicchio di Mugello, and died February 18, 1455 in Rome, Italy

Six of Coins

Top: Still Life *with Wafer Bisquits* (ca. 1630), Musée du Louvre, Paris; Lubin Baugin, born ca. 1610 in Pithiviers, died 1663 in Paris, France.
Bottom: *St. Lawrence Distributing Alms* (1447-49), Cappella Niccolina, Vatican Museum; Fra Angelico—also known as Fra Giovanni da Fiesole—was born Guido di Pietro ca. 1395 in Vicchio di Mugello, and died February 18, 1455 in Rome, Italy

Ass der Münzen

Die Hand aus *Bildnis der Johanna von Aragón* (1518), Musée du Louvre, Paris
Raffaello Santi (Raffael), * 06.04.1483 Urbino, † 06.04.1520 Rom

Zwei der Münzen

Der Nordwind. Graduale vom Sonntag Septuagesima bis zum dritten Fastensonntag (1470), Dom zu Siena
Liberale da Verona, eigentlich Liberale de Jacopo della Biava, * 1445, † 1526 oder 1529

Drei der Münzen

Weitere Angaben erwünscht *

Vier der Münzen

Unten links: *Der Heilige Laurentius erteilt Almosen* (1447-1449, Fresko)
Unten Mitte und rechts: *Sixtus II. übergibt Laurentius die Schätze der Kirche* (1447-1449, Fresko) Cappella Niccolina, Vatikanische Museen
Fra Angelico, eigentlich Guido di Pietro, Ordensname Fra Giovanni da Fiesole, * um 1400 Vicchio di Mugello, † 1455 Rom

Fünf der Münzen

Der Heilige Dominikus erweckt Napoleone Orsini (um 1434), Predella des Altars der Klosterkirche San Domenico, Florenz, Musée du Louvre, Paris
Fra Angelico, eigentlich Guido di Pietro, Ordensname Fra Giovanni da Fiesole, * um 1400 Vicchio di Mugello, † 1455 Rom

Sechs der Münzen

Oben: *Der Nachtisch* (um 1630), Musée du Louvre, Paris; Lubin Baugin, * um 1610 Pithiviers, † 1663 Paris
Unten: *Der Heilige Laurentius erteilt Almosen* (1447-1449), Cappella Niccolina, Vatikanische Museen
Fra Angelico, eigentlich Guido di Pietro, Ordensname Fra Giovanni da Fiesole, * um 1400 Vicchio di Mugello, † 1455 Rom

Sieben der Münzen

Tod Mariae (1605/1606), Musée du Louvre, Paris
Michelangelo Caravaggio, eigentlich: Michelangelo Merisi, * 29.09.1571 Mailand, † 18.07.1610 Port' Ercole bei Civitavecchia

Acht der Münzen

Das Atelier des Malers (1855), Musée du Louvre, Paris

Franz Xaver Winterhalter, né à Menzenschwand le 20 avril 1805, mort à Francfort-sur-le-Main (Allemagne) le 8 juillet 1873

Roi de Denier

Dalí, nouvelle création pour son tarot
Le Maître est assis personnellement sur son trône. À sa droite, il tient un ocelot en laisse. Lors de ses promenades avec ce compagnon, Dalí avait semé la perturbation parmi le personnel de l'hôtel Meurice à Paris.

Cavalier de Denier

Le Cortège des Rois mages (1459)
Fresque de la chapelle du Palais Medici-Riccardi, Florence
Benozzo Gozzoli, né Benozzo di Lese di Sandro à Florence en 1420, mort à Pistoia (Italie) en 1497

Valet de Denier

Master Hare (1788-1789)
Musée National du Louvre, Paris
Sir Joshua Reynolds, né à Plympton, Devon, le 16 juillet 1723, mort à Londres le 23 février 1792

As de Denier

La main est issue du *Portrait de Jeanne d'Aragon* (1518)
Musée Nationaldu Louvre, Paris
Raffaello Santi (Raphaël), né à Urbin le 6 avril 1483, mort à Rome le 6 avril 1520

Deux de Denier

Le Vent du nord. Du dimanche de la Septuagésime au troisième dimanche de Carême (1470)
Cathédrale de Sienne (Italie)
Liberale da Verona (Jacopo della Biava) né en 1445, mort en 1526 ou 1529

Trois de Denier

Informations supplémentaires souhaitées *

Quatre de Denier

En bas à gauche : *Saint Laurent distribuant des aumônes* (1447-1449, fresque)
En bas, au centre et à droite : *Saint Laurent recevant de Sixte II les trésors de l'Église* (1447-1449, fresque)
Chapelle Nicoline (Vatican)
Fra Angelico, né Guido di Pietro à Vicchio di Mugello vers 1400, mort à Rome en 1455

Cinq de Denier

Résurrection de Napoleone Orsini par saint Dominique (vers 1434)

Seven of Coins
Death of the Virgin (1605-06), Musée du Louvre, Paris; Caravaggio, born Michelangelo Merisi on September 29, 1573, in Milan, died July 18, 1610, in Porto Ercole near Civitavecchia, Italy

Eight of Coins
The Artist's Studio (1855), Musée du Louvre, Paris; Gustave Courbet, born June 10, 1819, in Ornans near Besançon, died December 31, 1877, in La Tour-de-Peilz, France

Nine of Coins
Portrait of Count Stanislas Potocki (1780), National Museum, Warsaw, Poland; Jacques-Louis David, born August 30, 1748, in Paris, died December 29, 1825, in Brussels, Belgium

Ten of Coins
The Turkish Bath (1862), Musée du Louvre, Paris; Jean Auguste Dominique Ingres, born August 29, 1780, in Montauban, died January 14, 1867, in Paris, France

* No scientific research on these cards has yielded any findings to date. The author would be happy to receive any further information on deciphering the cards. Please send your suggestions to j.fiebig@hotmail.de.

Gustave Courbet, * 10.06.1819 Ornans bei Besançon, † 31.12.1877 La Tour-de-Peilz

Neun der Münzen
Porträt des Herzogs Stanislas Potocki (1780), Muzeum Narodowe, Warschau
Jacques-Louis David, * 30.08.1748 Paris, † 29.12.1825 Brüssel

Zehn der Münzen
Das Türkische Bad (1863), Musée du Louvre, Paris
Jean-Auguste-Dominique Ingres, * 29.08.1780 Montauban, † 14.01.1867 Paris

* Zu diesen Karten liegen bisher noch keine Forschungsergebnisse vor. Weitere Angaben zum Entschlüsseln der Karten nimmt der Autor gerne entgegen. Bitte schicken Sie Ihre Anregungen an j.fiebig@hotmail.de.

Prédelle sur le maître-autel du couvent San Domenico, Florence
Musée National du Louvre, Paris
Fra Angelico, Guido di Pietro, à Vicchio di Mugello vers 1400, mort à Rome en 1455

Six de Denier
En haut : *Le Dessert de Gaufrettes* (vers 1630)
Musée National du Louvre, Paris
Lubin Baugin, né à Pithiviers vers 1610, mort à Paris en 1663
En bas : *Saint Laurent distribuant des aumônes* (1447-1449)
Chapelle Nicoline (Vatican)
Fra Angelico, de son vrai nom Guido di Pietro, en religion Fra Giovanni da Fiesole, né à Vicchio di Mugello vers 1400, mort à Rome (Italie) en 1455.

Sept de Denier
Mort de la Vierge Marie (1605/1606)
Musée National du Louvre, Paris
Michelangelo Caravaggio, dit Le Caravage, né Michelangelo Merisi à Milan le 29 septembre 1571, mort à Porte Ercole près de Civitavecchia (Italie) le 18 juillet 1610

Huit de Denier
L'Atelier du peintre (1855)
Musée National du Louvre, Paris
Gustave Courbet, né à Ornans près de Besançon le 10 juin 1819, mort à La Tour-de-Peilz (Suisse) le 31 décembre 1877

Neuf de Denier
Portrait du comte Stanislas Potocki (1780)
Muzeum Narodowe w Warszawie, Varsovie (Pologne)
Jacques-Louis David, né à Paris le 30 août 1748, mort à Bruxelles (Belgique) le 29 décembre 1825

Dix de Denier
Le Bain turc (1863)
Musée National du Louvre, Paris
Jean-Auguste-Dominique Ingres, né à Montauban le 29 août 1780, mort à Paris le 14 janvier 1867

* La recherche n'ayant pas encore livré d'interprétation pour cette carte, l'auteur vous remercie d'envoyer vos suggestions à j.fiebig@hotmail.de.

Bibliography

Dalí, Salvador. The Secret Life of Salvador Dalí.
[First edition 1942.] Dover Publications 1993
Dietrich, Margot, and Detlef Hoffmann (eds.). Tarot-Art /
Zeitgenössische Künstler gestalten das alte Tarock.
Exhibition catalogue of the German Playing Card
Museum. Leinfelden-Echterdingen 1989
Etherington-Smith, Meredith. Dalí: A Biography.
Sinclair-Stevenson 1992
Fiebig, Johannes. The Salvador Dalí Tarot. Krummwisch
2004
Gibson, Ian. The Shameful Life of Salvador Dalí. Faber
and Faber 1997
Graak, Karl. Künstler-Spielkarten des 20. Jahrhunderts /
Kunst zum Spielen. DuMont 1985

Imprint
© 2014 EVERGREEN GmbH, Köln

Photo page 2: Salvador Dalí, 1946
© philippe halsman / Magnum Photos / Agentur Focus
For the illustrations of the tarot cards: © Salvador Dalí,
Fundació Gala-Salvador Dalí, VG Bild-Kunst, Bonn 2014

Texts © 2013 by Johannes Fiebig,
www.johannes-fiebig.de
Special thanks for investigating the pictorial sources of
the Dalí Tarot to Annegret Boelke-Heinrichs,
Evelin Burger, Harald Joesten, Dr. Annette Koeger,
Margit Krysta, Pedro E. Seiler, Peer Zietz.
English translation: Manfred Miethe, Peter Meygen

Design: Sense/Net Art Direction, Andy Disl and
Birgit Eichwede, Cologne
www.sense-net.net

Printed in China
ISBN 978-3-8365-4387-3

Literaturhinweise

Dalí, Salvador, *Das geheime Leben des Salvador Dalí*. 3.
Aufl., München 1990
Descharnes, Robert, *Salvador Dalí. Das malerische Werk*.
Köln 2013
Dietrich, Margot und Detlef Hoffmann (Hg.), *Tarot-Art.
Zeitgenössische Künstler gestalten das alte Tarock*. Aus-
stellungskatalog des Deutschen Spielkartenmuseums.
Leinfelden-Echterdingen 1989
Etherington-Smith, Meredith, *Dalí. Eine Biographie*.
Frankfurt/Main 1996
Fiebig, Johannes, *Dalí Tarot*. Krummwisch 2003
Gibson Ian, *Salvador Dalí. Die Biographie*. Stuttgart 1998
Graak Karl, *Künstler-Spielkarten des 20. Jahrhunderts.
Kunst zum Spielen*. Köln 1985
Néret, Gilles, *Dalí*, Köln 2011

Impressum
© 2014 EVERGREEN GmbH, Köln

Für die Abbildung S. 2: Salvador Dalí, 1946
© philippe halsman / Magnum Photos / Agentur Focus
Für die Abbildungen der Tarotkarten: © Salavador Dalí,
Fundació Gala-Salvador Dalí, VG Bild-Kunst, Bonn 2014

Texte © 2013 von Johannes Fiebig,
www.johannes-fiebig.de
Bei der Ermittlung der Bildzitate in den einzelnen
Karten haben mitgewirkt: Annegret Bölke-Heinrichs,
Evelin Bürger, Harald Jösten, Dr. Annette Köger,
Margit Krysta, Pedro E. Seiler, Peer Zietz.

Design: Sense/Net Art Direction, Andy Disl und
Birgit Eichwede, Köln
www.sense-net.net

Printed in China
ISBN 978-3-8365-4387-3

Bibliographie

Salvador Dalí: *La Vie secrète de Salvador Dalí.* Éditions diverses

Robert Descharnes: *Salvador Dalí. Das malerische Werk.* Taschen 2013, Cologne

Margot Dietrich et Detlef Hoffmann (éd.): *Tarot-Art. Zeitgenössische Künstler gestalten das alte Tarock.* Catalogue de l'exposition du Musée allemand de cartes à jouer. 1989, Leinfelden-Echterdingen

Meredith Etherington-Smith: *Dalí. Biographie.* Archipoche 2012, Paris

Johannes Fiebig: *Tarot Dalí.* Koenigsfurt Verlag, en allemand (2003) et en anglais (2004), Krummwisch. En espagnol (2004), Madrid

Ian Gibson: *The Shameful Life of Salvador Dalí.* Faber and Faber 1997, Londres

Karl Graak: *Künstler-Spielkarten des 20. Jahrhunderts. Kunst zum Spielen.* Dumont 1985, Cologne

Gilles Néret: *Dalí.* Taschen 2011, Cologne

Mentions légales

© 2014 EVERGREEN GmbH, Köln

Pour la illustration page 2: Salvador Dalí, 1946
© philippe halsman / Magnum Photos / Agentur Focus
Pour les illustrations des cartes de tarot:
© Salavador Dalí, Fundació Gala-Salvador Dalí,
VG Bild-Kunst, Bonn 2014

Textes © 2013 par Johannes Fiebig,
www.johannes-fiebig.de
Contributeurs à l'identification des références artistiques de certaines cartes: Annegret Boelke-Heinrichs, Evelin Burger, Harald Joesten, Dr. Annette Koeger, Margit Krysta, Pedro E. Seiler, Peer Zietz.

Traduction française: Nathalie Debuly, Annick Schmidt
Design: Sense/Net Art Direction, Andy Disl et
Birgit Eichwede, Cologne
www.sense-net.net

Printed in China
ISBN 978-3-8365-4387-3

LA MUERTE

XIII

XIII

DEATH